Understanding Eastern Philos

Understanding Eastern Philosophy is a clear, introductory, yet critical study of Eastern thought and its differences and relationships with the Western religious tradition. Written without jargon or technical terms, this book is an excellent introduction to anyone coming to philosophy or religion for the first time, clearly setting out the main principles of Hinduism, Buddhism, Taoism, Jainism and Confucianism.

This book strikes a note midway between the many devotional but intellectually undemanding books in the field, and the more abstruse writings on specific issues, which assume considerable knowledge on the reader's part. Ray Billington initially discusses the nature of religion, concluding that a belief in the numinous, or spiritual, is essential. He goes on to explore the expression of the spiritual dimension in Hinduism, Jainism and Buddhism; and then to the schools of Confucianism, Yin and Yang, and Taoism from China. Finally the author draws out the central themes of religious philosophy, and compares Eastern views with those held in the West, particularly Christianity, such as belief in God, the soul, moral decision-making, nature, faith and authority. His conclusion is that Eastern thought with its expression of universal mysticism is the most fruitful route to experience the spiritual dimension.

Written in a direct, non-specialist style, this book will be the perfect introduction for readers new to the area, as well as to those studying philosophy, religion or cultural studies. For those interested in spirituality, or current debates on religion, it will be an ideal guide.

Ray Billington was Principal Lecturer in Philosophy at the University of the West of England for twenty-five years, where he now lectures part-time. Well-known for his writing on religious themes in the *Guardian* newspaper, he has also made numerous television and radio appearances. He is the author of *Living Philosophy* and *East of Existentialism*, both published by Routledge.

Understanding Eastern Philosophy

Ray Billington

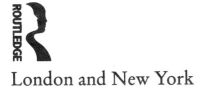

London and New York

First published 1997
by Routledge
11 New Fetter Lane, London EC4P 4EE

Simultaneously published in the USA and Canada
by Routledge
29 West 35th Street, New York, NY 10001

Typeset in Garamond by
Ponting–Green Publishing Services,
Chesham, Buckinghamshire
Printed and bound in Great Britain by
Mackays of Chatham PLC, Chatham, Kent

British Library Cataloguing in Publication Data
A catalogue record for this book is available from the
British Library

Library of Congress Cataloging in Publication Data
A catalog record for this book has been requested

ISBN 0–415–12964–8 (hbk)
ISBN 0–415–12965–6 (pbk)

Contents

Preface   vii

1   Eastern philosophy or Eastern religion?   1
2   The concept of God   9
3   Hinduism I: Its scriptures and systems   19
4   Hinduism II: Its basic teaching   31
5   The heterodox systems I   43
6   The heterodox systems II: Buddhism 1: Philosophy   51
7   The heterodox systems III: Buddhism 2: The way of Buddha   61
8   The heterodox systems IV: Buddhism 3: Mahayana Buddhism   71
9   Chinese philosophy I: Taoism   85
10 Later developments in Taoism   97
11 Chinese philosophy II: The Yin–Yang School   107
12 Chinese philosophy III: Confucianism   118
13 Metaphysics without theology I: The ground of being   134
14 Metaphysics without theology II: Human nature and destiny   142
15 Ethics and human behaviour   151
16 Nature and community   161
17 Authority and faith   169
18 Coexistence or coinherence?   178

Bibliography   188
Index   190

TO HATTI

motivator and mover in mysterious ways

Preface

Ours is the age of the publications explosion. Every six minutes, week in, week out, a new book is published in the UK alone: almost 90,000 a year. The indigestion among readers brought about by this eruption is perhaps illustrated by the findings of the *Independent* newspaper in September 1996, that the average readership for each of these new offerings – in the academic sphere, at least – was *eight* (other readers being, presumably, absorbed in catching up on the output of earlier years, or centuries). How accurate this conclusion is, it is impossible to say, but it suggests that there must be a sound reason for adding to the cornucopia.

Books about Eastern religion or philosophy are certainly not an exception to the pattern. Not a week goes by when some Western publishing house does not announce the latest expositions of Asian thought, whether on Hinduism, Sikhism, Jainism, Shintoism, Zen, Taoism, Confucianism or, especially, Buddhism. This outpouring of literature on the subject is mirrored in courses on Asian beliefs that have sprung up in universities, colleges and schools throughout the Western world: 'Religious Education', which not too long ago would have been confined to Christian teaching and biblical studies, is now usually broadened out to include at least some basic information about the more exotic religions.

This must be viewed as a thoroughly healthy situation. In the global village that we have now become, in which East and West increasingly recognise and explore their interdependence commercially and socially, it will no longer do to be in ignorance of each other's basic beliefs. In Western classrooms, as children of different religions are taught together, the implications of the different belief patterns have to be understood and, where necessary, accommodation made for them. Western nurses may well tend dying Hindus, whose approach to death is likely to be dominated by their distinctive beliefs: and again some accommodation may have to be made. If the explosion in writing, and the pursuit of courses, about the East can help to break down prejudice by overcoming ignorance, then this is an outcome greatly to be welcomed, even at the expense of yet another book in the ring.

The fact is that in this field there is a peculiar dilemma that springs from the two types of literature on the subject into which most books fall. The books are either devotional in content, aimed at enhancing the reader's spiritual life; or they are ultra-academic, concerned with minutiae of a particular school, so erudite as to cater only for advanced students. The first category serves a useful purpose but is ultimately unsatisfying for anyone who wishes to explore Eastern thought critically. 'My aunt has no trouble with her yoga,' wrote one of my students: 'she fits it in between her sauna and her bridge.' This is of course an extreme example of the indiscriminate approach to Eastern ideas for which much of this literature caters, but it serves as an indication of the facileness that can easily characterise the encounter, where the 'feel-good' factor outweighs the 'think- or work-hard'. If this is all there is to it, then those critics who describe the phrase 'Eastern philosophy' as an oxymoron, like military intelligence or global security, have a point to make.

At the other extreme, in their attempt to defend Eastern philosophy from this charge, many of its Western proponents have embraced an esotericism of Wittgensteinian proportions (Wittgenstein of the *Tractatus*, it should be said, not of the *Investigations*). It is as if, in their determination to confound the critics, they must prove themselves at least as recondite as their colleagues in the Western field, with their field of enquiry potentially just as arcane. These are admirable aims, but they are singularly unhelpful to anyone lacking considerable relevant knowledge. The kind of linguistic analysis required of specialists in Eastern thought – as in any area of philosophical enquiry – can be conducted only on the sure foundation of familiarity with the basic, sometimes intricate, teachings of Eastern philosophy and religion.

It is this foundation which, it is hoped, the following chapters will provide. The aim is to steer a middle course between, on the one hand, sentimental devotionalism (though this theme cannot be ignored) and, on the other, inscrutable obscurantism (though it cannot be guaranteed that this will always be avoided). The first section of the book therefore provides an outline of the beliefs held in the chosen areas of Eastern thought, together with the practices associated with them. Where necessary, information is provided about the origins and historical developments of certain schools, but this aspect is secondary to the main concern of the book, which is to present and critically examine Eastern *ideas*. (Other books are mentioned that concentrate on historical developments.)

The most difficult problem here arises from the need to limit the number of religions, or schools, that are studied. Any encyclopaedia of the world's religions will indicate that there are scores, even hundreds, of these open to consideration if the net is cast wide enough. The guiding factor in reducing this plethora to the required amenable proportions springs from my first reflection: the extent to which East and West are increasingly interacting, not only in general, but by an interest in, even to the point of being committed to, each other's religious beliefs. The key factor determining the choice of schools has therefore been: which of them have ideas about the world, about humanity, about the so-called spiritual dimension, about the purpose, if any, of existence, with which the West may empathise? Inevitably this guideline means excluding those religions, like Shintoism or Sikhism, that, on the whole, are limited to people of a particular national or cultural background. If this were a book on cultural studies, they might well have been included; as it is, the areas chosen are either those which are already making an impact on the West (such as Buddhism) or seem likely to do so in the near future (such as Taoism).

The second part of the book (Chapters 13–18) relates even more directly to this purpose. In these chapters, several key ideas expressed in the Eastern philosophies are extrapolated and compared with the way they are viewed in the West. Sometimes the comparison is with Western philosophy, and, where necessary, a brief outline of a particular school is given. More often, the comparison is with Western religions, particularly the Christian religion, since this has for almost two millennia dominated the English-speaking world. One cannot ignore the influence of both Judaism and Islam, and they are referred to whenever either of their teachings contributes distinctively to a discussion, but to dwell on either of these at any length would be beyond both the purpose and the constraints of the book. Like Christianity, they are Middle-Eastern religions rather than Eastern, Semitic rather than Asian; and, since all share a similar theistic basis, it would usually be repetitive to outline their metaphysical ideas alongside those of the – to most Western readers – more familiar religion.

I appreciate that that last phrase can, for many, be no more than relative. Readers who have specialised in religious studies, or are students of theology, should have little problem in understanding the issues raised, and comparisons and contrasts made, in the latter half of the book (which does not mean they will necessarily agree with all the conclusions reached). But for other readers, even undergraduates, it is impossible to be so sanguine. Despite compulsory religious education in the UK (to take just one example), there still seems to be an amazing ignorance about the basics of Christianity. Perhaps the RE syllabus mentioned earlier has been so broadened out that little has been studied in more than the shallowest fashion, with the apparent aim of knowing less and less about more and more until nothing is known about everything (the precise opposite of the cynic's definition of academic research). Whatever the reason, it is certainly alarming to be approached by an intelligent second-year undergraduate who admits to having had nine years of religious instruction, yet still asks the difference between the Old and New Testaments.

With this cautionary consideration in mind, it seems that some explanation of some of the basic ideas of Christianity is needed at appropriate points. Since many Christians – eminent as well as prominent – often show themselves to be divided on these matters, this should in any case turn out to be a profitable exercise. Some of the matters discussed may seem contentious, so it may be worth pointing out that I was for twenty years a Methodist minister, worked for some time on the Dead Sea Scrolls in Germany, and was for several years tutor in worship and preaching for the local (lay) preachers of Methodism. If I am critical of the theistic religions, and, in particular, say some harsh things about Christianity, it is not, I hope, from a state of prejudice or total ignorance.

I had reached early middle age before starting to teach and write about philosophy, and not till fifteen years later did I turn to Eastern thought with any seriousness of purpose. I take heart – though no invidious comparison is implied – that Kant himself was in his mid-fifties before Hume 'awakened him from his dogmatic slumbers'. Perhaps there is truth after all in Browning's heroic optimism: 'the best is yet to be'.

It would be impossible to thank all who have been influential in the production of this book. My erstwhile colleague at UWE, Glyn Davies, first persuaded me that Eastern philosophy was not an oxymoron, or contradiction in terms. Ken Bruder, who taught the subject at California State University, compelled me to teach it when we changed places for a year: the surest way to learn anything. I am grateful for the safe house offered me regularly by the monks of the Ramakrishna Order at Bourne End; the research being done there by Swami Tripurananda to find expressions of Advaita Vedanta philosophy in English, besides the idiosyncratic Hindu, literature is, I believe, a ground-breaking activity of crucial importance for the West. I am particularly grateful to my friend John Clarke (himself a more scholarly writer in the field than I) for his encouragement in general and his comments on the Buddhist section of the book in particular.

I shall not be forgiven in years to come if I do not thank my grandson, James (then 3½), who undertook to run off the script on the printer, and made a pleasure of a chore. If this publicity makes his sister Ami envious, she will simply have to come to terms with the fact that she was not around at the time. This is fortunately also the case for Mufti the cat, who would have ensured that the book did not get written in the first place.

1 Eastern philosophy or Eastern religion?

What makes a religion a religion? Is there an essential difference between a religion and a philosophy, and, if so, what is it? The word is often used loosely about individuals to describe an enthusiasm in their lives which seems to control everything they say or do: thus football, or gardening, or committee work, may be described as a person's religion. More broadly, but along similar lines, the dominant ideology of a community, or nation, has been similarly characterised. When Hitler seized power in Germany, Mussolini, the Italian dictator, said, 'Fascism is a religion; the twentieth century will be known in history as the century of Fascism.' From the other political extreme, Aneurin Bevan, Minister of Health in Britain's post-war Labour Government, remarked, 'The language of priorities is the religion of Socialism.' John Keats, in a letter to Fanny Brawne, described love as his religion, adding, 'I could die for that'; and, even more comprehensively, Samuel Butler, author of *The Way of All Flesh*, asserted, 'To be at all is to be religious more or less.'

The trouble with these all-embracing usages is that they reduce religion to little more than what people are keen on: anything that occupies their minds and fills their time to the exclusion of other interests and activities. But if this is religion, how are we to explain the fact that the word is used in a special way and about specific conglomerations of people worldwide? Why do we speak freely of the Christian, or Jewish, or Muslim religions, but not of the religions of Capitalism, or Marxism, or Feminism? To explain this phenomenon will require more careful analysis than the popular usage assumes; and this will not be inapposite, since such disciplined enquiry is the bread and butter of philosophy.

CHARACTERISTICS OF A RELIGION

In the comprehensive analysis contained in his book *The World's Religions*, Ninian Smart discusses the subject around seven categories, which may serve to begin the task of defining what is meant by religion. His seven are these:

A The practical and ritualistic.
B The experiential and emotional.

C Narrative and the mythic.
D The doctrinal and philosophical.
E The ethical and legal.
F The social and institutional.
G The material, primarily the buildings.

Smart does not suggest that all religions have all these categories, but he illustrates throughout his book how all religions have at least some of these. Nor does he lay any significance on the order of his list: he is not trying to establish priorities, or present any kind of logical sequence: A, F and G are normally found in close conjunction with each other; B and E will no doubt often inter-connect; and it will not be unusual to use C when embarking on D. But other combinations are commonly found, so that no generalisations as to which are essential can validly be made without exploring further the nature of religion.

To help in this, here is another list of characteristics often associated with the word. It is taken from *Introduction to Philosophical Analysis* by John Hospers (p.76f), though Hospers is himself quoting from W.P. Alston's *Philosophy of Language* (p.88):

1 Beliefs in supernatural beings (gods).
2 A distinction between sacred and profane objects.
3 Ritual acts focused around sacred objects.
4 A moral code believed to be sanctioned by the gods.
5 Characteristically religious feelings (awe, sense of mystery, sense of guilt, adoration, etc.), which tend to be aroused in the presence of sacred objects, and during the practice of ritual, and which are associated with the gods.
6 Prayer and other forms of communication with gods.
7 A world view, that is, a general picture of the world as a whole and of the place of the individual in it, including a specification of its overall significance.
8 A more or less total organisation of one's life based on the world view.
9 A social organisation bound together by the previous characteristics.

There are, not surprisingly, obvious parallels between this list of categories and the one on which Smart bases his discussion. 1, 2 and 7 reflect D in the earlier list; 3 and A refer to the same activity; E is represented in 4 and, perhaps, 8, though this feature may also be found in F. and in any case the second list makes no reference to the legal aspect of religion (though this may be contained in 7); 5 and 6 are found in B, 7 in D, while 9 correlates with F and probably with G, since any social organisation would normally pre-suppose a permanent meeting place for its activities.

There are two important differences between these lists, which may or may not be significant (even eminent authors sometimes overlook or underestimate aspects of their field of study). First, there is no place in the Hospers/Alston proposals for Smart's narrative/mythic category, though the latter may be found in the world view (7) of certain religious groups. For example, the myth of creation, recounted in the early chapters of Genesis in the Old Testament, is a distinct feature of the world view of numerous fundamentalist denominations in the Christian religion (with parallels in other religions). It is strange, however, that the second list makes no reference to sacred writings, or scriptures, since these feature, with varying degrees of authority, in virtually all of the major world religions. (This issue is discussed in Chapter 17.)

The second difference between the two sets of proposals is the more explicit reference to the holy, or the divine, in Hospers/Alston than in Smart. Each one of their first six categories mentions either the gods or the sacred. Clearly, this element is implied by a number of Smart's categories also, but the explicit references in the second list must be viewed as significant apropos of the question we are exploring. The most direct way to draw out the significance of the divine in religion is to consider what would remain if any, or some, or perhaps even all of the other suggested features were present, but the element of the spiritual, or the transcendental – or the 'numinous', as Rudolf Otto termed it in his seminal *Das Heilige* (*The Idea of the Holy*) – were missing. To put the question plainly: are any of Smart's seven features necessary or sufficient, *in the absence of the spiritual dimension*, for any set of ideas, or practices, or attitudes to certain objects, buildings or places, to constitute a religion? (This is, as will emerge, different from asking whether any of these may be termed religious.)

Smart's first, sixth and seventh categories refer to buildings, to objects found in them, and to events that occur in them. There is no difficulty in associating any of these with a religion: there can be hardly a village, let alone a city, anywhere in the world which does not boast its sanctuary: church or shrine, temple or mosque, chapel or cathedral; they stand as tangible evidence of the religious affiliations and beliefs of the local citizens. The importance of these objects of wood and stone, bricks and mortar is indicated by the fact that, for the vast majority of adherents of any religion, the practices associated with their beliefs take place in one of these material objects to the exclusion of all others. (It was, after all, in the 1990s, not the 1590s with their blatant religious intolerance, that the British Lord Chancellor was expelled from office in his strict Presbyterian community because he attended a funeral in a Roman Catholic church.)

Buildings, then, are important to most religious people (though perhaps of less importance to the religion), but this is also the case for any number of secular organisations. Political parties have their headquarters, to which members regularly repair; scouts, guides and other youth organisations have their meeting places, as do clubs of various kinds, for sports, physical exercise, hobbies, discussion. Arts centres and folk houses (for a wide range of activities) are regular features of modern town life; societies such as the Masonic Order, or military veterans, or self-help organisations all have their own rooms or buildings, and it is a natural human quality, having become familiar with a place, to feel attached to it.

So it is not unique to a religion to have a building where its activities are centred. Nor is it unique that most religious buildings (not all: the Christian denomination, the Society of Friends, is one exception) contain objects, such as particular forms of literature, that are held in the highest regard. In synagogues there will be readings from the Torah, in churches from the Bible, in mosques from the Qur'an, and these books will have a place of honour in the building. However, religions are not unique in this expression of reverence: meetings of Alcoholics Anonymous begin with readings from the so-called 'Big Book', scouts and guides from their respective codes, military veterans from their rolls of honour; but this process does not make a religion of them. There are similar parallels in secular groupings to other features of religious centres. Altars, icons, pulpits and all the other paraphernalia of churches, synagogues, mosques and temples are in themselves no more than what naturally becomes revered in any organisation if it is central to its activities and *raison d'être*. There are symbolic objects in masonic meeting places, images of its heroes in any football club's social centre, and activities in any assembled group of people which, when regularly repeated, take on the form of what in religious circles would be described as ritual. Whether they are concerned with the so-called sacred or so-called secular, the whole tends to become more than the sum of its parts. Familiar objects assume an aura, recurrent corporate activities a mystique, which singles them out from the commonplace.

When examining the remainder of Smart's categories of religion, we shall not find it difficult to make similar comparisons. Inner experiences and emotions, which often result in deeply held beliefs in religious circles, are reflected in non-religious contexts. Political rallies in the United States (and, though less often, in Britain) have all the fervour of a religious revivalist meeting. It may be argued that this is a poor example of the similarity, since religious and political conviction have much in common, not least that each is asking supporters to bet their lives, so to speak, on a proposition that cannot be verified. A less obvious example, but equally valid, is the football supporters' club. There one will encounter an enthusiasm which could challenge that of any religious assembly: the certainty that this is the right side to support; the adulation of current stars and the mythology about the deeds of stars of old; the commitment to victory for the cause and the sense that each person's loyalty will contribute to this; the willingness to sacrifice time and money in support of the team; and a sense of joy through uniting with fellow supporters: all these reflect many activities associated with religion yet, except in the most general of senses discussed earlier, membership of a football supporters' club could hardly be described as belonging to a religion.

This leaves us with the doctrinal/philosophical and the ethical/legal. The first refers to the creeds, the accepted beliefs, of a particular religious group, to the way its members approach the basic questions of existence: why are we here? what is our destiny? is there meaning in the cosmos? We shall explore these questions in later chapters, both singly in relation to specific religous bodies, and comparatively between bodies. Here it need only be stated that any group of people committed to a cause will be found to have its corporate credo. This is true not only of political parties but also of any kind of pressure group, such as animal rights groups, the Life organisation or the Green movement.

This last has a world view which can boldly stand alongside that of any body of religion, without specifically introducing any kind of religious considerations. The movement bases its case on compassion, common sense and even self-interest. Its philosophy is founded on the concept of what in the 1970s was termed 'spaceship Earth'. We are asked to see the planet as a complex inter-relationship of forces which, left to operate naturally, produce a harmonious relationship between, on the one hand, the many forms of life that have come into being and, on the other, the resources to sustain them. It consequently warns of the dangers of interfering in this process by the use of 'unnatural' farming methods or by introducing technology which, while increasing so-called efficiency, has the by-product of polluting the land, the sea and the air. We are therefore urged to revere the Earth, to cooperate with it rather than exploit it for personal material gain. The devotion that supporters of the movement express leads to a commitment which demands great sacrifices and sometimes, as when the vessel of the Greenpeace Organisation, *Rainbow Warrior*, was sunk by the French government in 1984 while being deployed to prevent nuclear tests, the surrender of lives. There is a sense of vision here that can compare with the Christian or Jewish view of the world as God's Kingdom ('He holds the whole world in His hands', as the popular song of the 1950s expressed it). But the Green movement is not a religion.

We are led to the same conclusion if we consider the final, ethical, category in Smart's analysis. The world's religions all provide admonitions about personal behaviour and, by extension, how society should conduct itself. We have the Ten Commandments, the Sermon on the Mount, directions from the Prophet Muhammad in the Qur'an. 'Love thy neighbour as thyself' is probably the most familiar moral injunction to be found in any of the world's scriptures, and it is not unknown for Christians to claim this as a religious, even a Christian, commandment (in fact it is first found in Leviticus 19:18, so it is strictly Jewish in the biblical context). Any debate about its origin is, however, rendered superfluous by the fact that this injunction, or parallels to it such as the 'golden rule' ('do unto others as you would they should do unto you') can be found in any number of moral guidelines based not on religious but on humanitarian considerations. Confucius, in the sixth century BCE, expressed the golden rule in reverse: 'don't do to others what you would not wish them to do to you' – which is probably a more comprehensive guide to behaviour than the positive version. Humanists and other secularists, not noted for their religious convictions, accept this admonition as the basis for human behaviour. So far as social ethics are concerned, religions are not at all unique in portraying the perfect society. Marxism and socialism both offer ideals of relationships between human beings that are based on cooperation rather than competition. Ayn Rand (not forgotten in some circles), in her philosophy of Objectivism, presents an alternative ideal based on her vision of a pyramidical society in which the ablest and fittest naturally assume the key primary roles. The debate about how the disparate forces in human society should be brought into a harmonious form of coexistence is one that has been conducted equally dedicatedly by religious and non-religious writers and thinkers alike.

There is, then, nothing distinctively religious about moral codes, which have, as a matter of fact, been in existence since well before the advent of the present world monotheistic religions. The code of Hammurabi, for instance, was penned, or, more accurately, inscribed on stone, in Babylon four millennia ago, and was itself based on earlier codes of Sumer and Akkad. Even in those earliest periods of human civilisation, the need seems to have presented itself to establish guidelines and sanctions regarding individual and social behaviour (including, in Hammurabi's code, the death penalty for doctors who carelessly allowed patients to die, and for builders whose shoddy homes collapsed: no *caveat emptor* there). It is of some interest, and a key factor in our present enquiry, that Hammurabi offered the code to his people as having been presented to him by Shamash, the sun god, rather as Moses, about a millennium later, described his receiving of the Ten Commandments on Mount Sinai.

What emerges from this brief survey of Smart's seven categories or facets of religions may seem startling: *not one of them is in itself either necessary or sufficient to bring about a religion.* We may encounter the most resplendent building, in which is conducted a ritual of the most devout and absorbing kind, with participants experiencing deep emotion, feeling that their whole lives are given direction by the experience; they may give up the bulk of their time and a high proportion of their income and energy in its service; they may live for it and die for it alongside many others of their kind; we may even describe their devotion as religious, in the sense that it absorbs them to the exclusion of all other considerations: but none of these factors on their own make such persons members or adherents of a particular religion. If that were the case, we could number the religious in billions.

There seems to be an unavoidable conclusion to this discussion, indicated by an unambiguous emphasis in both Alston and Hospers. This is that all the characteristics we have identified give unambiguous expression to a religion *only* when they are infused with the spiritual, or the numinous, or even – though this word is often misused or misunderstood – the supernatural, in the strict sense of being that which is other than or beyond the natural, or physical. Perhaps the least ambiguous word to express what is virtually inexpressible is the metaphysical, which literally means 'that which is beyond (or after) the physical', and dates from the time of Aristotle, whose followers used it when, after his death, they were cataloguing his enquiries into the nature of the soul, the afterlife, God and purposiveness.

Aristotle maintained a philosophically neutral stance on these matters, although the devoutly Christian philosopher, Thomas Aquinas, for whom he was simply The Philosopher, found in him the intellectual mainstay of many of his theological arguments. The world's monotheistic religions understandably lay neutrality aside and express a total commitment to the reality of God and all that this implies: the assurance that there is a spiritual dimension in the universe, besides the material; that *Homo sapiens* is more than just a physical body, and that in some form this element which is more will survive after the body's demise.

It is this acceptance of the reality, the actuality, of God, the soul, the afterlife, which, in all the world's religions, provides an answer to the key metaphysical questions (crucial to everyone, not just to those affiliated to a religion): is there a purpose to life? was the universe intended? Without a belief in a purpose established by some kind of almighty being who created and sustains the universe, all of the seven facets are no more than outward trimmings of religion, lacking a rationale for their existence. Buildings are just that, no more, no less; and all that takes place in them, however solemn, no more than a piece of drama. Without a belief in God, 'religious' ethics are no more prescriptive than those of any political or social group, or even of any individual who acts, shall we say, existentially. The emotion felt during acts of worship or in private prayer would be no different in kind from that felt by any enthusiastic band of followers of any cause, or of any individual in deep reflection. The authority for any set of religious beliefs or view of the world would be no greater than that of any parallel set, or view, in any secular sphere; and the scriptures used by any religion would be simply examples of the kind of texts, cultural or otherwise, that tend to assume an authority among any body of people who share a common cause.

It is quite feasible in universities these days to study religion in its psychological, social, philosophical and, above all, cultural contexts; and these are valid areas of study, in the sense that they require students to identify problems and attempt to resolve them. These aspects of religion will all have a contribution to make, explicitly or tacitly, in what follows. But the central conviction remains: for a religion to be a religion it must express a belief in the reality of the spiritual dimension in the universe: this, in philosophical terms, is a *necessary* condition of its nature. Whether it is (again in philosophical terms) a *sufficient* condition is another matter. Spiritualism (or, to be more accurate, spiritism) obviously declares the reality of the spiritual, but, since many of its followers believe in the naturalness of the spirit world (some would even define it as an aspect of the natural world capable of being explored through the discipline of physics), it is a moot point whether it constitutes a religion or not.

To return to the title of this chapter: we face the question of whether the schools of Eastern thought that are to be examined should be regarded as religions or as philosophies. No definitive answer to this can be found until further study on the schools' teachings has been undertaken; and it may be that, even then, an attitude of agnosticism will be the wisest one to hold. In any case, it will be found impossible to generalise about this, since both Hinduism and Buddhism embrace a wide range of approaches to metaphysical and ontological questions, so that both have found expression in what must – if the above analysis is correct – be termed religions, while both have also found expression (for example, in certain forms of yoga in Hinduism, and in a wide range of manifestations of Theravada Buddhism) in what, by the same token, cannot be termed religions. Zen may, or may not, be a religion (probably not), while, of the Chinese schools, it would be difficult, though not impossible, to designate Confucianism as a religion, and Taoism appears to solve the problem for us by expressly dividing its teaching into the philosophical form, *tao chia*, and the religious form, *tao chiao*. Whether or not we shall go along with these designations remains to be seen. Meanwhile we may at least have some idea of what it is we are looking for.

2 The concept of God

If the initial hypothesis is sound, and the *sine qua non* of a religion is a belief in what may loosely be termed the spiritual dimension, whether 'alongside' or 'within' the universe, it follows that, so far as the so-called Western religions are concerned (Judaism, Christianity and, though 'Western' in a much looser sense, Islam), this understanding is generally epitomised in a belief in God. It may therefore be useful at this early stage to consider what it is to which this item of faith commits the believer, together with the grounds for believing it. When we then turn to the Eastern schools of thought (where 'knowledge' in any case tends to replace 'faith', as will be illustrated in Chapter 17) we should then be better equipped to interpret the spiritual, or numinous, as they perceive it. In particular, we should be able to see why the typically Western idea of God is absent from the majority of expressions of Eastern religion or philosophy.

For the distinction between 'God' and 'spirituality' to be more than a vague glimmer in the mind, we need to outline the variants that are possible when discussing the concept of God, with particular reference to 'His' relationship with the universe (the significance of those inverted commas will be discussed later). We may start – and there is no 'hidden agenda' in the order of categorisation – with **pantheism**. This is derived from two Greek words: *pan*, meaning 'all', and *theos*, meaning 'God'; thus pantheism affirms that everything is God, and God is everywhere; or, alternatively (and more succinctly), that God and the universe are one. The emphasis in most expressions of pantheism, of which we shall find examples in both India and China, is on God's presence in living things: in human beings, animals, birds, fish, insects, trees and plants of all kinds. God and Nature are identical. The philosopher Spinoza in fact used the formula 'God or Nature' (*Deus sive Natura*), with the implication that the two are interchangeable. There is a good deal of pantheistic thought to be found in poetry, as in the English Romantics. Shelley's words on the death of his friend, Keats, are an unambiguous example:

> He is made one with Nature: there is heard
> His voice in all her music, from the moan
> Of thunder, to the song of night's sweet bird.

Some expressions of Western mysticism verge on pantheism, even if they do not explicitly embrace it. Mystics such as Eckhart and Jacob Boehme sought passionately to find God in Nature in their desire for union with the Divine. Because they seemed to place themselves outside, rather than alongside, the mainstream doctrines of their faith, they were viewed with suspicion by a number of their contemporaries and successors; but, as we shall see, many modern representatives of Eastern thought view them as exemplars of those who seek the non-dualistic experience of total absorption in the Infinite (or by whatever term this state, which is beyond the power of words to describe, is designated). The extent to which Eastern philosophy is pantheistic is one of the key issues to be discussed, both in terms of the relationship between the human and the divine, and of the affinity between human beings and the natural world.

Often linked with pantheism, but in fact having different emphases and being much more primitive, is **animism**. This is the belief that certain objects, such as trees, stones or waterfalls, are possessed of their own individual spirits. These give the objects their own characteristic qualities and cause their distinctive movements. Sometimes, perhaps because they have an unusual shape or size, occupy a distinctive location, or are closely associated with a certain individual or group, these objects assume an extraordinary significance in people's minds. Thus trees, rocks or rivers come to be looked upon as sacred, and believers may attribute magical qualities to them. There are echoes of animism in all the world's religions, not least in the Old Testament, such as the incident at Bethel where Jacob treats as divine the stone on which he had laid his head while he had his vision of the ladder set up from Earth to Heaven (Genesis 28:10–22). Critics of Christianity have been known to designate as animistic Christians worshipping of God in what are believed to be holy places, and of course the doctrine of transubstantiation lays itself open to this accusation. In fact, there are probably elements of animism wherever the word 'sacred' is introduced in contradistinction to 'secular' or 'profane' (the Society of Friends bases itself on the belief that no place and no thing is *per se* either sacred or profane), but, in most modern usages, the word 'sacred' reflects the more sophisticated beliefs of much later periods, which virtually eliminate the animistic elements. But those elements survive, and we shall note them in Eastern thought.

We turn next to **deism**, from the Latin *deus*, meaning 'God'. Prior to the late seventeenth century, this term was interchangeable with theism, to be discussed below; but with the advent of the Enlightenment, the Age of Reason, the word, in England at least, took on a connotation (or, since there were several schools, connotations), that gave it an emphasis quite distinguishable from, and, in its extreme form, inimical to, what has now become the more familiar term.

The basic mark of deism in its purest form (that is, unmixed with elements of theism), is its expression of what is known technically as religion without revelation. Belief in God is not discarded, but it is belief in an impersonal, omnipotent being, responsible for the creation of the universe, but not otherwise involved in its affairs. Indeed, since He *is* omnipotent, it follows logically that there is no further need for His intervention. Being perfect, He has made all things good (how could that which is perfect do otherwise?), so that, in Isaac Newton's famous image, like a flawless clock which needs no rewinding, the cosmos and its creatures can proceed to function immaculately for the remainder of time. God is thus the great Mathematician, the Architect of the universe, the uncaused First Cause.

It could be (and has often been) argued that this theory reduces God to no more than part of an equation – a theoretical explanation of what is otherwise inexplicable: how did anything come into being? It also makes of Him an absentee God. After all, if this theory is correct, it means that, having created the universe (whether in six days or six zillion years), He has since retired for a well-earned rest, lasting for what remains of eternity. This is a *deus ex machina*, introduced in order to fill a large lacuna, or black hole, in people's knowledge; and, like any other *deus ex machina* (such as the woodman who turns up in the nick of time to save Little Red Riding Hood from the wolf), this explanation has the stamp of being contrived.

There were eighteenth-century deists who retained some of the more personal attributes of God in their thinking. Some accepted the concept of divine providence, but only in the material world; others added a belief in God's intervention in human affairs, at both a moral and spiritual level; others added a continuing belief (rejected by many deists) in a life after death. But it was what some might describe as the more negative aspects of deism that finally triumphed. Those who followed this path felt that it was demeaning to God's perfection, including His unchangeableness, to envisage His intervening in human affairs, which, as we have seen, were part of His perfect creation. Deism effectively declares God redundant.

It should be noted at this stage that, between them, pantheism and deism introduce us to two key concepts apropos of God: the immanent and the transcendent. The former refers to God's presence in the world and in human lives; the latter to His status above and beyond the ephemeral: immutable amidst change and decay (though these are not necessarily synonymous, as we shall see in Chapter 11 with the discussion of yin and yang). The immanent God is the God within: comforter, counsellor, strengthener; the transcendent God is the object of awe and worship, before whom human beings are as nothing. Rudolf Otto, in his book *The Idea of the Holy (Des Heilige)*, described these facets as *mysterium fascinans* and *mysterium tremendens*, the God who draws human beings to Himself, and the God who instils a sense of dread: two concepts that we shall occasionally find expressed in Eastern thought.

In the West, we are likely to be more familiar with **theism**, a word now normally used to characterise, in chronological order, Judaism, Christianity and Islam. Some scholars claim that Zoroastrianism, founded in what was then Persia in the sixth or seventh century BCE, was the first theistic religion, although it would be more accurate to describe it as possibly the first expression of monotheism, in contrast to polytheism (see below).

Theism was originally used to express the opposite of atheism, the belief that there is no God. It was later used in contrast to pantheism and, since the Enlightenment, to deism. It is this last usage which gives theism its distinctive character. In contrast to deism's emphasis on the transcendental, effectively absentee God, it stresses the personal side of God's nature (God as immanent) while not ceasing to emphasise the 'Holy Other', the almighty creator of all things and all beings. Thus it holds together the central themes of both pantheism and deism. In this philosophical system, God's continuing intervention in the world through preachers, priests or prophets – even, according to Christianity, His incarnation in it in the person of Jesus Christ – in order to keep it on, or restore it to, the right path is not, as in deism, viewed as illogical. Human beings have been granted free will, and, by exercising their freedom wrongly (the theological term is sinfully) have strayed from His ways. Even miracles, events which seem extra-natural (or supernatural), which are totally alien to the deist perspective (as the philosopher Hume illustrated in his *Essay upon Miracles*), are quite feasible from this viewpoint. Thus, to return to Newton's metaphor, while the world may have begun as a perfect clock, it had within it the potential to run down: and God enters as the great rewinder.

These three terms, pantheism, deism and theism, between them contain the major theories of the nature of God and His relationship with the universe. Four other terms should, however, be noted, since they reflect certain historical developments in human views of the divine. The first of these is **polytheism** (literally 'many gods'), which is the acceptance of a plurality of gods. Like animism, with which this view has, at least on the face of it, parallels, this is a primitive concept. In the Graeco-Roman classical world we find a belief in a multitude of gods and goddesses, each having responsibility for different aspects of life, and receiving worship accordingly. There was a hierarchy among these gods based on the weight of their responsibilities: for instance, the Roman goddess of the hearth and household, Vesta, ranked lower on the heavenly scale than Mars, the god of war, and Saturn, the god of agriculture; while Jupiter, the counterpart of the Greek Zeus, was chief of all the gods. There are classical gods who represent or epitomise a wide range of facets of the human character, including those that some representatives of the theistic religions regard as sinful. Thus there is Bacchus, the god of wine, or drunkenness, and Venus, goddess of love (interesting that the former is male and the latter female).

Other civilisations also had their pantheons. There were dozens of Nordic gods (Odin, Thor, and so on), Egyptian gods (including Isis and Osiris), Celtic gods and goddesses, of whom Grannos and Brigit are probably the most famous, and Mexican gods with exotic names like Xochiquetzal, Mictlantecuhtli and, god of the planets, Tlauizcalpantecuhtli. We shall find in the next chapter that Hinduism, which embraces an enormous range of contrasting belief systems, the effect of developments over two or more millennia, includes a frankly polytheistic perspective, with belief in such gods as Rama, Vishnu, Krishna, Shiva and his consort, Kali. The Semitic neighbours of the Jews, held polytheistic beliefs in Old Testament times, and we find reference to them in the Jewish scriptures: Baal, Moloch, Rimmon and so on.

In earliest times, the Jews may well have held polytheistic beliefs, but, at least from the time of Moses in the second millennium BC, they held a view that, in two parallel manifestations, represented a stark modification of polytheism and led ultimately to its total denial as a valid expression of religious belief. The modification was seen in the twin concepts of **monolatry** and **henotheism**. The first of these, from the Greek *monos*, meaning 'single' and *latreia*, meaning 'worship', reflects the belief that, while other gods may well exist, there is only one God who should be worshipped. We find this approach in the second commandment (Exodus 20:5), where, condemning the worship of 'graven images' which are representations of other gods, it is stated: '. . . you shall not bow down to them or serve them; for I the Lord your God am a jealous God. . . .'

The word henotheism (Greek *heno* means 'one') has a slightly different connotation but can easily coexist with monolatry. Whereas the latter emphasises the restriction of worship to a single god, this theory, while similarly recognising the existence of several gods, regards one god as the particular deity of a specific tribe or nation. Reflection of this is seen in the first commandment (Exodus 20:3): 'You shall have no other gods before me.' The tendency among those who held either of these stances was to scorn the gods of other tribes or nations, implying that only their own tribal god was *worth* worshipping. This is expressed vividly in the account of Elijah's championship of Jehovah (more accurately, Yahweh) against the priests of Baal (I Kings 18:20–29).

From the historical point of view, both monolatry and henotheism can be considered as halfway houses to a full-blooded belief in only one God, **monotheism** (although some scholars argue that such an evolutionary account of the development of religious belief is difficult to sustain). The three theistic religions are thus by implication monotheistic, although the Christian doctrine of the Trinity – God the Father, God the Son and God the Holy Ghost – has by some critics been alleged to reflect polytheism. The Christian answer is that the belief is in one godhead with three Persons. A more challenging issue for all the monotheistic religions arises from their different perceptions of the godhead (see Chapter 13).

One further expression of God's relationship with the universe should be mentioned, not least because, while receiving little attention since it was coined early in the nineteenth century, it has been resuscitated in a book by John Robinson, author of the cult theological book of the 1960s, *Honest to God*. In a later book, *Explorations into God* (1967), he indicated that he had come to find the most satisfying philosophical stance concerning the deity to be not theism (which one might expect to hear from an Anglican bishop) but **panentheism**, or all-in-God. Effectively, this doctrine combines the central affirmations of the three major theories, pantheism, deism and theism. Like pantheism, it accepts the concept that God exists throughout the whole of Nature. But, if this is all that can be affirmed, we are left inexorably with a finite God, since all life on this planet (which is what the term 'Nature' here connotes) will, sooner or later, cease: it will be either frozen or burned into non-existence. So, if God is identified solely with Nature, He will likewise cease to be. Panentheism rescues God from this dilemma by declaring, along deistic lines, His omnipresence throughout the universe and, if need be, beyond: He is not limited by what He has created. Add to this the interventionist theology of theism, and, Robinson believed, we have the most comprehensive picture possible of the relationship between God, the universe and all forms of life, human or otherwise.

There are two words in common use to express a denial of God's existence, or, at least, scepticism on the matter. The first, already mentioned, is **atheism**, meaning, literally, 'no God', or 'without God'. In classical Greece, the word was used to describe anyone who, whether he believed in 'God' or not, disbelieved in the gods of the state, which was the equivalent of treason. Socrates was executed on these grounds. In the Roman Empire, the term was used similarly against Christians: a letter from the Church in Smyrna, for instance, written in 155 CE, describes how the mob, seeking the blood of the local bishop, cried out, 'Away with the atheists; let search be made for Polycarp.' Over subsequent centuries, the term came to mean the rejection of any kind of belief in God or gods, though, for a lengthy period up to the Darwinian controversy of the nineteenth century, its meaning was mixed with that of the second term: **agnosticism**.

Literally, this means 'having no knowledge' (Greek *gnosis*, knowledge, with the prefix *a-* giving its opposite). The sense conveyed is not of ignorance but of lack of verification, or proof. It was probably first used by T. H. Huxley when defending Darwinism, after he and his fellow evolutionists had been accused of being atheists. An agnostic is one who refuses to be committed to any form of belief – or disbelief – about which there is no conclusive evidence. As opposed to those who are prepared to act on 'blind faith', he/she remains firmly sceptical (a 'definite don't-know', as the opinion polls would put it): reluctant to go all the way along the atheist path by declaring unequivocally that there is no God. The jury, as the saying goes, is still out on that one, and, pending a verdict one way or the other, agnostics remain firmly on the fence.

As suggested earlier, the distinction between atheism and agnosticism is often blurred. The philosophical sceptic who demands further proof of God's existence before becoming a believer (though the term 'believer' would hardly be apposite if such proof were possible) remains in the agnostic camp unless, as in the school of logical positivism, he affirms that all talk about God is in any case meaningless. The philosophical materialist who asserts that the universe can be summed up in the phrase 'matter in motion' could well be taking a stance no bolder than that of agnosticism unless he/she adds the word 'only' after the word 'up'. Even a devout theist will agree that anyone *can* define the universe in materialistic terms: the issue is whether or not a religious interpretation is also possible without abandoning one's intellectual capacities. To deny this would stamp a person as a thorough-going atheist.

The question of where the great Eastern schools stand on this issue will be explored, along with other issues, in the ensuing chapters. We may expect to find parallels to the foregoing categories in most of the schools, but whether any of them is a central as opposed to merely a subordinate feature of their thought- or belief-patterns is, as will emerge, open to question. Those who wish to pursue the kind of enquiry initiated above may profitably turn to Karen Armstrong's *A History of God*; but it should not be read by any religious fundamentalist on an empty stomach.

The use of the male pronoun in reference to God throughout the foregoing discussion should not be left without comment. The societies in which all these theories about God flourished were, at least at the time when their beliefs were being committed to writing, patriarchal. It is not therefore surprising that their image of a perfect being should turn out to be male rather than female, and that the spiritual leaders who spoke of Him, from Moses to Zoroaster, Jesus to Muhammad, were, like the authors of their scriptures, men and not women. Modern Christians affirm that the doctrine of the Fatherhood of God includes the concept of the Motherhood of God but, admirable though the intention may be, many critics view it as a concession to modern thinking rather than a radical modification of the received belief (which is reflected in the continuing opposition to female priests among a fair percentage of Christians, as there is among followers of the other theistic religions).

There has been considerable exploration, in recent times, of the Earth goddess culture. Writers like Marija Gimbutas in *The Civilisation of the Goddess* and Elinor Gadon in *The Once and Future Goddess* have propounded the theory, backed by substantial archaeological and anthropological research, that the worship of the Earth goddess underlies the male-dominated theistic beliefs. Over the course of time, these beliefs, which flourished in prehistory – perhaps as far distant as 9,000 years ago – were swamped by (in Gimbutas's words) 'horse-riding, patriarchal, sky-god-worshipping warriors from the east.' She suggests that the successors of these warriors have, over the past 4,000–5,000 years, imposed the concept of God's masculinity.

It is instructive to note that the words 'pagan' and 'heathen' relate to the idea of the Earth, and this leaves open at least the possibility that it was indeed the case that worship of the female goddess, earthy and fertile, was abandoned – some might say smothered – by those who sought in their godhead a reflection of the typically masculine qualities of combativeness and aggression. It gives a new reference to the phrase 'make love, not war', which might be viewed as the epitome of the dispute between matriarchy and patriarchy.

It leaves open the question of the extent to which developments in beliefs about God reflected male fear of female sexuality. We shall return to this issue with reference to the yin and the yang.

Before leaving this discussion of what is effectively the history of God, it may be helpful to outline briefly the philosophical arguments for His existence. The first, and perhaps basic, is the **cosmological argument** (Greek *cosmos* means 'world'), the argument from First Cause. It is linked closely with the medieval Catholic philosopher Thomas Aquinas (1225–74) and his monumental work *Summa Theologica*, though, as Aquinas acknowledged, it owes much to Aristotle. It is based on a syllogism: nothing happens without being caused; the universe has 'happened'; therefore the universe was caused. God is then the cause of the universe. In the words of an earlier theologian/ philosopher, St Anselm (1033–1109): 'There never was a time when He was not, and there never will be a time when He will not be.'

Leaving aside modern developments in quantum mechanics and the notion of acausality (which challenge the basic premise about the inevitability of causation) this argument leaves unanswered the question 'Who or what caused God?' As it stands, the phrase 'uncaused first cause' is an oxymoron. We can circumlocute the problem with the idea that time is itself not eternal: it actually had a beginning before which, quite literally, there was nothing; but this concept requires us to pass beyond the capacities of the human mind, a creature of time. The idea of anything, whether God (spirit) or the universe (matter), coming into being out of nothing is, and I suspect will always be, beyond our capacity to imagine.

The second is the **teleological argument** (Greek *telos* means 'end' or 'purpose'). It is founded on the evidence of design in the universe and, in particular, in the forms of life that the universe contains. Each species is apparently designed in such a way that its individual needs are met, with the implication that an intelligent creator planned it so. The eye of a moth, for instance, has precisely the number of cells it requires in order to function as a moth, while the human eye has a more complex structure. This argument was much in vogue in the eighteenth century but was felt by many scholars to have been undermined by Darwin's theory that the cells reproduced in any creature were those that enabled it to adapt to its environment. For Darwin, survivability was the dominant, all-controlling drive of all species: this certainly allows for a teleological perspective, but seems pantheistic rather than theistic in its reference to God.

The third is the **ontological argument** (Greek *to on*, from the present participle of the verb 'to be'), associated again with St Anselm, together with René Descartes (1596–1650). It offers the view that God is a logical necessity. Anselm argued that, since God is, by definition, perfect ('that than which nothing greater can be conceived': *id quo nihil maius cogitare est*), then it follows that if He does not exist we should arrive at a contradiction, because we should then be able to conceive of an entity greater than (because this new entity *existed*) this non-existent God. Since we began by defining God as 'that than which ... etc.', we are now in the position of describing an entity who or which is more perfect than perfect: which is impossible.

Immanuel Kant (1724–1804) criticised this argument on the grounds that existence is not a predicate of any creature or object: the very fact that one describes, say, an animal, does not necessarily mean that it exists, as is illustrated by the drawing of a unicorn which I have just made for my grandson. The difference between 'to be' and 'to exist' is raised here and is a central feature of ontological discussion. The fact is that, if 'God' is synonymous with 'being', then the phrase 'God is' is a tautology. In any case, as Kant emphasised, we are no nearer to proving that God *exists*. For German speakers this ontological problem is facilitated by the presence in their language of the two phrases '*es ist*' (there is/are) and '*es gibt*' (there exists): thus, '*es ist ein Mann im Monde*' (there is a man in the moon); '*aber es gibt keinen Mann im Monde*' (no man exists in the moon).

The fourth 'proof' is the **moral argument**, which was the only defence of God's existence that Kant would accept as valid. It is linked to his central ethical theory that the essence of morality lies in the pursuit of duty, which was to be identified, as his famous 'categorical imperative' stated it, by a process of universalising one's proposed moral decisions. Good behaviour in an individual is not that which aims to produce happiness for those involved, as the Utilitarian school was later to assert, but that which is in accord with what is conceived to be the universal ideal. But where do the principles arise from which this ideal is gleaned? And how can one explain away the demonstrable fact that those who conduct their lives in this way do not necessarily prosper, or even achieve any long-lasting fulfilment?

Kant recognised both problems as real and argued that the answer lay in the fact of God's presence: He is the essence of moral goodness and the rectifier, in heaven, of moral injustice, or unfairness. Thus a group of religious beliefs – in God, the afterlife, the existence and survival of the soul, heaven – are necessitated by a prevenient ethical theory: a case, it seems, of putting the cart before the horse. The question of *why* things should be fair, or of how to cope with a clash of strongly felt moral duties (where social pressures may be a significant factor), is an insuperable problem only if one starts with a belief in a benevolent God who has revealed His will and purpose. Kant was in any case writing before the theory of evolution had been widely disseminated; and, according to that theory, our sense of right and wrong is linked to the basic drive towards survival. (See on the problem of evil in Chapter 16.)

All four of these arguments attempt to prove God's existence through a process of rational deduction. Independently of the fact that none of them is conclusive, one wonders both how many people have actually believed in God because of them, and how deeply He has featured in the lives of those who arrive at belief via this deductive route. It seems more representative of the human condition that the process of attaining a belief is an inductive one, based on the human feeling of insecurity and uncertainty in a complex universe. This was certainly the viewpoint of Schleiermacher (1768–1834), who argued that it was a feeling of dependence that created a need for God. We shall consider, in the chapters that follow, the extent to which Eastern schools of thought ignore the deductive arguments and rest their case on the experience of the numinous, to which testimony has been made over the centuries. In other words, as we shall explore specifically in Chapter 13, we move from what Martin Buber termed the world of 'I–it' to one of 'I–Thou'.

3 Hinduism I: Its scriptures and systems

The word 'Hinduism' is often misunderstood by Westerners, who interpret it to mean a specific religion, like Islam or Judaism. In fact, it is derived from the Hindi word for 'India' (Hindi being the official administrative language of India today) and refers to the traditional socio-religious structure of the Indian people. Within this structure are six main orthodox schools and countless local cults and traditions of worship and belief. So, while there are a number of basic ideas common to all Hindus (which will be our main consideration), to undertake a comprehensive study in the field would mean coming to terms with an enormous range of religious ideas, embracing all the concepts outlined in the previous chapter – and more.

Hinduism is based on mythology rather than on history and therefore, unlike Buddhism, Christianity and Islam, has no founder. There have been numerous **rishis**, or seers, but no single religious luminary around whom beliefs and practices have arisen. There is, probably as a consequence, no fixed code of beliefs and no equivalent to the Ten Commandments or the Sermon on the Mount. To make matters even harder for anyone trying to be specific in a typically 'rational' Western way, little attention is paid to historical detail. Hinduism always directs its followers towards eternity, with the result that there is a certain casualness about the temporal, whether in terms of the sequence of events or of the evolution of beliefs. It is possible to give a broad chronology of the unfolding process, but the dates given for accounts of *gurus*, philosophers, schools of thought and so on may diverge by as much as centuries (no small problem for those who insist that no idea or belief should be discussed in isolation from its historical cultural context).

We can identify four main periods of Hinduism, mainly by the writings that they produced. The first is the **Vedic period**, dating from at least 1500 BCE, and maybe much earlier. This is the period of the Vedas, meaning 'knowledge', 'sacred teaching', which may well be the oldest writings in the world (though Egyptologists are likely to disagree). They culminate with the Upanishads around the sixth century BCE (all texts are discussed below) and are accepted as the most authoritative Hindu texts.

The second is the **Epic period**, from about the sixth/fifth century BCE until the third or fourth centuries CE. The writings of this period were not accorded the same authoritative status as the Vedas, but their influence and wide usage over the centuries give them a unique standing in Hinduism. The two great epics are the *Ramayana* and the *Mahabharata*, the latter containing what is generally acknowledged to be the peak of Hindu writing, the *Bhagavad-Gita*.

The third is the **Classical period**, dating from around the fourth to the twelfth centuries CE. This was the period in which the teachings of the Vedas and the epic writings, which were not always easy for simple people to comprehend, were commented on and presented in a more popular foim. Typical writings of this period were the Puranas, which later became the chief texts of the religious, as opposed to philosophical, forms of Hinduism: Vaishnavism, Shaivism and Brahmanism.

The fourth period dates from the end of the classical period to the advent of the 'modern' period in the nineteenth century. It is known as the **Scholastic period**: one in which there was no original, creative writing, but much learned (and, to be frank, often pedantic) commentary on the received texts or scriptures, followed by commentaries on the commentaries, even commentaries on the commentaries on the commentaries. This period ended with the emergence of a number of dynamic spiritual leaders in the nineteenth and twentieth centuries: Ramakrishna, Vivekananda, Sri Aurobindo, Gandhi, Meher Baba; this was a period of increasing apperception of Hinduism in the West.

HINDU SCRIPTURES

To describe in detail the writings of an entire subcontinent over two or three millennia is beyond our present scope, but some broad indications can be given. An initial mention should be made of the language in which the sacred texts, from the Vedas to the *Bhagavad-Gita*, were written. This is **Sanskrit**, which literally means 'perfect, complete'. Over the course of the centuries, this language, which arrived in India with the Aryan races of the northwestern regions, was honed and refined so as to be able to express, through its earlier vedic to its later classical forms, the spiritual truths that were revealed to the writers of the texts – the *rishis*, or seers – in their meditations. It thus has a highly sophisticated vocabulary that can express with clarity the minutiae and nuances of spiritual experiences. Most of the terms have no equivalent in any European language, which means that, strictly speaking, any student of Hinduism should begin by learning Sanskrit. (This is, of course, the case for the study of any literature: only in the original language can the intuitive associations be made that are linked with the words and phrases employed.) The difficulty with Sanskrit is increased if we attempt to speak it, since, being a 'dead' language (like Latin), we cannot be sure how the words were pronounced. As the present exercise is one of writing and reading, this problem should not afflict us unduly, but we need to be conscious that for many Hindus Sanskrit is the 'language of the gods'. The Dominican mystic Meister Eckhart (1260–1327), whose spiritual experiences will be discussed in Chapter 13, said that 'to see God is to see as He sees.' Hindus offer a parallel conviction in relation to Sanskrit: an enlightened being speaks like God because he/she has attained divine consciousness.

As we have seen, the earliest Hindu writings were the Vedas. Because they are accepted as the highest peak in the hierarchy of sacred texts, any school of thought that does not accept this ranking is judged to be *nastika*, or unorthodox (Buddhism and Jainism are examples of this designation). The Vedas are complex in structure and enormous in length (six times the bulk of the Bible). They are divided into four parts: the *Rigveda*, or Veda of poetry; the *Samaveda*, or Veda of songs; the *Yajurveda*, or Veda of sacrificial texts; and the *Atharvaveda*, which is associated with the ancient Indian priesthood, the Atharvan.

The *Rigveda* is the oldest and most extensive of the four, comprising 1,028 hymns arranged in ten 'song cycles', or *mandalas*. Most of these are associated with the name of a particular *rishi* (seer) and are directed to personifications of natural forces such as Agni (fire), Indra (the atmosphere) and Soma (an intoxicating juice). It has been described as 'one of the most important linguistic, mythological–religious, literary, and cultural documents of human-ity. It has maintained its vital religious force in presentday Hinduism ... and is still held as binding by the people of India today' (W. Halbfass, quoted in *The Rider Encyclopedia of Eastern Philosophy and Religion*, henceforth *EPR*, 290).

The *Rigveda* is the source of most of the *Samaveda*, songs that accompany the offering of the sacrifice of *soma* in worship, and the *Yajurveda* is a series of sacrificial formulas chanted during the sacred rite. The *Atharvaveda*, written considerably later than the others, preserves many traditions of folk belief, together with marriage and burial songs. It is seen as the oldest document of Indian medicine, since it contains 'magical' spells against illness.

The four Vedas can be further subdivided in a variety of ways (for instance, into Vedas of knowledge and Vedas of liturgical practices), so it will be apparent that the task of becoming thoroughly familiar with them is at least as complex as that of coming to terms with the Bible. Each of them includes a **Brahmana**, a manual of instruction for the practical use of the material found in the collection (**Samhita**). Added to these are explanatory texts, which have served as a link to any philosophical discussion that might ensue. These discussions, the so-called **Aranyakas**, were added as supplementary texts under the name 'Vedanta', or 'crown of the Vedas' (see page 29). From these were later derived the Upanishads.

The word **Upanishad** means literally 'to sit down near to': that is, to sit at the feet of a *guru* in order to hear the secret, or confidential, message. Twelve Upanishads are particularly revered and generally viewed as the highest peaks of the Vedas. They are the most philosophical of the Vedas, less dependent on priestly dogma, and viewed by the Vedanta school as the point to which all the other Vedas were moving. We could say that they are in the Vedas but not of them; or, as Hindus themselves describe them, they are like creeping plants, attached to the main tree but maintaining their own independence and freedom. They are divided among the four Vedas and date from between c. 800 BCE and the time of Buddha (563–483 BCE).

The next great writings are examples of a distinctly Indian genre: the Itihasa (literally 'so it was'). These are heroic sagas, legends or mythological tales and are often in poetical form. The best-known examples are the two epics, the *Ramayana* and the *Mahabharata*, dating from about 400 BCE. They are long: the *Ramayana* has 24,000 couplets, while the *Mahabharata* has 106,000 verses in eighteen books. These epics tell of great adventures among super-heroes, virtual demi-gods, outlined in bold strokes that have gripped readers, both in India and beyond, to the present day. The *Ramayana* is the less well known of the two in the West, but the respect in which it is still held reflects the claim made in one of its early verses: 'He who reads and repeats the holy, life-giving Ramayana is liberated from all sin and attains heaven.'

The *Mahabharata*'s main theme is the battle for the kingdom of Bharata, which is waged between two families, the evil Kauravas and the virtuous Pandavas. The most important section, from the philosophical and religious points of view, is in Book 6, which contains the instructions of the god Krishna to Arjuna, one of the five Pandava brothers, prior to the battle. This may seem a strange context for one of the profoundest pieces of writing that the world contains, but we are here describing the *Bhagavad-Gita*, literally 'the song of the exalted one'. The battle in fact symbolises the age-old conflicts that are waged in every invidual between 'ego' and 'higher nature'. In the dialogue, Krishna outlines the central themes to be examined later under the schools of Sankhya, Yoga and Advaita Vedanta, all focusing on the union of the individual with *brahman*, the highest reality, or ground of being. The *Bhagavad-Gita* is known as the 'Gospel' of Hinduism and has influenced Indian religious life more than any other writing. It has eighteen chapters with 700 verses: Mahatma Gandhi and his family used to read it through monthly before meals, and many Indians know it by heart. There are numerous translations in English, some with commentaries by Hindu religious leaders, past and contemporary.

Similar in style to the Itihasas are the Puranas (literally 'ancient narratives'). Their content is different, in that they present legends of the gods, rather than of human heroes. Their main theme is devotional (*bhakti*), and they express the essence of worship in a simpler, more direct way than is to be found in the Vedas generally. They date from around the fifth century CE, and have been, and still are, used by Hindu worshippers whose devotion is directed towards the three great gods: Brahma (the creator), Vishnu (the sustainer) and Shiva (the destroyer, including the destroyer of ignorance and evil). These mythical, devotional writings are at a level that most Hindus can comprehend, and they have been described by Mario Vallauri as 'a kind of encyclopedia of Hindu religious forms and their countless traditions, which interweave, cross, and overlap one another' (quoted in *EPR*, p.280).

Slightly later than the Puranas, around the sixth century CE, there appeared a further set of writings which have played an important role among one stream of Hindus, whose beliefs and worship have followed a distinctive path. This is **Tantra**, meaning 'weft, context, continuum'. This bland translation disguises what for many in the West has seemed to be an exotic expression of Hinduism. Its central theme is that the divine energy or creative power is encountered and represented through Shakti, the feminine aspect of divinity in general, and of the various gods in particular. She is chiefly portrayed as the wife of Shiva: he is symbolised by the *linga*, she by the *yoni*. She may be one who brings good fortune, such as Maheshvari, or terror and destruction, such as Kail, with her necklace of skulls.

Most Tantric texts take the form of a dialogue between Shiva and his Shakti, indicating how worshippers may attain perfection by awakening cosmic forces (*chakra*) located in (and, in one case, just above) the body. It may be mentioned here that Tantra calls for the observance of rites and forms of meditation using five elements: wine, meat, fish, grain and sexual intercourse. Perhaps not surprisingly, this has led to what some might judge to be abuse: alongside the so-called 'right-hand path', or Dakshinachara – worshippers who seek purification and spiritual discipline by ritually surrendering to the 'divine Mother' in her many and varied forms – there has also arisen a 'left-hand path', Vamachara – those who practise licentious rites and sexual debauchery. We return to Tantra on page 82.

One final group of Hindu writings may be mentioned: the **Sutras**. The word literally means 'threads'; in the context of Hindu religion, it refers to short, often pithy, writings, either on specific subjects or as a summary of the Brahmanas, mentioned above. Some describe the performance of major sacrifices; others deal with household customs relating to birth, marriage and death; and a third group, the Dharma-Sutras, indicate the duties of the various castes and life-stations. These *Sutras* later gave rise to law books, such as the so-designated *Manu-Samhita*, allegedly emanating from Manu, the human progenitor. All systems of Hindu philosophy (*darshanas*) were originally written in *sutra* form, which perhaps helps to explain why some Western critics of Eastern philosophy, accustomed to logical, carefully shaped, 'rationally' structured presentations of arguments, are inclined to describe 'Eastern philosophy' as an oxymoron. However, the most famous Sutras, such as the Vedanta- or Brahma-Sutras and the Yoga-Sutras of Patanjali – to each of which we shall refer later – offer, it could be argued, depth of meaning to which the epithet 'philosophical' seems no misnomer.

These, then, are the writings to which Hindus refer, whether on a regular or occasional basis. They illustrate how far Hinduism is, as was remarked earlier, a many-sided philosophy, and not easily defined. So to move more closely towards an understanding of its central beliefs, we now need to indicate the six schools (*darshanas*, or systems) through which these beliefs have taken expression.

THE ORTHODOX SYSTEMS

The Sanskrit word for 'orthodox' is *astika*, and the key to the orthodoxy of the six systems is, as we have seen, their exponents' acceptance of the authority of the Vedas. Hindu scholars have always felt the need to debate the *meaning* of these writings, but their antiquity alone gives them a unique *status*. All six systems are, however, represented later in the *Bhagavad-Gita*, and this matter of fact should serve as a caution to anyone approaching the subject bearing Western prejudices: in particular, that schools of philosophy tend to contend with one another. The six schools certainly have different emphases, and some deal with issues that others leave alone, but none claims to have exclusive access to the truth, despite the fact that many Western enthusiasts look upon Advaita Vedanta, the sixth school, as the pinnacle of Hindu thought.

The systems are introduced here in no particularly significant order, but we may well start with **Nyaya**. This means, literally, 'to investigate fully' and relates to the science of discussion or debate. It is believed to have been founded by one Gotama (not to be confused with Gautama, the Buddha), whose dates are variously given as between the sixth and third centuries BC. He is credited with the authorship of the twelve-volume *Dharma-Shastra*, one of the classical Hindu law tomes, in which the themes of creation, transmigration and liberation are discussed. With these last two themes, we are already face-to-face with two of Hinduism's central tenets: reincarnation and enlightenment. Gotama expressed the basic principles of this school in the Nyaya-Sutras. What these principles affirm is that the process of exploring the great metaphysical questions, which could easily become one of vague and vapid generalities, must be accompanied by strict academic discipline, guided by logic and rationality. Consequently, the student should seek to understand the true nature of various categories of thought. These categories are right knowledge, the object of right knowledge, doubt, purpose, familiar example, established tenet, syllogisms, confutation, ascertainment, discussion, controversy, cavil, fallacy, equivocation, futility, and disagreement in principle.

Thus Nyaya can be seen as the analytical groundwork that underlies subsequent philosophical or religious enquiry; it is not unknown for Indian students of Eastern philosophy to spend four years studying it before proceeding to their chosen specialism. The classical commentator on the Nyaya-Sutras was Vatsyayana (*c.* fourth century CE), who described the system as 'the critical testing of the objects of knowledge, by means of logical proof'. (He is, however, probably better known as the author of the even more famous Hindu classic, the *Kama-Sutra*.)

The second school, and the oldest of the six systems, is **Vaisheshika**. It was founded in the second century BCE by a sage and, probably, priest named Kanada. Its name means, literally, 'referring to the distinctions' and is one of the earliest delineations of the different categories in nature (*padarthas*). It is often described as being scientifically rather than philosophically oriented, but this begs the question as to what is meant by science and what by philosophy. In the Vaisheshika-Sutra, Kanada listed the *padarthas* as sixfold: matter or substance (*dravya*); quality or characteristic (*guna*); activity (*karma*); universality (*samanya*); distinctiveness (*vishesha*); and inherence (*samavaya*), the relation between the whole and its parts, between the general and the particular, or between essence and substance.

There is a distinctly Western philosophical flavour in this account, which includes, among other issues, what we in the West would term linguistic analysis and epistemology. But Vaisheshika gives these matters a singular significance by affirming both that the fulfilment of certain duties leads to knowledge of the *padarthas*, and that this knowledge leads to enlightenment (*moksha*, to be discussed in Chapter 4). Thus again, by however improbable a route, we arrive at a central Hindu doctrine: and Kanada reinforced this by his assurance that the state of enlightenment was one in which the human affliction brought about by *maya*, or illusion, could be destroyed through a direct experience of the Self, with which all individual selves would finally be at one. This is the heart of Hinduism, and its unique contribution to religion.

The third and fourth systems should be studied in conjunction with each other, since one may be seen as the theoretical foundation of the procedures that the other advocates. The two are **Sankhya** and **Yoga**. The school of Sankhya was founded by a *rishi* called Kapila, about whom nothing else is known. No confirmed writings of his have survived, although a short text of fifty-four words called 'a summary of the truth' is ascribed to him. The earliest authentic Sankhya text, the Sankhya-Karika, dates from about the fifth century CE. However, despite these uncertainties, Sankhya emerges as a clear-cut, self-contained philosophy, with issues thoroughly explored and systematically developed. It cannot be accused of conceptual torpor.

Its basic thesis is that the universe comes into being (note the present tense) as a result of the union between two forms of reality: *purusha*, or consciousness, and *prakriti*, or nature. *Purusha* literally means 'man', or 'person', but in the context of Sankhya thought it refers to the original, eternal person, the highest Being, the Self, the Absolute, equivalent to the *atman* or self, particularly as this concept is expressed in Advaita Vedanta (see Chapter 4). As with the *atman*, there are as many *purushas* as there are living beings; and as with the *atman*, the end is union between the highest being and *brahman*, which is absolute being, absolute consciousness, the ground of all being. The spiritual reality that underlies the universe also permeates all creatures.

Prakriti is literally 'nature', or 'matter', and refers to the primal matter of which the universe consists. The structure of this matter is determined by three *gunas*, or fundamental qualities, which affect all objects of the world as we encounter it. The gunas are *sattva*, *rajas* and *tamas*. In the physical world, *sattva* embodies what is pure and expressive, such as sunlight; *rajas*, activity, such as lightning; *tamas*, immobility, such as a rock. In human terms they are expressed respectively as peace and serenity, activity and restlessness, laziness and stupidity. Sankhya taught that a person's character and mood were determined at any given time by the dominant *guna*. Most people might be expected to hope that this would be *sattva*, but Sankhya affirmed what is central in all the major systems of Hinduism: if the union of the Self and the individual selves is to be realised, even *sattva* must be superseded.

Sankhya teaches a fascinating, but highly complex, theory of evolution, called *parinamavada*. According to this theory (to express it with a simplicity that will cause Sankhya scholars to wince) there is a continuous process of evolution and involution in the universe. Evolution, or the emergence of the universe, occurs when *purusha* and *prakriti* are, for whatever reason, out of harmony with each other; involution is the reverse process, leading to a condition in which there is no universe, which happens when *purusha* and *prakriti* are in perfect accord. There has been, therefore, according to Sankhya teaching, an eternal process of the coming-into-being and the ceasing-to-be of universes. A universe now exists because the causal process, or interaction, between *purusha* and *prakriti* has entered a state of disharmony. But the ideal is the reverse situation, in which no universe exists at all: and, difficult though this concept is, we need to come to terms with it if our understanding of Hinduism is to be any more than skin-deep. How the basic theory of *parinamavada* is to be judged from a scientific perspective must be left to those with the knowledge and authority to be able to pronounce on the matter. Many may well feel, however, that it is no more beyond the bounds of human comprehension than are the pronouncements of contemporary astrophysicists.

The fourth system, Yoga, leaves aside these great imponderables and explores the philosophy of Sankhya in relation to the present human condition. It concerns itself with the here and now, and how to facilitate the process of harmonisation described in the Sankhya system. This approach, with its application at numerous levels, makes it the most accessible of all the Hindu systems, as many in the West have come to appreciate.

The name is derived from the Sanskrit word 'to yoke'. In this context, it is a question of yoking, or uniting, within oneself the twin forces of *purusha* and *prakriti*. As we have just seen in Sankhya, this means harmonising the physical body with the higher self (Atman) and, ultimately, uniting Atman with the absolute Self (Brahman, the ground of being). In some schools of Yoga, this is expressed in theistic terms, as union with God; in others, the philosophy of pantheism seems to emerge (although not in so many words). The significant factor is that, whatever the theological or non-theological thought patterns, its message is unambiguous: all people, of whatever religious persuasion, who seek union with the divine, however this is identified, can be described as being on the yogic path, if not actually *yogis* (those who have attained the highest spiritual levels, or sainthood). Thus Christian, Jewish or Islamic mystics, Tibetan Tantrists or Chinese Taoists, may join Hindu *gurus* or Zen Buddhist teachers in being designated *yogis*.

There is a universalise here that raises key issues, which will be discussed in Chapter 18.

As one of the six orthodox Hindu systems, Yoga originates in the Yoga-Sutras of **Patanjali**, who is dated variously between the fourth and second centuries BC. As a philosophy of life and means of spiritual growth, it predates the actual system by many centuries. Archaeological excavations in what is now Pakistan have unearthed statues of Lord Shiva and Parvan his wife performing different yoga positions: these statues are earlier than the Vedic age and the onset of Aryan civilisation. It seems that, from primeval times, there have been men and women who, while others were exploring the world around them, preferred to live alone in the mountains and forests and explore the world within themselves. Patanjali defined yoga as a means of mastering and uniting every aspect of the person. The physical body, the active will, the restless mind: all must be brought into a state of tranquillity in order to achieve spiritual harmony. He wrote these words, which will be a central idea of this book:

> Yoga is the settling of the mind into silence. When the mind has settled, we are established in our essential nature which is unbounded Consciousness. Our essential nature is usually overshadowed by the activity of the mind.

In the Yoga-Sutra, Patanjali outlined eight steps (known as the eight limbs) whereby this settled state may be achieved. These are:

yama — the laws of life.
niyama — the rules for living.
asana — the physical posture.
pranayama — rhythmic control of the breath.
pratyahara — withdrawal of the mind from sense objects.
dharana — concentration (on a single object).
dhyana — meditation.
samadhi (also known as *turiya*) — entry into the supraconscious state.

This is known as the path of Raja Yoga, or 'royal' yoga. The first two limbs are prerequisites for anyone who wishes to follow the path. *Yama* means self-control and consists of five ethical practices: non-violence (*ahimsa*); truthfulness (*satya*); not stealing (*asteya*); self-control (*brahmacharya*); and non-attachment, or non-covetousness (*aparigraha*). *Niyama* states the general principles from which the *yama* rules arise: outward and inward purity; contentment, or simplicity; strict concern about personal behaviour; reading the scriptures; and submission to God, however this concept is understood.

The next two limbs are related to the physical body. The purpose of *asana* is to find a position in which one can concentrate without the distraction that any discomfort would inevitably cause; rhythmic breathing, *pranayama*, is practised because the breath influences both thoughts and emotions. In the

West, these two steps tend to dominate the teaching of Yoga and are often viewed as the sole ends to be achieved. Patanjali's opinion was that they were in themselves beneficial, and his successors have, on the whole, held the same view: better to take a few steps than none at all.

Steps five and six complement each other: *pratyahara* means stilling the mind, emptying it of all daily cares and concerns; this helps to facilitate progress to the sixth step, *dharana*: concentration, usually on a particular object, such as a flower or the flame of a candle, to the exclusion of all other thoughts. With the mind disencumbered of superfluous matters, and fixed on a single goal, the way is prepared for *dhyana*, the *sine qua non* of the higher states of consciousness epitomised in *samadhi*. At the level of *dhyana*, the mind is no longer conscious of itself independently of the object of meditation but is, so to speak, absorbed in that object. The final state of *samadhi* is supraconscious, in which duality (the consciousness of the subject in relation to an object) ceases, and the world perceived by the senses no longer exists. It is equivalent to the 'Fourth State' of Vedanta, which will be described later.

There are a number of different types of *samadhi*, expressing different degrees of spiritual absorption, and of interest mainly to those who are far advanced in the Yogic path. This path, it should be emphasised, is open to all, whatever their strengths and weaknesses, their predilections and 'turn-offs': it is impossible to fail in Yoga, because there is a path for everyone. For those whose concern is for physical health (or, to give that word its derivative, wholeness) there is Hatha Yoga, the form normally taught in the West. *Ha* means 'sun', or positive energy, and *tha* means 'moon', or negative energy. The aim is to bring the two into harmony, causing equilibrium of body and mind. For those with strong social inclinations, there is Karma Yoga, the Yoga of action; for those with a bent towards abstract thought, Jnana Yoga, the Yoga of knowledge; those who seek what may be described as 'a closer walk with God' may turn to Bhakti Yoga, the Yoga of devotion; and we have already noted (page 23) Tantric Yoga, or Kundalini Yoga, the quest for spiritual growth through the awakening of certain centres of powerful energy in the body. There is yoga of music, of chanting, of visual imagery, and many more. Raja Yoga remains, however, the central and all-embracing expression of this system, linking it with the final two *darshanas*, which will receive only brief mention here, since they, particularly the second of them, will form the basis of much of the next chapter.

The fifth and sixth systems are both designated by the word **Mimamsa**, meaning 'investigation'. The first of these is **Purva-Mimamsa**, or 'earlier investigation'; the second is **Uttara-Mimamsa**, or 'later investigation'. The latter is generally known simply as Vedanta, meaning the end, or climax, of the Vedas; as a consequence, Purva-Mimamsa has, by a natural process of ellipsis, become known simply as Mimamsa.

Its teaching is based on the Mimamsa-Sutra, written by a *rishi* named Jaimini around the fourth century BCE. It is primarily concerned with ritual, since it was believed that the study and realisation of the philosophical and spiritual ideas expressed in Vedanta could be possible only after the cleansing experienced in the sacrifice of worship. Here arose a Catch-22 situation: it was deemed essential that the ritual be conducted correctly, yet the Vedas (in the Brahmanas) outlined these in a style that many would-be worshippers found virtually incomprehensible. Jaimini wrote his *sutra* as a commentary aimed at clarifying these complexities. How successfully it fulfilled this aim is indicated by the central role in Hindu life and worship still played by Purva-Mimamsa. Kurt Friedrichs (*EPR* 227) eulogises it in these words:

> The light of spiritual truth held in the Vedas finds its expression in the rhythmic perfection, the consummate style and the sublime poetry of the verses that are recited within the framework of Purva-Mimamsa.

Some scholars claim that they are the basis for the Greek mystery rites performed by Orphic and Eleusinian cults, which in turn prepared the way for the teaching of Pythagoras and Plato.

The sixth system, technically known as Uttara-Mimamsa but generally known as Vedanta, 'the end of the Vedas', is widely accepted, both in India and beyond, as representative of the highest peaks of spiritual experience. S. Radhakrishnan, the Hindu scholar (among other activities), wrote in *Indian Philosophy* (1962):

> Of all the Hindu systems of thought, the Vedantic philosophy is the most closely connected to Indian religion, and in one or another form it influences the worldview of every Hindu thinker of the present time.

The strength of this claim will be examined in the next chapter. Here we need finally to outline the three branches into which Vedanta can be divided: Dvaita Vedanta, Advaita Vedanta and Vishishtadvaita Vedanta. The key word is *dvaita*, or dualism: the experience of being aware of oneself as subject and the world, in whatever form, as object. In a religious context, *dvaita* expresses the belief that God and the believer are two, and will remain so for ever. This is a basic assumption of all theistic religions, of course, but is here expressed in Hinduism, which we shall see can hardly in general be characterised in that way.

Dvaita Vedanta's chief representative, Madhva (also known as Madhva-charya, or Anandatirtha), lived from 1199 to 1278. He suggested that there were five distinctions encapsulated in the term dualism: (1) between God and the individual soul; (2) between God and matter; (3) between the individual soul and matter; (4) between individual souls; and (5) between the individual elements of matter. Madhva therefore taught that there were in fact three realities, which would remain eternally separate – God, the soul, and the world – and this proposition takes us to the heart of religious enquiry. Madhva identified Brahman as the creator of the universe and the ultimate reality to which the world and the soul are subordinate. He equated Brahman with Vishnu, the divine being who has appeared in the world in various forms and moments in history. This sequence of divine incarnations is known as

avatars, or 'descents', and we shall look more closely at their significance in Hindu thought in the next chapter.

The school of Advaita Vedanta took a more radical view of the relationship between *brahman*, the individual soul (*atman*) and the world. Advaita means 'non-dualistic' and its central theme is that, since there is only one universal consciousness, *brahman* and *atman* are identical. Just as particle physicists have discovered that matter consists of continously moving fields of energy, so the *rishis* of this school have identified reality as energy in the form of consciousness (*chit*). The external world seems real to us only because of our ego, ensnared in our physical bodies. This state of illusion (*maya*) will be dispelled only when we attain enlightenment (*moksha*). The main protagonist of Advaita Vedanta was Shankara (788–820), whose teaching is the guiding feature of Chapter 4.

A lesser-known expression of Vedanta, midway between Dvaita and Advaita Vedanta, is *Vivishtadvaita Vedanta*, meaning 'qualified non-dualism'. It was founded by a South Indian philosopher and saint, **Ramanuja** (1055–1137). His ideal was *bhakti*, devotion, or the love of God, and he believed that all creatures, animate or inanimate, were what he termed 'forms of God'. This represents a more radical position than that of Dvaita Vedanta, but he was not prepared to accept the Advaita position. He believed that individual souls were, and must always be, dependent on, rather than identified with, *brahman*; and he viewed the world, with its qualities of truth, beauty and goodness, as possessing a reality of its own that he could not reconcile with the personal abstractions (as he saw them) of Advaita, although he continued to maintain a close, spiritually intimate relationship with those who could.

4   Hinduism II: Its basic teaching

As the preceding chapter should have indicated, there are many ramifications in Hinduism, both philosophical and religious, which have well-nigh overwhelmed many a novice in the field. To explore its labyrinthine paths comprehensively requires both a fixed resolve and virtually a lifetime of study and experience: here we can only assume the former and anticipate the latter. It is nonetheless possible to extrapolate some central ideas to which most, if not all, who call themselves Hindus are likely to subscribe; between them, they give Hinduism its essential and unique character.

The central drive of Hinduism, its view of the underlying aim of all life's activities, decisions, relationships and commitments, is the attainment of *moksha*. This word literally means 'enlightenment', in the sense of 'seeing the light'. It is the moment when scales are removed from the eyes, so that one recognises as real what had always been there to be seen, but to which one had previously been blind.

There are two parallel revelations which lead to *moksha*, one negative, the other positive (what Taoists would describe as *yin* and *yang*). The negative is the realisation that the world and all it has to offer is an illusion, *maya*: not in the sense that it does not really exist, but because its ability to satisfy human needs can never be other than temporary. Material objects will either decay or lose their appeal; skills and talents will decline with advancing years; relationships will either fall apart or end in death; not even the pursuit of scholarship can last for ever. As the Hebrew text Ecclesiastes, written in the second century BC, states repeatedly: 'All is vanity'; and the writer's words are echoed in an ancient Hindu saying: 'This world is a bridge: pass over it, and do not build your house upon it.'

This philosophy may sound pessimistic, but to those whose goal is *moksha* this would be a blinkered assessment, arrived at only by cushioning oneself from reality and living in a permanent state of delusion; as artificial and transitory as the euphoria gained from a bottle or a needle. *Maya* is held to be so all-pervasive that any goal in life that seeks to overcome its threat must be seen in a positive light. Of the four goals that Hindus recognise, *moksha* alone achieves this absolutely. This becomes apparent when it is compared with the other three goals: *artha* (wealth), *kama* (pleasure) and *dharma* (duty).

None of these is viewed as reprehensible *per se*, but if they become ends in themselves (which, as experience shows, they tend to do), *maya* triumphs.

It is important to be clear about the Hindu attitude here, since otherwise we might be identifying it, wrongly, with the ultra-asceticism and world-hating self-denial of the Jains (to be discussed in Chapter 5). The pursuit of *artha* is viewed as natural and, if it does not involve the destruction of other people in the process, even laudable. Wealth is neither good nor evil in itself: used for the benefit of others, it may be spiritually advantageous to its possessor. Only when it induces greed and leads its owner to lose sight of the ultimate end does it become a hindrance on the religious path: and, sadly, this is its propensity.

The fact that Hindus can make the same concession about *kama* is more significant. The word (not to be confused with *karma*, 'action', a concept that will feature later in this account) means 'pleasure', in the sense of sensual desire, and, in particular, sexual delight. We have noted (page 23) how sexual intercourse is used in Tantrism as a foretaste, if not actual experience, of the divine: and this is indicated in the *Rigveda*, which describes *kama* as the first stage by which the Absolute reveals itself:

> Desire [*kama*] arose in him who is the source of consciousness, whom the sages by examination have found in their hearts and who unites absolute being with the manifest world.

This seems to be making explicit what is implicit in the description of Jesus as 'the Son of God': to have a son, there must be *kama* on the part of the father. But Hindus are no less aware than are the Jains that the pursuit of *kama*, even more than *artha* (which is often directed toward *kama*), can divert people from the spiritual path. As in many religions, there is considerable ambivalence on this issue.

The third goal, *dharma*, refers to the basis of moral behaviour in the world, its underlying principles, such as justice, righteousness, benevolence. So far as the individual is concerned, it means the kind of behaviour that is viewed as a person's religious duty. Even more than *artha* and *kama*, it may be recognised that *dharma* can be observed without being deceived by *maya*; but, just as obviously, it can become an end in itself, so that *moksha* remains remote, eclipsed by the myopia often found among believers in duty for duty's sake. For Hindus, the extent to which *dharma* might lead to *moksha*, rather than be obscured by *maya*, depends on the individual's karmic situation, that is, his or her current position on the spiritual quest (see pages 37–40).

Maya is, then, a condition of cosmic ignorance (*avidya*), which is reflected in any individual who is deceived by it. It is the equivalent of what is known in Sanskrit as *ajnana*, the state of one whose eyes have yet to be opened by attaining *moksha*. Its opposite is *vidya*, or knowledge (equivalent, *jnana*), which can be interpreted both at a low level, in the sense of garnering information and experience, and at a higher, intuitive level, as a faculty that leads to liberation from *maya* and the acquisition of spiritual enlightenment. So far as Hindus of the Advaita-Vedanta school are concerned, however, even *vidya* needs to be transcended, since, like its opposite, *avidya*, it operates in the sphere of time, place and causality, and is consequently, and inevitably, an aspect of the world of the relative, not of the absolute. What this means brings us to the heart of Hinduism.

We could condense the positive aspect of *moksha* (positive, that is, in the sense of what is turned to, or embraced, rather than what is turned away from, or rejected – though the one, of necessity, cannot occur without the other) into the single succinct statement that may be made by anyone who has reached the state of *moksha*: *I am God*. For any Western reader, however, (and for not a few Hindus) the baldness of this assertion is likely to jar, and it must be tempered with an account of Hindu ontology, with particular reference to the teachings of Advaita Vedanta.

The key words are, as we have seen, *atman* and **brahman**, and it is necessary both to understand their meanings and to appreciate how they differ in implication from their Western counterparts. *Atman* is often translated as 'the soul', and, in the sense that it refers to an immortal element in human beings, contrasted with the mortal body, it is a reasonable starting point. In the West, however, the word 'soul' is used in so wide a range of senses that its meaning is often (and no pun is intended here) nebulous. Sometimes it means an alternative self to that represented by the body, as in Wordsworth's 'Ode on the Intimations of Immortality':

> The Soul that rises with us, our life's Star,
> Hath had elsewhere its setting,
> And cometh from afar.

Sometimes it means a human being, no more, no less, as when we describe a person as a 'poor soul', or in David Lodge's description of the British post-graduate student as 'a lonely, forlorn soul'. In other expressions the word implies the basic 'real' self, exemplified in Simone Weil's words in *The Need for Roots*: 'To be rooted is perhaps the most important and least recognised need of the human soul.'

Because of the confusion that is therefore inevitable if we translate *atman* as 'soul', it seems preferable to use the word 'self', in the sense of the underlying person represented by his or her physical actions, mental de-liberations and spiritual reflections; however, since all of these, including the last, are likely to be subject to *maya*, the word 'represented' could well be replaced by 'camouflaged'. The *atman* is the essential self, universally acknowledged to be a mystery, in the literal sense of 'that which is waiting to be unfolded, or revealed'. Hindus would argue that this condition is inevitable in the pre-*moksha* stage because only with enlightenment and the release from *maya* comes awareness of who or what one basically is.

The other key word, *brahman*, occurs throughout the Vedas and describes a number of related but contrasting ideas. Derived from a verb meaning 'to grow' or 'to expand', it literally means 'vast expanse', but is commonly translated as 'the Absolute' (note the upper-case: having no capitals, Sanskrit transliterations into European languages may be found with or without them). In the earliest Upanishads, the word refers to the primal creative (or procreative) source of the cosmos, the world that is made manifest. In this sense, there is little to distinguish *brahman* from the Creator God of other religions. Later, a pantheistic element was introduced, when it was taught that the universe and *brahman* were identical: 'All this is the brahman', it is stated (Chandogya-Upanishad III.14); *brahman* subsists in everything 'as a razor is hidden in a razor case' (Brihad-Aranyaka-Upanishad I.4.7).

The ultimate and essential theme of Upanishadic literature, however, gives a new and unique perspective to the debate: *brahman is identified with atman*. As the air inside a jar is substantially the same as that on the outside, though separated artificially by the glass, so the absolute ground of being is one with the basic self of every individual, but seemingly separated because of the blinkers brought about by *maya*. Once those blinkers have been removed through the experience of *moksha*, it becomes possible to make, with absolute assurance, the great affirmation (*mahavakya*) from the third Veda, '*Tat tvam asi*': 'Thou art that.' Each of the four Vedas contains a similar *mahavakya*; the other three are: 'I am that' (or 'I am *brahman*'); 'Consciousness is *brahman*'; and 'This self is *brahman*' (*Ayam atman Brahma*). All have overtones of the Hebrew word for God, Yahweh, meaning 'I am that I am', but they diverge from the Hebrew affirmation by discarding the implicit dualism of that word (since it refers only to God, not to human beings) in favour of *advaita*, or non-dualism. '*Tat tvam asi*' can be addressed to both the *brahman* and the *atman* because, as salt dissolved in water flavours all the water, so does *atman* pervade *brahman*:

> That which is the finest essence – this whole world has that as its soul. That is reality. That is *Atman*. That art Thou.
>
> (Shvetashvatara Upanishad VI.9.4.)

As we shall see in Chapter 9, there is a parallel here with the teaching of Taoism: the *Tao* is the 'Way', the equivalent of *brahman*; and the *Te* is the manifestation of the *Tao* in the life of any individual human being.

The affirmation '*tat tvam asi*' can be made authentically (that is, with the authority which comes from experience) only after the attainment of *samadhi*, the final limb of Yoga. In order to give those – and there are, of course, many of them – who are still on the path towards this an idea of what to expect when they arrive, Vedanta uses the phrase *sat-chit-ananda*, literally 'Being-consciousness-bliss'. It is an attempt to put into words what is ultimately inexpressible: the bliss referred to is not that which can be enjoyed through worldly activities since, worthy though these often are, they are inevitably clouded by *maya*. Rather, it is the unaffected absolute bliss found only when one is free from thoughts, anxieties, hopes, fears and suffering: in other words, as the word *samadhi* indicates, only when one has experienced divine consciousness. For this reason, every member of a certain monastic tradition in Vedanta who has become a *sannyasin* (that is, has surrendered all worldly concerns in the pursuit of *moksha*, and, having attained it, spends the rest of his or her days facilitating the path for others) is given a name ending in -ananda, such as (and probably the most famous) Vivekananda (1863–1902).

The 'certain tradition' referred to is that of **Adi Shankara** (788–820), who, more than any other Hindu teacher, drew out the teaching of *advaita* from the Upanishads and expounded it with wisdom and deep insight. Tradition has it that, from a very early age, he exhibited such deep spirituality that he was seen as the incarnation of Shiva, after whom his name is derived. He founded numerous monasteries, several of which still survive, and was a man of great versatility, being not only a mystic and a saint but also a philosopher, a poet, a scholar and a reformer (an earlier Martin Luther, perhaps, with saintliness added).

It was Shankara who first used the image of the air and the jar, mentioned earlier. The state of non-dual unity that this image illustrates was described by Shankara as the final state to which all human beings aspire, if not at present, then eventually. He was referring to one of the most famous sections of the Vedas, the Mandukya-Upanishad, where the view is propounded that human beings experience four states of consciousness (*avasthas*): the waking state (*jagrat*, or *vaishvanara*); dreaming sleep (*svapna*); deep, or dreamless sleep (*sushupti*); and *turiya*, which means, quite literally, 'the fourth'. *Jagrat* is the normal state of consciousness, both of oneself as subject and of the outside world as object: it is therefore a dualistic state. *Svapna* is also dualistic: in dreams, one is conscious still of oneself as subject and of the dream's characters as objects of that consciousness. With *sushupti*, however, we enter into a different state of consciousness, in which there is no longer mind or ego, and we cease to be aware either of ourselves or of the universe; it should accurately be described as a state in which all thought has ceased, rather than one of unconsciousness.

Turiya is also non-dualistic, but in a way quite different and, in Shankara's view, infinitely beyond *sushupti*. It is a state of absolute consciousness that defeats any attempt at description; effectively (though this statement is tautologous) only those who have known *turiya* can know it. Even the verb 'to know', with its connotation of *jagrat*, the dualistic state of awareness, is misleading. It must be understood in terms of *jnana* or *vidya*: knowledge that springs from insight, closer to intuition than to reasoning. The Mandukya-Upanishad is in fact more comprehensible when describing what it is not than what it is:

Neither subjective nor objective experience, neither knowledge of the senses, nor relative knowledge, nor derived knowledge ... [it is] pure, unified consciousness, unspeakable peace, nondualistic [*advaitam*] ... the nature of the *atman*.

This fourth state is also described as **brahma-chaitanya**, '*brahman*-consciousness', and, whatever afterwards may happen to one who has attained it, he or she can never be disabused about its reality. Shankara, in a famous image, describes the situation before and after achieving *moksha* as like a man in a darkened room who spends his time in terror because he believes a deadly poisonous snake to be over by the window. A moment arrives, however, when a gleam of light reveals to him that it is no snake, but simply the window-sash. From that moment his terror evaporates and will never return. Others may call out to warn him that he is risking his life by remaining in that room, but their fear does not touch him. He can laugh at his former terror for he now knows, absolutely, that it was based on an illusion. Now he has experienced *moksha*, and *maya* can no longer deceive him.

The first three states are symbolised in Vedanta by the letters A, U and M, making the sound 'OM'. This indicates that the *atman* combines the waking state, the dreaming state and the state of dreamless sleep. But the *atman* is more than these, since they do not include *turiya*, the fourth, the state of enlightenment. This is a state of silence, so no sound needs to be added to the A, U and M: OM therefore represents all four states of consciousness, and together they describe the *atman*. Ultimately, according to the Upanishad, the silence of the fourth state makes the other three redundant, so that the sound of OM can no longer be heard:

> The fourth is soundless: unutterable, a quieting down of the differentiated manifestations, blissful-peaceful, nondual. Thus OM is *atman*, verily. He who knows thus merges his Self in the Self – yea, he who knows thus.

OM is referred to in the Maitrayaniya-Upanishad as 'the sound of the soundless Absolute', and for this reason it is the most fundamental of all Hindu (and Buddhist) **mantras**: words or phrases repeated (or, in the case of OM, hummed) in meditation in order to bring the *yogin* or *yogini* (male or female practitioners of yoga) to a state beyond that of finite consciousness. Because the aim is to experience the numinous, the sound of OM has no literation; it is written as a symbol which, rightly understood, expresses and reinforces the meaning of the four states. OM, both as a sound and as a symbol, represents the Absolute, beyond time and space. As the Upanishad states:

> The past, the present, and the future – everything is but the sound *om*. And whatever else that transcends triple time – that, too, is but the sound *om*.

The sacred sentence *OM tat sat* – 'OM, that is Being', where 'that' refers to *brahman* – is found at the beginning of many books, and is written at the end of every chapter in the *Bhagavad-Gita*.

The poet Shelley, in his 'Adonais', already quoted, expresses a similar idea:

> The one remains, the many change and pass;
> Heaven's light forever shines, Earth's shadows fly;
> Life, like a dome of many-coloured glass,
> Stains the white radiance of Eternity.

It should be emphasised that entry into the fourth state does not mean that thereafter the *yogin/yogini* excludes the other three from his or her life. Most of them carry out their daily work, often, but not exclusively, as teachers: their entry into *turiya* is then a continual reminder of what, to them, eternity has in store. Heinrich Zimmer, in *The Philosophies of India* (p.376) states:

> The self-transforming change of emphasis becomes a well-known and controllable experience for the skilled practitioner of yoga. He can make the states come and go, their spheres appear and disappear, according to his will ... he can produce the subtle, fluid forms of the inward state of vision whenever he likes, fix them and retain them as long as he requires, and after that, again according to his wish, come temporarily back into touch with the exterior world. Such a virtuoso is not subject and exposed helplessly to the waking state, but enters it only when and as he wishes – his real abode, or homestead, meanwhile, being the 'fourth' at the opposite end of the series.

KARMA AND REINCARNATION

Having attempted to describe the significance of *moksha*, we need now to examine how Hindus perceive the hindrances to the arrival at this state, and the life-long, or, to be more accurate, lives-long process by which progress is generally made. One concept here is central, and we shall not understand the Hindu mind until we have come to terms with it: that of *karma*, or *karman*.

Its basic meaning is 'deed', or 'action'. It can mean ritualistic actions, but in Hindu thought it refers typically to the accumulated effect of moral behaviour, and the intentions that direct it. Everything we do creates *karma*, which we bear with us as part of an inexorable cycle of cause and effect, extending from the past through the present and into the future. What we do now has been affected by previous deeds, because the situations in which we now find ourselves, with their broad or narrow range of options, are themselves the product of earlier decisions, as they in their turn were products of decisions before them, and so on. Similarly, what we do now will fix the range of options open to us in the future, and, according to the action then taken, those available in situations beyond that, and so on. Furthermore, because the thoughts and actions that produce *karma* relate to concerns of the material world, the world of *maya*, it follows that, while the notion of 'good' *karma* versus 'bad' is not unheard-of, all *karma* is ultimately bad because it binds us to this world of illusion: it is the mechanism by which conditional existence maintains itself: existence, that is, which gains meaning only through activities characterised by *maya*, and therefore, by definition, ultimately unrewarding; so long as anyone remains subject to *maya*, this binding mechanism continues to operate.

The name for this process is *samskara*, meaning 'impression' or 'consequence'. It describes the tendencies in each person's character that have arisen as a result of thoughts, intentions and related actions throughout his or her existence: and for Hindus this includes not only this present life but also an indeterminate number of previous lives, or cycles of experience. That is to say, the concept of *karma* is linked with what Western theology describes as the transmigration of souls; in Hinduism the word is *samsara* (not to be confused with *samskara*, mentioned above). So long as one is subject to *karma*, the process of *samsara* is inevitable.

The word literally means 'journeying' and refers to the journey through many incarnations that is the lot of everyone until he or she achieves deliverance (see below). The view is that everyone experiences birth, or rebirth (the Sanskrit word is *punar-janman*) with the *karma* he or she accumulated in previous existences; throughout this present life, either deliverance is found or further *karma*, 'good' or 'bad', is added: and this in turn determines the starting conditions for the next cycle of experience. Thus *samsara* may be described as the domain of *karma*: the Varaha-Upanishad characterises it as 'a long dream (*svapna*), a delusion of the mind, a sea of sorrow'(II.64); the Maitrayaniya-Upanishad states that 'those who are liberated look down upon the samsara as upon a dizzily revolving wheel' (VI.28). *Samsara* is a state similar to that of drug dependency, with *karma* the drug on which it feeds: and as with many people so dependent, it is possible to have an attitude of mind that not only does not look beyond this state for what passes as fulfilment, but has no desire to do so.

Karma, then, spreads its tentacles timelessly, over the past, present and future, working itself out according to the laws of causality. These laws are illustrated by the three types of *karma* identified in the Vedas. The first of these is **prarabda-karma**, literally, *karma* that is the consequence of deeds (*karma*) begun (*arabdha*) before (*pra*): that is, *karma* borne in this life as a result of deeds performed in an earlier existence, the consequences of which are still working themselves out. As the arrow that has left the bow cannot be recalled, so, by a similar natural law, the effects of the earlier deed cannot be wiped out. (Our bodily constitution is a good example of this type of *karma*.)

Second, there is **sanchita-karma**, the accumulated *samskaras* or 'karmic deposits' (*ashaya*) that we built up in past lives and await fruition in some future life: these deposits are the network of subliminal *samskaras* (or activators) that form the subconscious or depth memory (*smriti*). This may or may not be the equivalent of the 'collective unconscious' described by the Western psychologist (and amateur orientalist) C. G. Jung, but Hindu teaching is that it affects our life span and life experience.

The third type of karma is **agami-karma**. This is the *karma* arising from actions in this present life, which will work themselves out, according to the same inexorable natural law of cause and effect, in some future existence. A distinction can be made between this and the other two types of *karma*: with them, there is absolutely nothing that can be done to bring about change: the natural law is operating, based on earlier decisions and inherited predilections. So far as *agami-karma* is concerned, however, we are dealing with future effects of present actions: actions, that is, which have either not yet been taken, or are only at the initial process of being taken. This means something that is absolutely basic and philosophically pivotal: we can influence our futures by our choice of present actions.

On the face of it, that statement sounds banal rather than pivotal, but the pivot is the word 'choice', which is redolent of implications for the whole theory. The doctrine of *karma* is often represented as deterministic, even fatalistic, and there are certainly elements of fatalism in the teaching. We are dealt a certain hand – through our parents, our genes, even our social background – and there is nothing we can do to change this. It is a harsh thing to say, but the sins, or the virtues, of one generation can be seen to have worked their way through 'unto the third and fourth generation', as the Old Testament frequently puts it: we simply have no choice over what we inherit from parents and grandparents. But at every point where we make a decision between alternative courses of action there is, according to the teachings of *karma*, genuine choice, and the same was true in the past when we made the decisions whose consequences we are experiencing now. The *karma* we get is the *karma* we have freely chosen, and nobody but ourselves is responsible for where or what we are. In Kierkegaard's words, we are, then, 'free to choose, free to be': the *agami-karma* we are about to accumulate will be the direct result of the choices we are about to make.

So there is both determinism and free will in this Hindu teaching, expressed succinctly by the first prime minister of independent India, Pandit Nehru, with the words, 'It's like a game of cards: determinism is the hand you're dealt: free will is how you play it.' Natural law fixes the hand: the rest is up to us. Just as Western existentialism, with its emphasis on libertarianism, or freedom of the will, emphasises our personal responsibility for the decisions we make by stressing our autonomy and the need for authenticity, so Hinduism affirms that where we are and what we are is the consequence, not of fate, but of our own freely made choices throughout aeons of existence. Thus an existentialist carries his own can, a Hindu his own *karma*.

This reflection may help to modify the critical attitude that Westerners usually adopt towards the Hindu **caste** system. This system, (in Sanskrit, *varna*) was first mentioned in the *Rigveda* and divides Hindus from birth into fixed social groups. The highest of these is the **brahmans** (*brahmanas*), or priestly caste; this comprises the educated class of religious and academic leaders: priests, scholars, philosophers. Then comes the caste of warriors (*kshatriyas*), comprising both military people and politicians and civil authorities. Third are the merchants and farmers (*vaishyas*): those who produce the nation's financial and economic resources, hence also known as the providers. The lowest of the four major castes is the **shudras**, the workers and servants. (Lower than these, however, are the untouchables, or outcasts (*pariahs*), who are outside the caste system: they are generally left to perform the most menial and undesirable tasks.

If this were a treatise on the sociology of India, a broad excursion would be needed here, along quite obvious lines. How rigidly the system stll operates is a matter for considerable (and often vituperative) debate. If it is becoming less rigid in its application (and the fact that an outcast became prime minister of independent India suggests that it may be) then it could be said that the system is returning to the original Vedic tradition, designed to order a complex society and to minimise rivalry and competition. The rigidity that we tend to associate with the system came about only after the Mogul invasion of India in the sixteenth century, with its introduction of stricter Islamic teaching, and it was not modified by subsequent colonial authorities. A reform movement in the nineteenth century set about dismantling the system gradually, and modern Indians such as Mahatma Gandhi have supported this process.

It is worth pausing to wonder, independently of the rights and wrongs of the system, whether there is any other country in the world that places its scholars and religious leaders in a higher category than that of its soldiers, politicians and businessmen: an affirmation of values that merits some reflection. Furthermore, while any defence of the system on the basis of the doctrine of *karma* may seem, on the face of it, to be an example of buck-passing, Vedanta teaches that *moksha* can be achieved by everybody, including the outcast. And even if enlightenment is not found in this present cycle of existence, the message is that all, of whatever background, will eventually find it: there is to be no final Day of Judgment, where the sheep are divided from the goats.

HINDU PHILOSOPHY – HINDU RELIGION

One final issue remains for consideration. Anyone who has visited India may feel justified in believing that the above, basically philosophical, outline of Hindu thought takes little account of the more popular expressions of Indian beliefs to be seen throughout the subcontinent, with individuals praying to their own private god or gods, and ritualistic acts taking place in temples and elsewhere, including rivers, streets and numerous other 'holy' places. We may start with the concept of the *avatara*, or avatar, meaning literally a 'descent', or incarnation of divine consciousness on Earth. An *avatara*, it is believed, occurs not because of *karma* (as we have seen to be the case with ordinary human beings) but through the free choice of one who, though enlightened, and therefore released from *samsara*, enters the world from time to time in order to give spiritual impetus to those struggling on the path to *moksha*. Precisely when an *avatara* has occurred is not a matter of chance but is related to the special needs arising from the circumstances of the time.

The traditional view is that only Vishnu, one of the Hindu trinity, or **trimurti** (alongside Brahma and Shiva: see below), is incarnated, and has appeared in ten forms, each relating to the era of the appearance: (1) Matsya, the fish; (2) Kurma, the tortoise; (3) Varaha, the boar; (4) Narasimha, the man–lion; (5) Vamana, the dwarf; (6) Parashu-Rama, or Rama the Axe-Wielder; (7) Rama of the Ramayana (see page 22); (8) Krishna; (9) Buddha; (10) Kalki, who has not yet appeared. A separate tradition includes Jesus as an *avatara* – a point that will be followed up in Chapter 18.

The other two divinities in the Hindu trinity are Brahma and Shiva. Brahma symbolises the principle of creation and the ontological necessity of being. Vishnu symbolises the sustaining force of the universe; hence it is logical that he should be seen as the one whose *avatara* is necessary when particular needs arise. Shiva, with his consort Shakti, or Kali, functions as the god of dissolution and destruction (that is, of *avidya*, or ignorance.) All three are interdependent, since everything in creation, after a period of sustained existence, experiences the process of destruction, to be followed by further creation, and so on. (We are again not far from the Chinese philosophy of *yin* and *yang*, to be discussed in Chapter 11.) The important point that links this more theistic approach with the non-dualism of Vedanta is that all three gods are viewed as manifestations of the One, with whom all Hindus expect ultimately to be united.

Modern Hindu worship divides itself into three main groupings, concentrated in different parts of India, and each of them holding different sections of the Vedas as central to its beliefs. On the one hand is Vaishnavism, followers of Vishnu, and subdivided according to which aspect of the god they worship. The followers of Shiva are the Shaivists, while the third group, believers in Shaktism, take their name from Shiva's consort, Shakti. This school is also called Tantrism, which was discussed on page 23. While Western writers often mention Brahmanism, after the third god in the trinity, it plays only a minor role in modern-day Hinduism.

In addition to the *avataras* there are Vedic hymns and prayers addressed to numerous *devas*, or minor gods, each with a special area of responsibility: thus there is Indra, the god of rain and thunder, Varuna, the god of sky, Usha, the goddess of dawn, Agni, the god of fire, and so on. Many of them are mentioned in the Vedas, and both Indra and Agni (for example) are described in different places as the greatest of all the gods. How can this be, and how does one accommodate the *devas* into the schema of the Six Systems?

It must be emphasised that, in a nation as large as India and a religion as widespread as Hinduism, it would be surprising to the point of miraculous if there were not a wide range of understanding of metaphysical issues between those with scholarly training at one extreme, and simple peasants at the other. There is a similar world of difference in Christianity between, say, Catholics in rural South America and Quakers in urban Britain.

I am grateful to Professor Sushanta Sen of Visva-Bharati University for the clarification he makes concerning the *devas* in relation to *brahman*. (*Concepts of the Ultimate*, ed. L.J. Tessier, ch. 11). He makes three points. The first is that the Vedas themselves acknowledge all gods and all *devas* to be no more than names or manifestations of *brahman*, the ground of being. For example: 'That which exists is one: sages call It by different names' (Rigveda I.90.3). Even more explicitly, a later Upanishadic text states: 'There is but One Being, not a second' (*op. cit.* p.91).

Sen's second argument is also aimed at dispelling the charge of polytheism sometimes made against Hinduism. He suggests that the *devas* are in fact presented as human beings who have built up such good *karma* (although without having yet attained *moksha*) that no earthly rebirth can compensate adequately; so 'after physical death he or she is reborn as a god [*deva*] in heaven to enjoy uninterrupted heavenly bliss'. Sometimes, when the saintliness of the individual on Earth has been exceptionally awe-inspiring, his or her reward may be to become the chief of these gods: Indra, Agni, or any other who had achieved that status at that time.

> But the lives of all these gods including Indra come to a definite end when their accumulated merits become exhausted by the enjoyment of heavenly pleasures and privileges; and after that they have to die from heaven as gods and be reborn again on earth as ordinary human beings within the process of . . . samsara.
>
> (*ibid.* p.89)

This explains, Sen suggests, why no god or *deva* remains as king of gods throughout the Vedas; and why Hinduism should not be equated with the polytheism of, say, the Greek or Roman theodicy.

Sen's final point is that the furthest the Vedas stray from monotheism is not into polytheism but to henotheism (see page 13). Whether this label fits a religion that hardly lends itself to Western delineations is a moot matter. The fact is that, so far as Hindus themselves are concerned, theirs is, quite simply, *sanatana-dharma*, 'the eternal religion': a claim to be tested in the latter part of this book.

5 The heterodox systems I

So far we have considered only the orthodox systems of Indian philosophy: those that acknowledge the authority of the Vedas and are designated *astika*. Besides these, however, India has given birth to an alternative group of systems, designated as **nastika**, or unorthodox (heterodox), because they reject that authority. This is not to say that they deliberately set out to deny the ideas and values expressed in the Vedas: only that they assert the right, where it seems appropriate, to modify them, disregard them, or add to them.

An important qualification must be made at this point. Although designated *nastika*, which can be translated as 'atheist', these systems have not, with the exception of Charvaka (see below), been viewed generally as alien to Hinduism. The most widespread example of a *nastika* system is in fact Buddhism, which will be studied in detail in the ensuing chapters. Yet Buddha, however heterodox in his beliefs, was held, as we saw in the last chapter (page 40), to be the ninth avatar (descent, or manifestation), of Vishnu. This means that we simply have to overcome our typically Western designation of different belief systems as 'true' or 'false': the Hindu view is that all roads lead to the mountain-top where *moksha* is to be experienced, and if some paths seem to stray widely from the most favoured routes, that is generally accepted as a matter for individual choice. (The mountain imagery of the spiritual quest is popular with Eastern teachers, reflecting the terrain in which it takes expression.)

CHARVAKA (CARVAKA)

In terms of the issues raised throughout this book, this system is important only because it affirms what all the others either ignore or deny. It is not mentioned in H. Zimmer's comprehensive *The Religions of India*, although it is included in the *Source-Book in Indian Philosophy* by Rhadhakrishnan and Moore. This is clearly because, while Eastern thought generally oscillates between being a religion and being a philosophy, Charvaka belongs unambiguously in the philosophy camp. Its importance as a catalyst for other Indian thought, however, will be apparent as we proceed.

Charvaka was a philosopher who lived around the sixth century BCE. We know nothing about him except that he is held to be the author of the Barhaspati-Sutra, on which his philosophy is based. This writing is lost: all we can glean about it is from references to it (mainly hostile) in much later works, particularly by Jainites and Buddhists. The philosophy that it expresses is called **Lokayata**, *loka* meaning 'this world', and *yata*, 'real' or 'existing'. It affirms that the only reality is the material world, the existence of which our senses confirm. The rest, including the so-called spiritual or numinous dimension, is illusion, not in the sense of *maya*, which, as we have seen, refers to the impermanent and ultimately unsatisfying nature of what the world has to offer, but, quite unreservedly, because it is based on self-deception, even wishful thinking. Perception is the sole basis or source of knowledge, and consequently only the objects of perception are real. All that the universe consists of, and ever will consist of, are the four elements: earth, air, fire and water.

A fourteenth-century CE work on Charvaka, entitled (rather dauntingly) *Sarvasiddhantasamgraha*, expresses this idea succinctly:

> Only the perceived exists; the unperceivable does not exist, by reason of its never having been perceived; even the believers in the invisible never say that the visible has been perceived ... If the rarely perceived be taken for the unperceived, how can they call it the unperceived? How can the ever-unperceived, like things such as the horns of a hare, be an existent?
>
> (2,3)

If matter is all that there is, it follows, according to Charvaka, that there is no soul and no afterlife. The soul has no existence apart from the body, and its apparent existence is accounted for as a manifestation of, variously, the body, the breath, the senses and the brain. And since there is no divine being, there can be no divine providence, or any form of morality based on the divine will. Those who look in this direction, with its alleged reward in the life beyond, are weaklings (there are anticipations of Nietzsche here):

> There is no world other than this; there is no heaven and no hell; the realm of Shiva and like regions are invented by stupid imposters.
>
> (*ibid.* 8)

The natural outcome of this philosophy is thoroughgoing hedonism, since there exists only the world of material things to be enjoyed. The obvious procedure is therefore to go ahead and enjoy; and, since life is short and one is a long time dead, one should grab all one can while one can. This is the philosophy characterised in the New Testament as 'eat, drink and be merry, for tomorrow we die'; the *Sarvasiddhantasamgraha* states:

> The enjoyment of heaven lies in eating delicious food, keeping company of young women, using fine clothes, perfumes, garlands, sandal paste etc. ... while liberation [*moksha*] is death which is the cessation of life-breath ... The wise therefore ought not to take pains on account of moksha;

it is only the fool who wears himself out by penances and fasts . . . Chastity and other such ordinances are laid down by clever weaklings.

(9,11,12)

We are here in an epistemological and axiological scene (that is, of theories of knowledge and assessment of values) set widely apart from that of not only the Six Systems but also the other two heterodox schools. The next of these that we shall consider is in fact as far removed from Charvaka as it is possible to imagine.

JAINISM

The name of the second heterodox system, **Jainism**, is derived from the word *jina*, meaning 'conqueror': the aim of Jainism is to conquer the evils of the world and achieve salvation, liberation, or *nirvana* – a key concept, as we shall see, in Buddhism, but given a different connotation by the Jains. They believe that, over many aeons, there have been twenty-four *jinas*, also termed *tirthankaras*, or 'ford-crossers', who have passed over from this stream of existence to the 'other shore'. From there they continuously facilitate the crossing for those who desire to follow them.

The last of the twenty-four *tirthankaras* was **Mahavira**, literally 'great hero', a contemporary of Buddha (Jains fix his dates as 599–527 BCE) who systematised the doctrines of Jainism and effectively established the direction it would take. His predecessor, the twenty-third *tirthankara*, was Parshva, who died nearly 250 years before Mahavira's birth; but Parshva's mythological predecessor is dated eighty-four millennia earlier, which indicates how deeply shrouded in antiquity Jains believe their religion to be.

Mahavira was himself raised as a Jain, withdrew around the age of thirty from the world of family (he had a wife and daughter) and financial commitments, and became a Jain monk. After twelve years of asceticism he achieved 'omniscience', which for him meant release from the bondage that the concerns of the world brought about. The rest of his days he spent in teaching and organising his followers, exhibiting a depth of self-denial and saintliness that appear to have marked him out from all the rest.

Not surprisingly, Jainism expresses certain beliefs that seem on the face of it to be not dissimilar to those of the surrounding Indian culture. Like Hinduism, Jainism holds that this world is an illusion, from the snares of which one needs to be freed if permanent fulfilment is to be found; like Hinduism, it expresses the doctrine of *samsara*, the transmigration of souls in a continuing round of reincarnations; like Hinduism, it teaches that each rebirth is the direct consequence of earlier lives and decisions then made; like Hinduism, it holds that the overcoming of *karma* is the key to enlightenment; and, like Hinduism, it offers yogic meditation as a positive way of achieving this.

When we look more deeply at Jainite teaching, however, it soon becomes apparent that all these ideas and beliefs, built into an elaborate system, are given a distinctive emphasis, which will emerge if we start with the Jainite view of the cosmos, and the nature and destiny of those who inhabit it. The image is of a gigantic human figure, with the world as we experience it situated roughly around the waist. Each person, with each successive incarnation, will rise higher or lower, through a succession of heavens or hells, according to his or her deeds. The aim is to reach the highest pinnacle, the temple, which is where perfect serenity and liberation are found. There the souls of those who have followed the ford-crossers will remain eternally motionless. In terminology that is generally associated with Buddha, this is *nirvana*, a state of perfect tranquillity, perfect knowledge and perfect power. The Jains describe this as *kevala*, the state in which one no longer has anything to do with the multifarious forms of the manifest world.

The important factor here, which differentiates Jainism from all systems of Hinduism, is that there is neither God nor *brahman*: Jainism is atheistic. Each person is held to be a duality of the immortal soul, or *jiva* (the conscious) and the mortal body, *ajiva* (the unconscious). Only by total rejection of the demands of the body can the *jiva* make progress; and this means, so far as Jains are concerned, that no distinction can be made between 'good' *karma* and 'bad'; since even good deeds require involvement in the world of *ajiva*, they cannot facilitate the *jiva*'s release from the cycle of *samsara*.

It may be argued that, if even the slightest dependence on *ajiva*, or material substances, is detrimental to the attainment of the omniscient state of *kevala*, which is what those at the highest peak of the cosmos are believed to have achieved, nobody can possibly make it, since, as King Lear cried in desperation, 'our basest beggars are in the poorest thing superfluous'. The Jains are conscious of this logistical problem but are unconcerned, for two reasons. The first is hinted at by the length of time that, in Jainite mythology, has elapsed before arriving at this moment: probably millions of aeons if the chronology of the *tirthankaras* is to be followed. Darwin defended the theory of evolution with the statement, 'Nature has all the time in the world'; and Jains take an equally long-term view of the soul's progress to perfection. The dimensions of the cosmic man also confirm the length of time to be contemplated: it is fourteen *rajjus* high, a *rajju* being the distance one could travel in six months at a speed of two million miles per micro-second.

The second Jainite reaction to King Lear's viewpoint is to accept the fact that it is bordering on the impossible to be totally free from all worldly attachments, but to demonstrate that it is possible to take radical steps towards total detachment. The Jain life-style, certainly for those who have entered the monastic order, has therefore become a byword for the most stringent form of asceticism that it is possible to imagine, demanding the renunciation of all physical comforts and, if necessary, social constraints. The Jains term this a life of *tapas*, or total austerity: all personal possessions are relinquished. For one group this includes any kind of clothing, since even the wearing of rags reflects an element of worldly attachment. Those who follow this way are called the **Digamambara**, or sky-clad; their numbers are fewer than in earlier centuries, most Jains now belonging to the **Svetambara**, or white-clad group, in which each monk or nun wears three pieces of simple white cloth.

This austerity is one of the five virtues that Jains practise in accordance with their 'great vow', or **Mahavrata**. Three other virtues specified in the Mahavrata find a parallel in numerous religious and secular contexts: truth-speaking, non-stealing and chastity; the fifth virtue has, however, become a hallmark of Jainism: *ahimsa*, or non-violence. The Jains were the first to make this a fundamental rule of life, and they apply it as totally and as consistently as is possible. The familiar picture of the Jain monk or nun is of one who wears a piece of gauze over the mouth, preventing the accidental inhalation of an insect, and brushes the ground ahead when walking to avoid accidentally treading on even as 'anti-social' an insect as a mosquito.

They are of course vegans; but even the eating of fruit, vegetables and nuts involves violence against living entities, so they drink only water, and eat only the minimum, chiefly grains, that is required in order to sustain life. Even this is accepted as being under the cloud of *karma*: the ultimate act of non-attachment is, as Mahavira is believed to have done, to cease taking any kind of sustenance whatsoever and effectively commit suicide. This happens occasionally in Jainite monasteries; it is normally, but not invariably, under-taken by the old, and is seen by fellow monks and nuns as a sign that the aspirant is psychologically and spiritually ready to take a great step forward.

It should be emphasised that, while lay Jains attempt to follow as far as possible the path taken by their monastic colleagues, modifications in the life-style have to be made, inevitable when they are committed to the natural processes of family life. Because no Jain can be involved in any profession that involves violence, many of them have become successful in business and commerce. This is recognised as being subject to karmic forces, but the income they earn allows them to help in alleviating the distress of sick and needy sentient beings, and to give alms to their monastic colleagues. In any case, if challenged about the apparent inconsistency of, on the one hand, believing in the virtue of non-attachment and, on the other, being successful in business, Jains would state that this is no more than an indication that they have further incarnations to experience before they may attain the higher spiritual levels. In many other ways lay Jains accept a discipline not dissimilar to that of their monastic colleagues: chastity (not to be confused with celibacy, although among monastic Jains there is is no physical contact at all between the sexes); vegetarianism; abstaining from intoxicants; regular attendance at religious festivals and worship; and the practice of *dhyana*, or deep medita-tion. This way of life, it is believed, enables lay Jains to move closer to the ideal of perfect knowledge (*kevala*) and may encourage non-Jains to take tentative steps towards it.

Jainism, however, is not a proselytising religion: not because of the harshness of their life-style (which might be expected to deter even earnest seekers after truth, as it did the young Buddha) but because of their view of history. They believe that there have been continual cycles of spiritual experience, up-cycles (in this sense) alternating with down-cycles, and each lasting for many aeons. We are at present, it is believed, approaching the end of a down-cycle, so that converts are likely to be rare in numbers, and the age one of spiritual shallowness. As it is, although relatively few in numbers (there are estimated to be between two and three million in India today), the influence of the Jains, like that of the Quakers in the United Kingdom (fewer than 50,000), far exceeds what might be expected of so small a percentage of the community.

If my suggestion in the first chapter is correct, that belief in a deity is essential for a religion to be so characterised, then Jainism is not a religion. However, the Jain belief in the immortal soul, the *jiva*, which is on its journey to the peak of the cosmos and the eternal state of motionless contentment, *kevala*, implies that, effectively, the Jainite aim is to become as gods are often described by adherents of movements that are acknowledged to be religious. The aim, to use familiar Hindu terminology, is to free the *atman* from the shackles of the physical body, which is attached to the material world of karmic forces. Vedanta teaches that this aim is achieved through *moksha*, the realisation that the *atman* and the *brahman* are one. Jainism teaches that *moksha* is the moment when the *atman* (*jiva*) is recognised as itself the ultimate reality.

The temptation is always present in the minds of some Jainite worshippers to promote the ford-crossers (the *tirthamkaras*), to the status of gods (as we shall see to be the case in some expressions of Buddhism). The most frequent objects of Jain veneration, however, are not these mythical or quasi-mythical figures but the ascetics of the present, those who have taken the great vow, *mahavrata*, and express extreme asceticism, *tapas*, in their daily lives. *Tapas* means, literally, 'heat', and those who have met these ascetics state that they do in fact generate a mysterious heat, together with power over both themselves and their surroundings. These *yogis* create a sense of awe to which even awe of the gods is subservient. It is typical of Indian thought generally (we have seen it in Hinduism and will discover it again in Buddhism) that ultimately salvation is to be found by following one's own path, using the powers, brought about by spiritual insight, that one builds up in oneself, rather than through any cult of the gods. Whether the personal self-mortification central to Jainism is in fact a necessary condition for the achievement of this state, or whether it is possible to attain this through a less rigorous life-style, will be an issue in the study of Buddhism that follows.

To demand a clear-cut answer (that is, either 'yes' or 'no') to the question of whether Jainism is a religion or not would, in any case, be a sign to the Jains that the questioner did not understand their view of logic. Although strictly a philosophical matter, this view has implications for issues raised in the second half of this book, and it needs to be decribed briefly at this point.

The central feature of the Jain attitude to logic is that knowledge – that is, human knowledge here on Earth – can never be more than partial, so that it is impossible to make an absolute statement about anything: only with the omniscience gained when *kevala* has been achieved (at the peak of the Cosmic Man) can that be possible. Meanwhile, we must content ourselves with what is always relative – to time, place, circumstances and, above all, perspective. This is the Jain doctrine of *syadvada*, literally 'it may be' (*syat*) 'teaching' (*vada*): the view that reality has many aspects (*anekantavada*, 'not-one teaching'), as opposed to *ekantavada*, the doctrine that reality has a single nature, about which absolute statements can be made.

For Jainism, the consequence of syadvada is that even the most affirmative statement about anyone or anything can only be provisional or concessionary. Implicit, if not explicit, in every statement is such a phrase as 'it may be', or 'in a certain sense': key words are 'somehow' and 'perhaps'. Everything depends on one's standpoint, or point of view (*naya*): the doctrine of *nayas* is that reality is many-sided, so that, when any statement about it is being discussed, the side from which it is being viewed, the speaker's premise, must be identified.

There are, according to *syadvada*, seven possible standpoints (*saptabhangi*), and only seven. These comprise the seven possible combinations of an affirmative statement, a negative statement, an either confirmative or negative statement, and a statement to the effect that the subject under discussion is indescribable. These give us seven forms:

1 Somehow a thing is.
2 Somehow it is not.
3 Somehow it both is and is not.
4 Somehow it is indescribable.
5 Somehow it is and is indescribable.
6 Somehow it is not and is indescribable.
7 Somehow it is, is not, and is indescribable.

This may seem an abstruse matter, hardly related to the issues of this book. But if it is the case that statements relating to issues raised in religious discussions, including those raised here, may be true from one point of view, but not from another, then this will profoundly affect any discussion of issues like the existence of God, the death of God, the immortality of the soul, the freedom of the will, the authority of religious texts, and so on. If there is no absolute, then all these matters are thrown, so to speak, into the melting-pot.

Critics of Jainism argue that the consequence of accepting this relativist stance is not only that nothing can be said 'for certain' about anything, but also that two self-contradictory statements can be made about the same thing. Whether this is the case or not, and, if so, whether it puts any kind of barrier on religious discussion, is a matter for later analysis. The Jainite answer is that contradictory statements cannot be made about the same thing if they are made at the same time and from the same perspective, but that normally this unity of perspective does not take place, so that contradictory statements need to be discussed in the light of the doctrine of *syadvada*.

If we do that, maybe the division between one who denies and one who affirms the existence of (for example) God may be found to be a difference in standpoint rather than of values and spiritual beliefs. The Jainite would simply ask: from what point of view does the self-confessed absolutist speak? We shall reflect in Chapter 18 on the extent to which this relativist perspective is the great contribution to the world's religions made by the Indian subcontinent.

6 The heterodox systems II
Buddhism 1: Philosophy

The literal meaning of the word **Buddha** is 'the awakened one', one who has gained enlightenment. **Buddhahood** is therefore a state, equivalent to the Hindu doctrine of *moksha*, that all sentient beings may seek with confidence. We tend to associate 'Buddha' primarily with one particular individual, but at the heart of Buddhist philosophy lies the assurance that we are all capable of achieving buddhahood because, whether we are aware of it or not, we all share 'Buddha nature'. What is needed, if we are to realise this truth for ourselves, is that our eyes should be opened, like those of the man described by Shankara concerning the snake and the rope (see page 36). However, the path taken by Buddha differed in several ways from that of his native Hinduism, so that his teaching came to be viewed by Hindus as unorthodox (*nastika*). How far this was a fair or reasonable assessment should emerge from what follows.

On the face of it, Buddhism is a straightforward philosophy and therefore easy enough to describe. If we were to concentrate entirely on Buddha's own teaching, as does many a short primer, this might well be the case, but the history of Buddhism is – unlike Hinduism – one of expansion, and cross-fertilisation with other Eastern cultures and belief systems. In this process, many of Buddha's original ideas were developed or modified to such an extent that it is difficult to draw a dividing line between 'basic Buddhism' and Buddhism as it is now variously taught worldwide.

The procedural method that I have adopted, therefore, is to consider first Buddhist *theory*, then, in Chapter 7, the Buddhist *way of life*. In Chapter 8 I outline some of the more important Buddhist ideas and practices expressed in China, Japan and Tibet. This procedure means that particular care must be taken with the chronology of this chapter and the next. Here we follow Buddhist philosophy from its earliest expression to some of its most significant later developments, particularly Nagarjuna, in the belief that, while Buddha did not state these later ideas explicitly, they are a natural extension of his philosophy (this is certainly how most Buddhists perceive them: students of Christianity should sympathise with the problem involved). This means that occasionally we leap ahead in the account of Buddha's development in order to pursue an issue to its conclusion (or, at least, to a major later development). We then return – and the start of Chapter 7 is a prime example of this procedure – to the point of departure. The approach is, therefore, thematic rather than chronographic.

BUDDHA

The man who is universally known simply as 'the Buddha' was born Siddhartha Gautama in northeastern India around 563 BCE and lived for eighty years. He was thus one of the many creative thinkers who between them made that century expressive of what has been termed 'the white heat of pure original thought, paralleled in human history only by the Enlightenment'. It was the century of Confucius and Lao Tzu, the Taoist, in China; of Zoroaster in Persia; of Mahavira, founder of Jainism, in India; of the great Jewish prophets – Jeremiah, Ezekiel and the so-called 'second Isaiah'; and, for the West most important of all, of many Greek philosophers and artists, such as Parmenides, Pythagoras, Xenophanes, Aeschylus, Aesop and Thespis; together with the 'seven wise men of Greece', creators in Athens of the embryo of democracy. The phenomenologist Jaspers described theirs as 'the Axial Age', and one wonders how they might have inter-related if modern means of communication had been open to them.

Siddhartha Gautama was born into a noble clan, the Shakya, from which another name by which he is known – **Shakyamuni** – is derived. This means 'silent sage of the Shakya clan', an epithet given to Siddhartha after he had left the clan to find the way to enlightenment for himself. ('Shakyamuni Buddha' is a title now used to distinguish the historical Buddha from other Buddhas.) Tradition tells of a man born into a prosperous family with a powerful position in the local community. Siddhartha was raised in a princely fashion, married at the age of sixteen, and had one son. It seems that his father did all he could to shield him from the poverty and general hardship that was prevalent in the state. He must have been vaguely aware of the divide between his own comfortable condition and the destitution of many of his fellow citizens, but this imbalance does not seem to have impressed itself upon him until he was 29. At this age he encountered what is known in Buddhist lore as the '**Four Signs**', and they were to change his life radically and, six years later, after his experience of total awakening (see page 53), permanently.

The four signs were encounters that Siddhartha had with four men who, between them, brought him face-to-face with poverty and destitution, awakening him to the pain of existence and the inescapable fact of the mortality from which nobody and nothing is exempt. They were:

- an old man;
- a mortally sick man;
- a dead man;
- a wandering ascetic.

These encounters brought home to him the pervading presence of suffering (*duhkha*) so profoundly that he decided that he could no longer continue to live the sheltered, privileged existence that he had till then experienced. He left his family home for ever and became a wandering mendicant, debating the problem of suffering with *yogis* and ascetics, most of whom had concluded that the way to counter it was by self-denial, to the point of the extreme self-mortification practised by the Jains, as described in Chapter 5.

None of this brought him the peace of mind he was seeking, although he spent six years in the quest. During this period he certainly learned to control the bodily appetites and thereby establish in himself an inner strength that was to add to the authority he would evince throughout his later ministry. What he found, however, was that his rigorous life-style made little difference to his inner sense of dissatisfaction: for all his self-denial, his life, as he perceived and assessed it, remained meaningless: self-denial for its own sake proved to be ineffectual (as, two millennia later, Luther was to find in his monastic cell) as a means of achieving inner harmony. As a result, Buddha spent these years feeling on the edge of a vital discovery but without being able to remove the blinkers that hid it from him.

Then came the event that was to provide the breakthrough and bring Buddhism as a philosophy, if not a religion, into being. Disillusioned with all that the ascetics had affirmed, Shakyamuni went to a remote place near Gaya, 60 miles south of Patna in northeast India. There, for forty-nine days, he sat in deep meditation under a fig tree. This is now known as the **Bodhi-tree**, meaning the tree of awakening, for it was there that Shakyamuni achieved perfect enlightenment and became a Buddha. The place is called Bodh-gaya, and the 'grandchild', a scion of the original tree, still stands near the Mahabodhi temple, a natural focal point of Buddhist pilgrimages.

An obvious comparison to make here is with the forty days and nights that Jesus spent in the wilderness prior to the beginning of his ministry. The difference is that we are simply not told anything about Jesus's reflections during that time, whereas we have, from Buddha's own subsequent teaching, an awareness of the condition to which his prolonged inner absorption brought him, indicated by the use and meaning of the word *bodhis*. This was a concept with which Buddha would have been familiar, since it was frequently spoken of in the prevailing Hindu tradition, in which the four stages of the supramundane path, *arya-marga*, the way to enlightenment, were referred to. These stages were defined in the Vedas as:

1 Freedom from doubt, and from dependence on rites and rules;
2 Freedom from the 'unwholesome roots': sensual desire, hatred and delusion;
3 Freedom from the chains of self (the ego);
4 Freedom from defilements and passions (*asrava*), and from the blindness of ignorance (*avidya*): the attaining, in a word, of *nirvana*, a state of 'no more learning' (because this is a state of perfection).

While, therefore, as we shall see below, Buddha's account of his Bodhi-tree experience was to create a new way of thinking in the world of philosophy and religion, it is important to recognise that, although his way was certainly a deviation from the surrounding Hinduism, it was not an attempt to uproot it. Some might say that, like Jesus apropos of Judaism, he came to fulfil rather than to destroy. It seems, for instance, that Buddha's experience under the Bodhi-tree included his passing through all the stages of the *arya-marga* as taught in Hinduism and outlined above. This may help to explain why it was that, though they held him to be unorthodox, the Hindus were eventually to accept Buddha as an incarnation of Vishnu.

NIRVANA

Where Buddha's account of the Bodh-gaya experience moves into a different form of thought from that of Hinduism is in his unequivocal claim: 'I have obtained *nirvana*.' Since all his subsequent teaching assumed this to be the ultimate goal of all seekers after enlightenment, its meaning should rightly be clarified at the start, and it might be thought that, with so well-used a word, this would be a straightforward task. This is not, however, the case: Buddha's statement is certainly simple enough, but this key word remains open to many interpretations.

In Sanskrit it means, quite literally, 'extinction': 'blowing out', as of a candle. In the Upanishads it is the same as *turiya*, the fourth state; in Yoga it is *nirbija-samadhi*, 'seedless *samadhi*', because all seeds of future *karma* have been destroyed; in Vedanta it is *nirvikalpa-samadhi*, 'changeless *samadhi*', the highest transcendent state, in which is realised the concept, 'I am *brahman*'. In the *Bhagavad-Gita* it is in fact termed **brahman-nirvana**.

Buddha's own interpretation is not easily summarised, since he declined to make any positive statement about the nature of *nirvana*. What can be affirmed is that it accords with the received Hindu view that its attainment brought release from *samsara*, the continuous cycle of reincarnations (or, to use his word, rebirths – see page 38) and entry into a different mode of existence. Further, Buddha agreed that it could not be achieved without experiencing the four stages of *bodhis*, and, in particular, the overcoming of the three unwholesome roots, desire, hatred and delusion: and that this could involve many rebirths. He agreed that *nirvana* required the coming to rest of all desire, or active volition (*samskara*); that it meant freedom from the inescapable effects of *karma*; and that it is *unconditioned* (*asamskrita*): in other words, it is beyond the world of causality, of things coming into existence, passing through existence, changing, and passing away. In many respects this teaching echoes the traditional Hindu concept of *maya*: but Buddha gave the concept of *asamskrita* a distinctive stamp with his affirmation of the three so-called **Marks of Existence**. These 'marks' will be discussed separately as we proceed but may conveniently be named at this point. According to Buddha, everything that is conditioned is:

1 insubstantial, or lacking soul (*anatman*);
2 impermanent (*anicca*);
3 characterised by suffering (*duhkha*).

What emerges from the discussion so far is an emphasis on what *nirvana* delivers us *from*: and, since this was Buddha's own main concern, it will occupy most of what remains in this chapter. What people also wish to know, however, is what it liberates us *to*: and here we reach an impasse, since subsequent schools of Buddhism have interpreted Buddha's own silence on the matter in a variety of ways. Taking the literal meaning of the word, blowing out, as of a candle-flame, it becomes immediately apparent that the question of *where nirvana* is located cannot be answered because it is a meaningless question: as meaningless as asking where a candle-flame goes when it is blown out. It cannot be described as going north or south or east or west, or up or down; nor can it be described as either one (or more) of these options or another one (or more) of them; nor can it be described as all of these, or a combination of them; and it cannot be described as none of these. All one can say is that, having been blown out, the flame, or what constitutes it, enters into a different mode of existence. All that Buddha would say about it was that it is a state in which the flames of desire have been eliminated; that some (like himself) might enter into this state during the present cycle of experience; that, having entered, they would know not only what it was but also that it was indescribable to those who had not yet found it; and that for most of his contemporaries this ultimate prize would be achieved not in the present but in a subsequent rebirth. If it happened, however, it would mean that all karmic effects had been annihilated, so that, as a direct consequence, no more rebirths would be required.

So is the state of *nirvana* similar to the bliss of union with *brahman* as expressed in Vedanta teaching? Hardly, since Buddhism was agnostic about God, whether thought of in theistic terms or as the ground of being. Is it a state of perpetual bliss, akin to the Jainite view of the eternal quiescence and perfect knowledge (*kevala*) experienced as the climax of the aeons-long spiritual quest? Or is it, quite simply, annihilation, for which the Sanskrit word, significantly, is *parinirvana*, the final release from this world of tragedy and frustration: to sleep with no chance to dream?

Buddha's answer to these and similar questions was: 'neither yes nor no'. For this, he, and his followers who spoke similarly, were described by their Hindu contemporaries as 'eel-wrigglers': they would not answer a straight question but wriggled out of it. We leave to Chapter 14 a discussion of how far this represented a deliberate silence on a matter about which all statements must be speculative rather than categorical. At this stage, the best way to understand Buddha's approach to *nirvana* is in relation to the Marks of Existence, to which we now turn, guided, perhaps, by these words written some five centuries after his death:

Nirvana is absolute ease, and nevertheless one cannot point to its form or shape, its duration or size, either by simile or explanation, by reason or by argument ... As a mountain peak is unshakeable, so is Nirvana. As a mountain peak is inaccessible, so is Nirvana inaccessible to the passions.

(Milanda's Questions 322)

THE MARKS OF EXISTENCE

After his experience at Bodh-gaya, Buddha was faced with the choice between either becoming a recluse or pursuing a teaching ministry. To the benefit of millions of followers throughout two-and-a-half millennia, he embarked on the latter course, starting, according to tradition, with the famous **Benares Sermon**, which he is said to have preached to five somewhat sceptical ascetics who had accompanied him on many of his earlier sojourns. Much of what is now held to be mainline Buddhist teaching is said to have originated in this sermon, but how true this is we cannot be sure. It may be that, like Jesus's Sermon on the Mount, it is an amalgam of teachings developed and given over a period of time.

The Marks of Existence (*trilakshana* or *tilakkhana*) lie at the heart of Buddhist philosophy. They are three features of earthly life that stamp our lives indelibly, so that, if we ignore their reality, we shall fail to achieve the goal as Buddha outlined it. The vernacular names for these are given first in Sanskrit, then in Pali, which is the dialect of Sanskrit held to have been used by Buddha (although there is considerable debate about the alleged Pali source of basic Buddhist writings, and where exactly it was spoken.

The three marks are, as we have seen, *anitya* (*anicca*), meaning 'impermanence'; *anatman* (*anatta*), meaning variously 'no-soul', 'non-self' or 'egolessness'; and *duhkha* (*dukkha*) meaning 'suffering' (though this word will need some discussion, as we shall see on pages 61–2). The first two are metaphysical concepts that are logically interconnected and will therefore be considered here in tandem; *duhkha*, as a description of the human experience of living, is a more empirical observation and is closely linked with two other central Buddhist affirmations, the 'Four Noble Truths' and the 'Noble Eightfold Path', and will be analysed in the next chapter apropos of these sets of teaching.

The concepts of *anicca* and *anatta* (using the Pali transliterations) are quintessentially Buddhist. As we saw in Chapter 4, Hinduism teaches that everything in the phenomenal world of *maya* is in a state of flux: only *brahman* is constant. Buddha accepted this as a truism: nobody steps into the same river twice, and even the Himalayas are not the same from one second to the next. Had he been able to study human biology, he would have found confirmation of this state of impermanence in the continuous destruction of old cells and creation of new ones; and, as Capra illustrates in *The Tao of Physics*, the study of subatomic physics confirms this. At one level, therefore, *anicca* is simply a description of the universe as we perceive it; and, as we shall see, this feature of Buddhist thought found ready confirmation when Buddhism moved into China, with its philosophy of *yin* and *yang* (see Chapter 11).

Buddha's doctrine of anicca was starker than this, however, because he linked it with the doctrine of *anatta*. Not only was there no permanence in the physical world, but the mental and so-called spiritual side of human beings was subject to the same all-embracing process. If *anicca* is a universal condition, *anatta* follows inexorably, and any talk about immortality, whether in relation to a god or to a human soul or self, is empty. The image that Buddha presents apropos of the human consciousness (*chitta*, or *citta*) is that of a row of unlit candles. The end one is lit, and from it the next one, after which the first is extinguished; the second then lights the third, and is itself extinguished: and so on along the row. Thus, said Buddha, is human existence: a series of discontinuous moments, each giving birth to the next and then ceasing to be, so that it cannot be said that any person is constant from one moment, even one micro-second, to the next.

It is clear that this description of the human condition accords with our experience in a general way. We know how moods change from one moment to the next, and how consciousness can alter over a long period of time, so that it can be confusing, even embarrassing, to meet people whom we knew in earlier years who relate to us as we were then, rather than as we have (for the time being) become. Yet amid this impermanence, we seem to sense a kind of thread that links all these 'persons' into an essential *me*; but it seems to be this idea of essence that Buddha rejects.

We are here at the epicentre of a debate that has occupied Buddhist scholars for centuries. Much depends, if we are to reach an understanding, on the interpretation of '*chitta*-consciousness'. It can be used as a synonym for the thinking mind (*manas*) and for consciousness in the sense of general awareness (*vijnana*). *Chitta* would then be equated with our general thought-processes, which certainly lack constancy. However, in one of the three books (the so-called *Tripitaka*, or 'Three Baskets') that together form the canon of Buddhist scriptures, the interpretation of *chitta* is different. This book is called the *Abidharma-pitaka*, or 'basket of the special teaching', and it describes *chitta* as a mental *substance* separate from these mental processes. As a substance it is therefore, to fall into tautology, substantial: that is, it is real and enduring.

What emerges from this discussion is that the issue remains unresolved, and those who wish to delve more deeply must consult the Bibliography. It may help our understanding of the matter if at this stage we move ahead to the second century CE and refer to two concepts associated with one of the greatest of all Buddhist scholars: **Nagarjuna**, and his theories of **conditioned arising**, or **dependent arising** (*pratitya samutapada*), sometimes translated as the 'causal nexus', and of *shunyata*, literally 'the void', or 'emptiness'.

The doctrine of conditioned arising states that all the phenomena that constitute human existence, whether physical or psychological, are inter-dependent and mutually condition each other. This interconnection creates the cycles of *samsara* that were described in relation to Hinduism: the endless round of birth, life, old age, death, rebirth, and so on either *ad infinitum* or until the achievement of enlightenment (*nirvana*). The twelve links (*nidana*) that form the chain of this 'causal nexus' connect previous existences with both the present life and those still to come. We arrive, Nagarjuna stated, bearing the *karma* accumulated in earlier cycles; we accumulate more *karma*, maybe better, maybe worse; and we are reborn in the new state of con-sciousness brought about by the changes which that *karma* effects.

On the face of it, the doctrine of conditioned arising as expounded by Nagarjuna points to a thread that seems to connect the totality of human experience, and so requires a reassessment of the meaning of *anicca*, 'im-permanence'. What Buddhism emphasises, however, is that connectedness does not mean continuity: parents and children are connected in a number of ways, but this does not mean the continuity of the one in the other, just as individual frames of a film, which seem to produce continuity on a screen, do not inhere in each other. The irony is, as we shall discover when discussing the third mark of existence, *duhkha* (suffering), that the apparent thread of continuity is created and sustained by *karma*, the undesirable cause of *samsara* in the first place. On this matter, Buddhism is at odds with Hindu thought, where *nicca*, or *nitya* (the opposites of *anicca* and *anitya*), meaning literally 'constant' or 'eternal', are held to be basic features of anyone who has experienced the ultimate reality, the union of *atman* with *brahman*.

The doctrine of *anicca*, then, if seen in the light of *pratitya-samutpada*, presents a picture of impermanence amid an illusion of permanence. Its central affirmation is that nothing that we encounter in life endures, however much we may wish otherwise. Faculties come to a peak and then decline, relationships develop and die, enthusiasms wax and wane: all is in a state of flux, and permanence can be found only in *bodhi* and the eternal non-dual condition of *nirvana*.

Here, however, Buddhism, especially as reflected in Nagarjuna's teaching about the void, presents us with a second problem. Included in the universal condition of impermanence is the second mark of existence, **anatman** (*anatta*), or non-self. As we have seen, to Buddha's Hindu contemporaries the key to *moksha* lay in discovering the eternity of *atman* in union with *brahman*. Yet here Buddha is presenting the opposite of this concept as the true reality: no self, no soul. What Hindus proclaimed (and still proclaim) to be eternal was, or so he and his successors seemed to imply, merely part of the process of conditioned arising, and so was illusory, since the con-sciousness (in the first of the interpretations outlined on page 57) that gives rise to the belief is itself insubstantial.

We may better understand what *anatman* implies if we examine Nagarjuna's concept of the void: **shunyata**, or **emptiness**. Nagarjuna argued that there is no such thing as the fundamental nature, or essence, of anything. Nothing exists in itself, but only in relation to something else: either to that with which it is linked chronologically, as in the process of conditioned arising, *pratitya-samutapada*, or with its opposite. Thus everything can be viewed only as either a middle way between two stages or as, so to speak, one side of a coin, which can exist only if the other side exists – and vice versa.

If anything has an essence, Nagarjuna argued, it would have no arising, changing, ageing and dying; rather, it would be unchanging, everlasting, independent of other essences. But the world that presents itself to our senses, whether physical (through sight, touch and so on) or psychological (through mental formations and perceptions), has none of these qualities; all things – ideas as well as atoms, mind as well as matter – arise and pass away. In a word, all is emptiness, *shunyata*; instead of essence, there is a void. Is there such a thing as coldness, or joy? Since we know the meaning of the former only because of its opposite, heat, and of the latter only because of its opposite, sorrow, the answer is that neither can have an independent essence, but each, like everything else in the manifest world (the world of appearance), is part of the universal void, a condition in which there is no independent existence, no essence, no eternity. In a void (and this is another tautology) everything is empty.

We may be tempted to ask the straightforward question: do things exist, or do they not? Nagarjuna's reply is that this is the wrong question. At one level, the level of 'conventional truth' (*samvriti-satya*) they do exist, as phenomena that are objects of the senses. But at another, deeper, level, the level of 'ultimate truth' (*paramartha-satya*), absolute truth compared with relative truth (akin, perhaps, to Plato's 'ideas'), they do not exist. So, from the point of view of conventional truth, the world and everything in it has validity; from the point of view of definitive truth, it has no validity, since it is only appearance, the object of human perception, that is itself subject to the inescapable law of *anicca*.

A similar distinction is made by Steven Collins in his scholarly discussion *Selfless Persons*, in which he argues that, in order to understand *anatman*, the difference between **conventional truth** and **ultimate truth** needs to be grasped. He argues that any talk about 'self' in Buddhism refers to the conventional and not the ultimate level; this includes even passages in one of the Buddhist scriptures, the *Dhammapada*, such as the phrase, 'the self is lord of the self'. Collins argues that this is a colloquial use of the word, often adopted by Buddhists when speaking on ethical matters; and this interpretation seems consistent with Buddhist metaphysics as a whole.

The question at issue, however, is not how the word *atman* is used apropos of this present existence, but what the implications of *anatman* are for one's view of future lives. Buddha speaks of rebirth; but, if there is no self, no soul, what is reborn? In particular, can there be any continuation of one's personal identity between this life and the next? Here, as Collins emphasises, the doctrine of dependent arising provides the key and, with it, the middle way between the Hindu doctrine of 'eternalism', the view that there is in each living being an eternal divine self that continues from one existence to the next, and 'annihilationism', the philosophy of Charvaka, which claims that whatever constitutes the self is destroyed at death.

The doctrine of dependent arising states, as we have seen (page 58), that at rebirth it is the *karma*, not the self, that is handed on; and this process continues until *nirvana* has been realised. The logical conclusion is that the one who reaps the karmic effect is not 'ultimately' the one who produced the karmic cause. There are, of course, problems with this doctrine, which Collins discusses in some detail (and, in any case, not all Buddhist schools follow this line – see Chapter 8). From the pragmatic point of view, however, this doctrine makes sense. Any beliefs about future existence or non-existence are purely speculative and, more to the point, bring suffering (what Heidegger termed anxiety): hence Buddha's comparative silence on the matter. If it is the case that the consequences of my present deeds are to be borne by someone in the next generation, then that gives – or should give – a strong motivation to me to ensure that the *karma* which I pass on will be the least possible burden to its recipient. This will affect present decision-making and the values that I express, and by which I live.

The important point for Buddhists – and it is impossible to over-emphasise this – is that alongside the world of appearance, conditioned and contingent, is *nirvana*, which is independent of all phenomena, is unconditioned and uncontingent. It would be wrong to describe it as something to be arrived at or attained, but rather as the realisation of the true nature of phenomena, in which manifoldness becomes dormant and is still.

As we shall see in the next chapter, the way of Buddhism involves primarily not a host of metaphysical speculations but a down-to-earth assessment of our present condition, and of how to cope with it. This may well imply that Buddhism must be looked on as basically a rule of life rather than as a philosophy or a religion: a decision that all who seek to learn from it must decide for themselves.

7 The heterodox systems III
Buddhism 2: The way of Buddha

If the study of Buddhism were simply an exercise in theory, like the scholastic debates of the Middle Ages, it would be generally viewed as the focus of a number of highly complex ideas leading to a variety of possible conclusions. This is partly because Buddha was not himself a systematic philosopher: in fact he often stated that his ideas were not intended to be a *darsana*, or philosophy, so that for a more comprehensive exposition of his theories we need to turn to later teachers, such as Nagarjuna (discussed in the last chapter), Vasubandhu (*c.* fourth/fifth century CE) and Buddhaghosa (fifth century). This is particularly necessary apropos of those theories that he quite deliberately (or so it seems) left cryptic.

His non-systematic doctrines, however, are best appreciated in the light of his declared aim, which was to be a *yana*, or vehicle for others in their pursuit of enlightenment. Rather than speculate on metaphysical matters, he chose to spend his years showing his followers how they might come to terms with *duhkha*, the product of a world characterised primarily by *anicca*. His main concern, therefore, was how to cope with this 'vale of tears', in which anything or anybody on which or on whom we may set our hearts will, sooner or later, pass away. He believed that under the Bodhi-tree he had found the answer to this conundrum, and millions over the centuries have testified to the truth as he stated it.

The basis of his teaching is, as we saw in Chapter 6, probably contained in the Benares Sermon or discourse, often referred to as 'the first turning of the wheel of *dharma* (teaching)', or *dharma-chakra*. (The *chakras*, meaning 'wheels of energy', were noted on page 23 apropos of Tantric meditation in Hinduism and, as will be seen in Chapter 8, are a key element in Tantrism in Tibetan Buddhism.) The discourse began with what are now known universally as the **Four Noble Truths** (*arya-satya*) and, along with the **Noble Eightfold Path**, to which they point, they provide the kernel of what may be described as 'the Buddhist Way'.

DUHKHA AND THE FOUR NOBLE TRUTHS

The first truth is that the world is permeated with suffering, or *duhkha*. This is the third 'mark of existence' referred to in the previous chapter, and its meaning is closely linked with theirs. From the fact of *anicca* (*anitya*), it can be interpreted as not just pain and sorrow (or 'suffering', as Western writers often characterise it) but as dissatisfaction and unfulfilment: ambitions unachieved, relationships severed. From *anatman* (*anatta*) it expresses the hopelessness of seeking permanence in the idea of immortality. Buddha taught that the human personality, for which immortality was sought, consists of five **aggregates**, or *skandhas*: corporeality or form (*rupa*), sensation (*vedana*), perception (*samjna*), mental formations (*samskara*) and consciousness (*vijnana*). But neither body nor mind, however rigorously disciplined or finely tuned, can survive death, and to believe or hope otherwise can only cause suffering.

The second truth is virtually contained in the first. The cause of *duhkha* is craving, or desire (***trishna***): the thirst for that which cannot satisfy. *Trishna* expresses itself not only in the direction of sensual pleasures but also by psychological motivations, such as the desire for fame, or wanting to be liked. The five *skandas* are frequently referred to as **aggregates of attachment** (*upadana-skanda*), since it is to them that *trishna* attaches itself. This attachment leads to the most poignant of all expressions of *duhkha*: the frustration of failing to find enlightenment, and so remaining bound to *samsara*. Buddha's own words about *trishna* are recorded in the *sutras*:

> But what, O monks, is the noble truth of the origin of suffering? It is that craving which gives rise to fresh rebirth and, bound up with lust and greed, now here, now there, finds ever fresh delight. It is the sensual craving, the craving for existence, the craving for nonexistence or self-annihilation.

The third truth takes the matter a further natural step in the argument. It is that *duhkha* can be ended only through the total elimination of *trishna*. Once craving has faded away and become extinct, it is possible to have a sense of detachment about the object of craving; and with this sense comes liberation and peace: the state of detachment towards any pleasure or luxury is one in which disappointment does not, cannot, occur.

The fourth truth concerns what was for Buddha (and for all Buddhists since) the supreme question: how can *trishna* be destroyed? How does one overcome this craving, which grips at every level? Buddha's answer was to offer his followers the way known universally as the Noble Eightfold Path (*ashtangika-marga*).

THE NOBLE EIGHTFOLD PATH

The eight parts of the *ashtangika-marga* are, in Buddhist teaching, the final step, or limb, of what are in fact thirty-seven 'limbs of enlightenment' (*bodhipakshika-dharma*), and they include all aspects of the threefold training (*trishiksha*) for Buddhist monks. We shall reflect on the training when considering the 'Three Jewels' of Buddhism, one of which is the Order, or *Sangha* (page 68). Here we shall consider the Eightfold Path as it affects all Buddhists, whether monks or lay people.

There has been considerable debate among Buddhist scholars about the translation of the adjective that precedes all eight steps of the path. In Sanskrit it is *samyag*, or *samkyak*; in the Pali dialect (used by Buddha), *samma*. This is often translated as 'right', but the problem with this is that the word can then be interpreted in contrast with 'wrong', and this is not the meaning of *samma*. A better word is 'perfect', in the sense of wholeness, or completeness, and this will be the word used here. The eight steps are:

Perfect view (*samma-ditti*)

This means the perspective on life brought about by accepting the Three Marks of Existence and the Four Noble Truths. That is, it means realising the impermanence of everything (*anicca*), so that any attempt to cling to what must pass away is recognised as craving for the unattainable, resulting only in pain and dissatisfaction (*duhkha*); and, since there is no self (*anatta*), it is equally pointless to take refuge in the hope of immortality.

Perfect resolve (*samma-sankappa*)

This means the resolve to live according to the Buddhist way: non-attachment to the world, with its transient delights; sympathy and good will to one's fellows; and empathy with all sentient beings so that one seeks never to cause them harm.

Perfect speech (*samma-vacha*)

Everything one says will be true and kind, avoiding lies, gossip and slander.

Perfect conduct (*samma-kammanta*)

This is epitomised in Buddhism as avoiding any kind of behaviour that conflicts with *shila* (Pali: *sila*), moral obligations or precepts. There are ten *shilas*, the first five being expected of monks, nuns and lay persons alike, the last five being expected only of monks and nuns except on certain days of fasting (*uposatha*), when lay people observe all but the last two. The *shilas* are (1) not killing; (2) not stealing; (3) not indulging in prohibited sexual activity; (4) refraining from unjust speech; (5) abstaining from intoxicating drinks and from (6) solid foods after noon; (7) forgoing music, dance, drama and similar forms of entertainment; (8) not wearing perfumes or ornamental jewellery; (9) sleeping in simple, hard beds; and (10) avoiding contact with money and other valuables.

Perfect livelihood (*samma-ajiva*)

This step is usually characterised negatively as which forms of livelihood to avoid rather than which to pursue. The strictures spring from the second step, and the resolve not to harm any sentient being. One could not, for example, live in a state of *samma-ajiva* and be a butcher, a hunter or a soldier, or deal in arms or narcotics. For many, though not all, Buddhists, this step leads to a pacifist or vegetarian life-style, but Buddha made no absolute rule about these issues. He considered, for instance, that a live animal was one entity and meat another, so that, while it would be wrong to actually butcher the animal, it would not necessarily be wrong to eat its carcass, which would otherwise simply decay.

Perfect effort (*samma-vayama*)

On the face of it, this step seems like a variation on earlier steps, but it contains a specific consideration that justifies it as a discrete step. The effort called for is the cultivation of actions that are karmically beneficial and avoiding those that are karmically injurious. On this matter, Buddha agreed with Hindu teaching that *karma* can be designated either 'good' or 'bad', as opposed to the Jainite view that all *karma* is bad. The important point that Buddha was making was, as we have already noted (page 58), that unwholesome *karma* strengthens the bonds of *samsara*, the cycle that binds people to the eternal round of conditioned arising.

Steps seven and eight take us to the heart of Buddhist meditation, without which *nirvana* cannot be achieved, and will therefore be discussed in greater detail.

Perfect mindfulness (*samma-sati*)

This means the control of all the mind's activities. These activities embrace what are termed the 'four awakenings (or foundations) of mindfulness' (*satipatthana*), and are essential steps in meditation if the final step is to be achieved.

The first 'awakening' is *awareness of the body*, such as one's breathing and posture, and of the different parts of the body individually. As a butcher speaks of 'meat' rather than 'cow', one has to learn mentally to dissect the body into its constituent parts, and so to realise that they are ultimately nothing but the four elements (*dhatu*): solid, liquid, heat and movement. The aim is to become more fully aware of *anatman*, to adandon the concept of an ego and recognise that the body, in which people take delight, is transitory, unreal, and subject to *duhkha*. One form of meditation, 'charnel ground contemplation', even calls for the meditator to imagine his or her body's parts to be strewn among rotting corpses and crumbling skeletons.

The second awakening relates to one's *sensations or feelings* (*vedana*, the second of the five *skandhas* described on page 62). The aim is to identify one's feelings as either pleasant, unpleasant or indifferent, worldly or transcendental, and to realise that, like the body, they are transitory, subject to *anicca*.

The third awakening is *mindfulness of one's thoughts* (*chitta*), which includes, as we saw on page 57, both the thinking mind (*manas*) and a person's consciousness as a whole (*vijnana*, the fifth of the *skandhas*). Here one seeks to recognise every state of consciousness: to be able to distinguish between those that are normally accompanied by deep emotion or a sense of aggression and those that are not; and, in particular, to discern those matters about which one may be deluded.

The fourth awakening takes further this process of deep self-exploration. It is awakening to the *objects of thoughts*, since it is by the ability to control these that deep meditation, facilitating the way to *nirvana*, becomes possible. The most important requirement is to overcome the 'five hindrances', or obstructions (*nivarana*), which may prevent a person from achieving the eighth step. The obstacles are:

- desire (*abhidya*);
- ill will (*pradosha*);
- sloth and torpor (*styana* and *middha*);
- restlessness and compunction (*anuddhatya* and *kaukritya*);
- doubt (*vichikitsa*).

It must readily be obvious that nobody will be able to enter into the deep meditation of the eighth step of the path if his or her mind is occupied by any of these distractions: even so apparently small a matter as wondering if one has remembered to lock the house door will be an insuperable barrier.

Perfect concentration (*samma-samadhi*)

We have encountered the word *samadhi* previously in relation to the Hindu school of Yoga, descriptive also of the fourth state in Advaita Vedanta. In Buddhism too it describes the highest state of meditation, one of total absorption, or ***dhyana***. (In fact '*dhyana* Buddhism' is a general name given to all schools of Buddhism that view meditation as the basic way to enlightenment. Its most unambiguous expression is in Zen, which we shall consider in Chapter 8.) The state of absorption is one in which all passions have died away and the practitioner is able to concentrate uninterruptedly on the object of meditation. It differs in emphasis from that of Yoga or Vedanta, since for Buddha there is no conception of union between *atman* and *brahman*: there is for him neither 'self' nor underlying ground of being. The absorption is found, not by discovering our 'real selves', but through the realisation of selflessness in the context of total transitoriness. There are four stages of absorption:

1 The surrender of personal desires: anything, that is, which is karmically unwholesome (*akushala*), bearing with it the seed of future suffering. At this stage there are still likely to be wandering thoughts.
2 This stage marks the coming to rest of thought-processes and the achieving of inner tranquillity, 'one-pointedness of mind' as it is called; it may well be brought about by concentrating on a particular object, such as a flower or a candle-flame.

Both these stages may be expected to be accompanied by a sense of joy (*priti*) from following the Buddhist way, and a consciousness of well-being (*sukha*).

3 At this stage, while the sense of well-being remains, joy is replaced by equanimity (*upeksha*), one of the most important Buddhist virtues. It is a state where the mind is lifted above the distinctions of joy and suffering to a condition of equilibrium, while still remaining alert and aware.
4 *Samadhi*, the goal of all Buddhist meditation: all that remains is a state of wakeful equilibrium beyond all distinctions and all 'pairs of opposites', such as good and bad, joy and sorrow. It is the gateway to *nirvana*, the state beyond desire.

THE THREE JEWELS

So far, in this and the previous chapter, we have studied the main philosophical concepts relating to Buddhist teaching. In so doing, we have been reflecting on one of what are known throughout the Buddhist world as the **Three Jewels** or 'precious ones' (*triratna*), which comprise the central components of Buddhism. They are:

• the Buddha;
• the teaching (*dharma*, Pali: *damma*);
• the order (*sangha*), or companions along the way.

The jewels are, then, the awakened one himself, the ideas he taught, and those who accept and live by these ideas.

ENTERING THE STREAM

The act of committing oneself to the three jewels is called 'entering the stream' (*shrota-apanna*). By taking this first step, stream-enterers affirm not only a general desire to follow the Buddhist path but also, in particular, indicate that they have overcome three of the fetters (*samyojana*) that bind them to the cycle of *samsara*. The fetters are:

1 **Belief in the ego** (*drishti*). This belief denies the truth of *anatta*, non-self, and accepts a philosophy of 'eternalism': the view that there is an immortal element in each person.
2 **Scepticism** (*vichikitsa*): doubt about the truths of Buddhist teaching,

which will inevitably cause a person to waver and be indecisive when confronted with alternative ideas.

3 **Clinging to rites and rules**: to enter the stream means throwing away these crutches, since (and this is particularly stressed in Zen Buddhism) these outward signs mask, rather than manifest, the inner reality.

There are seven further fetters to be overcome before final liberation may be achieved, in particular the fetters of **passion** (*klesha*). This means that there must be more rebirths before the last fetter, **ignorance** (*avidya*), is removed. Stream-enterers, however, take comfort in the knowledge that, by openly committing themselves to the Three Jewels, they ensure their rebirth in one of the higher modes of existence (**gati**). Since much Buddhist iconography depicts people and creatures existing, happily or unhappily, in these modes, we may outline them at this stage. The iconography is itself, as many Western Buddhists acknowledge, difficult to understand, bearing in mind that every detail has a pedagogic significance. Perhaps a Western form will eventually emerge alongside the exotic Eastern imagery.

There are three higher modes of existence: human beings, lower gods (*asuras*), and gods (*devas*), all of whom, it should be noted, remain subject to *karma*. That is, the gods are not to be viewed in the same light as Greek or Roman gods, enjoying immortality and supernatural powers. In Buddhist teaching, they are simply beings who are enjoying a particularly pleasant existence as a reward for past good deeds. The highest mode, it should be noted, is the human being, since this is the form that offers the best opportunity to escape from the cycle of *samsara*: gods are in fact specially prone to stray from the path, because of the comforts they enjoy. (The significance of this will be discussed in Chapter 13, but it must already be apparent that Buddhism is effectively an atheistic system.)

There are three lower modes of existence: first, animals; second, 'hungry ghosts' (*preta*), whose *karma* is bad because of greed, envy and so on, but not so bad as to land them in the third, the lowest mode of all: hell-beings (*naraka*), who suffer torment and retribution for past misdeeds. The torment is of limited duration, however, and there is always the chance for them to be reborn in a higher mode. We may feel that the lowest modes describe a mental state rather than a particular place, but the positioning of animals in the Buddhist hierarchy raises logistic and, for some, moral dilemmas: how does any creature lacking the power of choice build up good *karma*?

Confident, then, that by 'entering the stream' they ensure rebirth in a higher mode, Buddhists turn to the Three Jewels, the precious ones, as 'places of refuge' (*trisharana*). They affirm their commitment to the Buddhist path by pronouncing what is termed the threefold refuge formula: 'I take refuge in the Buddha, I take refuge in the teaching, I take refuge in the community.' (In Pali: *Buddham saranam gachchami, dammam saranam gachchami, sangham saranam gachchami.*) This affirmation is part of daily Buddhist practice. The second of the *trisharana* has been discussed throughout the last two chapters, so we turn to the first and the third.

THE FIRST JEWEL: BUDDHA

About the status of the historical Buddha in the eyes of his followers it is, like so much else in Buddhism, hard to generalise. (How hard will be clearer when the Mahayana and Theravada schools are discussed in Chapter 8). The most straightforward approach is to see him as Muslims see Muhammad: one who made a unique proclamation on many of the issues associated with a religion. He is not, at least according to the Theravada tradition, to be described as 'divine', or 'son of God', as Jesus is described by Christians. According to this tradition, Buddha is in *nirvana*, and is consequently no longer accessible to us. The problem with this simple statement is that it would not be accepted by most Buddhists outside the Theravada tradition. By many followers he is referred to as 'The Lord Buddha', with all the implications to which this designation may give rise. Bearing in mind the original meaning of 'Buddha' as 'the awakened one', he should perhaps be looked upon as one who, with a charisma rarely found throughout human history, through his teaching and example showed a way of living that millions have found to meet their deepest needs. Whatever designation is given him then becomes a matter for the individual concerned.

THE THIRD JEWEL: THE *SANGHA*

The *sangha* can mean either the order of Buddhist monks/nuns (*bhikshus/bhikshunis*) or the Buddhist community as a whole: monks, nuns, and laymen and women (*upasakas* and *upasikas*, literally 'those who sit close by'). We have seen already (page 63) that lay persons who have 'entered the stream' are normally expected to observe only the first five of the ten *shilas*, or precepts, apart from on special days of fasting (*uposatha*), which occur on days of the quarter moon. This special observance is less important in Mahayana than in Hinayana (Theravada) Buddhism, which lays greater emphasis on the strictness of the path to liberation. While in the Mahayana tradition this is held to be possible for all, monks and laity alike, in the Theravada tradition only monks can gain it. The laity, through their inevitable involvement in the worldly life and its pleasures, are viewed as having still a long distance to travel along the way to enlightenment, hence the compelling need for them to observe the three additional precepts on the *uposathas*. (In this respect, Theravada Buddhism is not dissimilar to Jainism.)

The aim of every devout Theravada lay person is, as a consequence of this teaching, to be reborn as a monk, and this aim provides a strong motivation to build up karmic merit (*punya*) by a variety of practices: not only the obervance of fast days, but the daily reciting of *sutras* such as the refuge formula, meditating, and, above all, giving alms (*dana*), particularly to monks, whose acceptance of the gifts complements and completes the meritorious act. In the Mahayana tradition, which lays great stress on care for the needy, *dana* is held to be karmically highly propitious, whether the gifts of food, clothing or money are made to monasteries or to the poor.

The Sanskrit word for a monk or a nun (*bhikshu* or *bhikshuni*) literally means 'beggar' and gives a hint of the life-style expected of one who has entered the *sangha*, in its narrower sense. To become a novitiate (*shramanera*) in a Buddhist order is described as entering a state of homelessness (*prav-rajya*): leaving one's family behind, and surrendering all social ties except with fellow monks. One description of homelessness also gives a picture of a Buddhist monk as he may be seen today:

> 'Full of hindrances is the life of a householder, a state of impurity; but like the open air is the life of homelessness. Not easy is it in the householder's state to lead an immaculate, holy life. What if I were now to shave hair and beard, put on the yellow robe, and go forth from the house into homelessness?' And after some time, giving up a small or a great fortune and a small or a large family, he shaves his hair and beard, dons the yellow robe, and goes forth from his house into homelessness.
>
> (Quoted in *EPR* 133)

As in monastic orders of many religions, Buddhist monks are called upon to live in poverty, chastity and obedience; to these is added the admonition to live peaceably. The poverty is expressed through the possession of only a few personal items, such as razor, toothbrush, sewing needle and – an essential commodity – alms-bowl. With this, monks originally spent all but the monsoon period wandering, begging and giving instruction along the way. Only during the rainy season did they live in monasteries, *vihara*, literally 'sojourning places'. Over the centuries they have tended to spend less time in wandering, more in the sedentary life-style of the monasteries.

The rules for the *vihara* are contained in one of the 'three baskets' (*tripitaka*) of the Pali canon, the *vinaya-tripitaka*, already referred to on page 57. Among other injunctions, these rules contain grounds for the final or provisional expulsion of monks, punishments for less serious faults, and directions for meal times, manners and the resolution of disputes. Any violation of these rules is expected to be confessed during the *uposatha* ceremony. There are many more rules for nuns than for monks, which raises an issue that needs to be mentioned.

If we seek a hint of equality of the sexes in the Buddhist way, we seek in vain. Buddha himself was reportedly opposed to the creation of an order of nuns on the grounds that they would create moral disorder. Whether as a consequence of this fear, or as a reflection on later developments in Buddhism generally, the number of nuns, compared with monks, has always been extremely small, and their orders have played only a minor role in comparison with those of monks. The ordination of nuns has to be repeated in the presence of monks, punishments are stricter and more numerous, and nuns, no matter how much older they may be than their male counterparts, must treat all monks with deference and never reprimand them. On the rights of women, it seems, Buddhism has little to teach other cultures.

Much of a monk's time is spent in meditation, because he will be required to follow all thirty-seven of the *ashtangika-marga*, the 'requirements for the attaining of enlightenment', of which, as we saw on page 62, the Noble Eightfold Path is the thirty-seventh. Younger monks are therefore normally placed under the direction of older colleagues, or Masters, whose task is to ensure that the complexities of the path are understood, and the way followed aright. This requirement of long periods of meditation gives Buddhism – as, in a different way, it gives Hinduism – a distinctive stamp, which may justifiably be described as being the essence of Eastern philosophy and religion.

The majority of Buddhists are lay people, however, and are content simply to follow the basic teaching, leaving the more complex matters to those equipped to cope with them. They are happy in the knowledge that, by 'entering the stream', they are committing themselves to the company of those who, at different levels, are pursuing basic goals in the name of Buddha. Thus they take refuge in the third jewel, the *sangha*. Like the climbing of a mountain, it is an individual quest; but, like the climbing of a mountain, it does not have to be pursued in isolation from others.

Buddhism is often described as 'the middle way'. What this means is straightforward enough: the life-style that it recommends represents a middle path between the extreme self-indulgence of the *Charvaka* philosophy and the extreme asceticism of the Jains. On the whole, Buddha seems to have concurred with the Hindu saying already quoted: 'This world is a bridge: pass over it, but do not build your house upon it.' The aim is to reach such a frame of mind about whatever the world has to offer that one can enjoy it without being dependent on it, much less addicted to it. There are no 'thou shalt nots' in Buddhist teaching: rather, there is the warning that certain things produce bad *karma*, thus delaying the achievement of one's ultimate aim. Perhaps the emphasis is on 'leave it' rather than 'take it', but the main impression is that Buddha is advocating a way of life not dissimilar to Aristotle's mean: moderation in all things.

The important point, which practising Buddhists continually affirm, is that the Buddhist way should not be seen as one of sacrifice but as one which gives a joy that is untouched by the absoluteness of *anicca*. Sooner or later, as everyone who has reflected on the matter comes to know to be true, any worldly pleasure either loses its appeal or is removed: to reach a state of mind in which this inevitable deprivation does not leave a sense of unendurable loss seems a goal worth pursuing. If that is *nirvana*, it should have a universal appeal.

8 The heterodox systems IV
Buddhism 3: Mahayana Buddhism

Over the previous two chapters, reference has from time to time been made to two variant expressions of Buddhism: Theravada (or Hinayana) and Mahayana. Generally, the descriptions of Buddhist teaching and practice have related to the former of these, and it is now necessary to look specifically at the latter. Before doing so, however, we need to be clear about three matters: what the names mean, where the two forms are to be found, and what the main differences are between them.

Hinayana and Mahayana literally mean 'lesser vehicle' and 'greater vehicle', a distinction that was introduced around the first century CE by members of what became the Mahayana tradition. As the names suggest, the bone of contention between them was the extent to which the teaching of Buddha, already stretching back over half a millennium, should continue to be expressed without modification or extension. This dilemma became increasingly acute as Buddhists began to take their message to countries beyond India, its native terrain. It was a similar dilemma to that faced by early Christianity, torn between being faithful to its Jewish roots and accommodating itself to the cultures it encountered as it spread abroad.

Originally there were many schools of Hinayana, but only one, the Theravada (literally 'Teaching of the Elders'), survives. Hence the two names are now effectively synonymous and, since this is understandably the preferred name of those who belong to it, 'Theravada' will be the term used in the discussions that follow. It is to be found mainly in southern Asia, in Thailand, Laos, Burma, Sri Lanka and Cambodia.

Mahayana Buddhism, not surprisingly, spread more widely afield, establishing itself, between the second and sixth centuries CE, in China, Japan, Vietnam and Korea, and, in the eighth century, in a much changed form (often termed Lamaism), in Tibet and Mongolia. In the process of extension, the Mahayana itself divided into a series of further schools, such as the Madhyamika ('Middle Way') school, founded by Nagarjuna (see Chapter 6), and the Yogachara school, which, as its name suggests, takes from Hinduism the belief that Yoga is a basic means of achieving enlightenment. Akin to Tantrism in Hinduism is the Vajrayana ('Diamond Vehicle') school, which flourishes primarily in Tibet. In China, two major schools became established: Ch'an, or Dhyana, expressed in Japanese as Zen, and the Pure Land school, which in Japan is found under the generic term Amidism (from Amitabha, its most famous exponent).

The main differences between the Mahayana and Theravada traditions arise essentially from a disagreement about the basic incentive of the Buddhist path, pinpointed in the contrasting images of the ideal person as delineated in the two traditions. In Theravada, this is the *arhat* ('worthy one'): one who has achieved the highest point of *aryamarga*, the supramundane path that he began, many lives earlier, as a 'stream-enterer'. For him there is 'no more learning'; all defilements and passions (*asrava* and *klesha*) have been finally extinguished: he enters *nirvana* confident of salvation, which is full extinction, achieved by his own efforts. (Note the male pronoun: there are no female *arhats*.) Ingrid Fischer-Schreiber describes him in these words (*EPR* 17):

> He is fully free of the ten fetters of the cycle of existence, to wit, belief in an individual entity, scepticism, clinging to rites and rules, sensual desire, resentment, craving for refined corporeality and non-corporeality, arrogance, excitement and ignorance. An arhat is seen as a person all of whose impurities are dissolved, whose wishes are fulfilled, who has laid down his burden, attained his goal, and freed his mind through perfect understanding.

In stark contrast is the Mahayana ideal, the **bodhisattva**, literally 'enlightenment being'. This is one who has gained enlightenment but voluntarily postpones his or her (there are female *bodhisattvas*) final entry into *nirvana* until all have been enlightened. He or she may be a person still living who exhibits great saintliness and wisdom, to whom others may come for guidance along the Eightfold Path. More frequently, the *bodhisattva* is thought of as supramundane, in a state just this side of the ultimate state of *nirvana*, offering compassion and understanding to all who seek it. The contrast with the *arhat*, who seeks only his own liberation, is stark: the *arhat* is an example for others to follow; the *bodhisattva* is both an example and a benefactor.

It would not be misleading to categorise *bodhisattvas* as a combination of guardian angels and saints in Christianity. There are some 'living saints', but the majority of them, having spent their lives arriving at a state of saintliness, are now in a supramundane sphere somewhere between Earth and Heaven, and are available, in a variety of capacities, to those on Earth who seek their aid. The parallel is not total, however, since the *bodhisattva* has many roles besides those of offering wisdom and compassion, such as taking upon him/herself the sufferings of all human beings (a role left, in Christianity at least, to Jesus, the Son of God) and, even more unlikely in a theistic, much less a Theravada context, transferring his or her karmic merit to others.

Buddhist iconography depicts the *bodhisattvas* in a variety of exotic forms that, to anyone raised in a Western culture, may seem bizarre. Thus one of the most important, Avalokiteshvara ('he who hears the outcries of the world') is depicted with a thousand arms (symbolising universal compassion), a thousand eyes (symbolising universal recognition of human needs) and eleven faces (symbolising, according to one tradition, the ten stages of a *bodhisattva*'s career plus the final step of Buddhahood). Another, Samantabhadra ('he who is all-pervadingly good') is depicted, though primarily in Tibetan Buddhism, in sexual union (*yab-yum*) with his female consort, expressing the view that meditative concentration can be intensified through the combination of both male and female energies in a single person. Other famous *bodhisattvas* are Manjushri ('he who is noble and gentle'), who is depicted with the sword of wisdom and the *sutra* of wisdom (Prajnaparamita-Sutra); Mahasthamaprapta ('one who has gained great power'), often depicted with a pagoda decorating his hair; and Kshitigarbha ('womb of the Earth'), the only *bodhisattva* portrayed as a monk.

The contrast in ideals between Theravada and Mahayana expresses itself in their attitude to the universal experiences of *duhkha*. In the Mahayana tradition, there is a deeper sense of compassion for the poor and needy, a greater attachment to what Christians would describe as 'the social gospel'; it is also considerably more liberal about the possibility of attaining Buddhahood. In the Theravada tradition, only monks can achieve this goal; in most expressions of Mahayana, the assumption is that it is open to all, since all possess Buddha-nature. Zen Buddhism even suggests that it is wrong to speak of *attaining* Buddhahood, since we already in fact possess it, the trouble being that most people are not aware of this reality. What we need, therefore, is not to find a new dimension outside ourselves, but for our eyes to be opened to the dimension latent within.

There are, then, echoes of the debate in early Christianity as to whether revelation is once and for all (and therefore confined to the original texts) or whether it is ongoing. Not surprisingly, there was considerable debate among Buddhist scholars about the authority of their scriptures, since many of the later developments in the Mahayana tradition could not be upheld without at the same time accepting that the *dharma*, or teaching, could be modified in relation to cultures with different traditions from its own. The Theravada view was that only the writings contained in the Pali canon, the so-called *tripitaka* or 'three baskets', mentioned on page 57, could be accorded this veneration. As we saw, the *tripitaka* represent the earliest writings of Buddha and his immediate disciples, written in the dialect that Buddha himself probably spoke. The Mahayana tradition accepts these as authoritative but adds to them a wide range of *sutras* and *shastras* (teachings) written over subsequent centuries; these contain both additions and changes to the *tripitaka*.

There are other, observable, differences between the two traditions. In Mahayana, there is more ritual, iconography, and (especially in Tibetan and Japanese Nichiren Buddhism) chanting; in Theravada there is more emphasis on meditation as the main path to enlightenment. As we saw on page 68, the view of the person of Buddha is different in the two traditions, ranging from the acceptance of a historical figure who is no longer accessible to human beings on Earth to one who is, or can be, present in the lives of all.

From the philosophical perspective, the Theravada tradition is the more profitable to the student; but for one who wishes to understand how Buddhism is most frequently expressed in the world, it is essential to study Mahayana in at least some of its forms. This we shall now do, mainly with reference to two traditions which have become familiar in the West: Ch'an/Zen in China and Japan, and Tibetan Buddhism, headed by the most famous Buddhist in the world, the Dalai Lama.

BUDDHISM IN CHINA

Buddhism arrived in China around the sixth/seventh century. Its emissary was Bodhidharma, the twenty-eighth Indian patriarch after Shakyamuni Buddha. He is said to have sailed to south China, where he was unsuccessful in spreading his teaching; he then travelled to Lo-yang in the northern province of Honan and settled there in the Shaolin monastery on Mount Sung. Tradition has it that he spent nine years facing a wall in deep meditation known as *zazen* (literally 'seated absorption'), a period known as *menpeki-kunen* ('nine years in front of a wall'), and in many Zen paintings he is shown seated, facing a cliff wall. He was thereafter visited by many enquirers, who were interested in the message of so remarkable a person, including Huiko, his ultimate successor and second patriarch of Ch'an (Zen) in China. Over the centuries, Buddhism in China has established itself alongside two other schools, Taoism and Confucianism, which are discussed in later chapters.

The Chinese word 'Ch'an', better known by its Japanese equivalent, 'Zen' (by which we shall now designate this school), is synonymous with the Sanskrit word *dhyana*, or absorption, although with a somewhat different emphasis from the Hindu. Its aim, as the name suggests, is enlightenment as experienced by the Buddha under the Bodhi-tree. More than any other school, whether of Buddhism or of Hinduism, it teaches the absolute centrality of deep meditation as the surest, albeit the steepest, path to enlightenment. Everything else, however strongly associated with religion, is viewed as little more than lumber, more a hindrance than a help along the way.

The word used in Zen for the enlightenment experience is *satori*, from the word *saturo*, to know. This is not knowledge gained empirically but intuitive knowledge, arrived at by no identifiable logical or rational steps. A word with a similar meaning to *satori* is *kensho*, literally 'seeing nature', although this often refers to beginners along the path rather than to Buddhist or Zen 'masters'. Because there are no 'well-worn steps' to *satori*, it is impossible to say how long one may have to spend in deep meditation before achieving it. What is certain is that the moment, when it comes, will be instantaneous, and awareness of its efficacy unshakeable (again, like Shankara's man with the rope and the snake).

Much play on the intuitive nature of *satori* was made by Zen masters. It was described as akin to an archer's hitting the target without taking aim: the more one tries consciously to do the right thing, the more impossible the task seems. Like the pursuit of happiness, it is best to let things take a natural course and act intuitively rather than follow rules or guidelines.

This aspect of Buddhist teaching arises from Shakyamuni Buddha's first encounter with his disciples, when, so tradition has it, he said nothing but simply held up a flower. One man in the company, Kashyapa, understood and smiled: he was to become Mahakashyapa, the first patriarch of Indian Buddhism. In China, the idea of *satori* found a ready response from many of those following the native Chinese way of Taoism, which similarly stressed the intuitive above the empirical. It meant that the enquirer was called upon to find resources within him- or herself, rather than relying on external, tangible aids.

We should be clear what this implied: what the 'lumber', referred to earlier, was that was to be treated with caution. First was *dependence on ritual*, and all other public forms of religion. A few might find them a means of attaining the awakened state, but, it was held, by their very nature they were more likely to be a stumbling-block, encouraging people to settle for outward observance rather than inner realisation. The trouble with ritual, or liturgy, according to Zen, is that it lacks spontaneity, which is the essence of *satori*: it is possible to be so concerned with performing the right act in the right time and place that one loses sight of the underlying purpose of the drama.

The same criticism applies to so-called *sacred writings*: one can hardly be trying to hit the target without taking aim if, in the process, one is depending on ancient authorities who have asserted in their writings what the aim should be. (There are overtones here of Nietzsche's *Übermensch*, following his own path without recourse to 'heavenly guidance', and, in fact, of existentialist thought generally: see my *East of Existentialism*). To rely on sacred writings, Zen teaches, is like asking a friend 'what is that?' while pointing at the Moon, and receiving the reply, 'that's your finger'.

Most importantly, Zen rejects *intellectual debate* as a way to finding enlightenment. This is often illustrated by the use of **koans** in meditation. These are illogical or meaningless statements or questions, indicating the limits of discursive reasoning and forcing the student to take an intuitive leap beyond logic and rationality. The most famous *koan* known in the West is 'What is the sound of one hand clapping?'; but there are hundreds of others, such as, 'If I have nothing, what should I do? Throw it away', and 'If you run away from the void, you can never be free of it. If you search for the void, you can never reach it.'

The *koan* is used particularly in the **Rinzai** school of Zen in Japan, one of two major schools still active. The other school, **Soto**, is sceptical about the use of any form of language in meditation, even this unusual use. In this school, emphasis is placed on **mokusho**, wordless meditation, and, even more extremely, on **shikantaza**, meaning 'nothing but sitting'. The aim is to meditate without any tangible, visible or mental aids, such as counting the breath, chanting a *mantra* or using a *koan*: rather, the mediator seeks to be free from all thoughts, directed to no object, attached to no particular content, like Bodhidharma facing the wall. In the Soto school it is in fact customary for monks to practise *zazen* facing a wall rather than the *zendo*, or hall, as in the Rinzai tradition. One Soto teacher said, 'Your own heart, that is the hall', so affirming that any outward context or environment should be transcended by Zen. The wall then becomes a metaphor for the problems encountered by anyone who relies on props like ritual or books: all that is needed is one intuitive leap whereby he breaks through the wall by realising that it never really existed. The leap is called *jikishi-ninshin*, 'direct pointing at the human heart', where everyone's *bussho*, or Buddha-nature, resides. This teaching, the Buddha-dharma, has, according to Zen tradition, been passed 'from heart-mind to heart-mind' through the centuries, and there are complex lineages outlining the Zen masters through whom the transmission has been effected (see *EPR* 445–450).

Whether Zen can be defined as a religion or not is a moot point. The Japanologist, Michael Diener, states (*EPR* 443):

> It is rather an indefinable, incommunicable root, free from all names, descriptions, and concepts, that can only be experienced by each individual for him- or herself.

The word 'incommunicable' is a translation of *fukasetsu*, meaning 'unsay-able', and this is characteristic of the mystical experience over the ages among followers of many religious paths. It is closely linked with the native Chinese philosophy of Taoism, to be explored in the next chapter, but its links with Zen can be illustrated here by these words of the Taoist sage Chuang Tzu:

> If the Tao were something that could be presented, each man would present it to his lord. If the Tao were something that could be handed to somebody, each man would give it to his parents. If the Tao were something that could be told to others, everybody would tell it to his brothers.

Zen does not really belong to any specific religion, not even to Buddhism. All the great religious leaders, sages, saints and *gurus*, of all cultures and nations, can be described as Zen masters; and *zazen* may be characterised, not so much as a means of helping people of a certain religious persuasion, as the realisation of the perfection, the spiritual nature, that is always latent in everyone.

PURE LAND BUDDHISM

We should not leave Buddhism in China without a brief mention of a Mahayana school that today, in both China and Japan, has more followers than any other school. Pure Land Buddhism, known also as 'Buddha-realms' or 'Buddha-paradises' (Chinese: *ching-t'u*), expresses the belief that there are a large number of transcendent states, each ruled or watched over by a Buddha, and designated as 'Pure Lands'. In folk belief they exist as blissful, geographically located places, but basically they represent aspects of the awakened state of mind. They are one step, but only one step, this side of *nirvana*, and it is believed that, once a person has entered a Pure Land, he or she will never regress, so that ultimate entry into *nirvana* is assured.

Out of all the Pure Lands, variously located according to directions of the compass, the most important is **Sukhaviti**, literally 'the blissful', the Pure Land of the West. Like all the Pure Lands, it was created from the karmic merit of a Buddha, in this case, **Amitabha**, meaning 'boundless light'. According to tradition, he was a king who became a monk after encountering Buddhist teaching. He vowed that if he achieved enlightenment he would free his karmic merit (*punya*) to others, so that, by calling on his name and envisaging his person, they too should be reborn in his Buddha-field. Having become a Buddha, he fulfilled his vow and remains one to whom any follower may still turn in order to be reborn in Sukhaviti. There he (nobody is reborn there as a woman) will awaken in a lotus-flower and will experience no sorrow, misfortune, pain or any other unpleasantness. He will hear Amitabha, abide by his teaching, and then proceed to enter *nirvana*.

What, then, must followers do in order to gain this assurance? First of all, Amitabha's name must be recited continually. This process, sustained for lengthy periods, enables them to concentrate the mind in preparation for the second stage, which is to visualise Amitabha and his companions in their blissful state. At first, this visualisation will be of the Buddha in separation from the follower, but this should lead to a higher point, at which separation ceases and he is contemplated in union with the follower. The final stage is to see Buddha Amitabha in a vision, after which rebirth in his Pure Land is guaranteed.

There is a world of difference between this teaching and that of Theravada Buddhism, where every step is to be made by one's personal decisions and efforts. Here, help comes from beyond through the liberating will of the Buddha. It is also, literally, an 'easier way': *tariki*, meaning 'power of the other', which was advocated by Amitabha himself for those unable to undertake the rigours of Theravada (or, being women, were not allowed to). Simply to call on Amitabha in the hour of death gives assurance of rebirth in his Pure Land. The formula of the invocation is 'Veneration to the Buddha Amitabha' (in Chinese, '*Namo o-mi-to-fo*').

The opposite of *tariki* is *jiriki*, meaning 'one's own power', which probably has its clearest manifestation in Zen: there is a difference again between the Zen monk practising *zazen* when facing a wall and the Pure Land Buddhist calling repeatedly on Amitabha in the hope of receiving some of his *punya*, or karmic merit (as big a difference, perhaps, as there is in Christianity between the Society of Friends and members of the charismatic movement). On the face of it, *tariki* and *jiriki* are poles apart, but the situation may not be as stark as it seems. Even on the *tariki* path, one's own efforts are required in order to make oneself receptive to the merit of the 'other', while one's 'own effort' on the *jiriki* path can be viewed as in part a discovery of the power of 'the other'. The important question of *punya*, merit, will be discussed in Chapter 15 with reference to human nature and motivation. Here it remains a value judgment (probably) whether enlightenment should be looked for with ease, or with difficulty; speedily, or slowly. Aldous Huxley, in *The Doors of Perception*, argued that the hallucinatory drug mescalin provided the surest, simplest and speediest way, although he did not comment on the meditational merits of its side-effect, schizophrenia.

TIBETAN BUDDHISM

Buddhism in Tibet is probably the form of this philosophy most famous in the West, partly, no doubt, because of the occupation of that country for around half a century by the Chinese, who have made continual – so far, unsuccessful – attempts to eradicate it since 1950, when they declared Tibet to be the Chinese province of Xizang (and accepted as such by the editors of, for example, the *Collins Atlas of the World*, first published in Edinburgh in 1983). It is not the purpose of this book to enter into political debate on this matter, except to say that, as so often where people have been persecuted for their beliefs, with whatever difficulty, Tibetan Buddhism survives, and Tibetan efforts to express their beliefs freely are supported by non-Tibetans throughout the world. It was Napoleon, not Buddha, who said that when ideas were confronted by the sword, ideas would always win; so far, the Tibetans have proved him right.

Buddhism took its hold in Tibet and in neighbouring Himalayan countries in the eighth century CE, mainly through the ministry of **Padmasambhava** (meaning 'the Lotus-born'), a Tantric master from Kashmir. He was venerated by his followers as the 'second Buddha' and to this day retains that veneration in Himalayan countries under the name Guru Rinpoche (Precious Guru). One school in particular, the Nyingmapa (literally 'School of the Ancients'), celebrates important events in his life on the tenth day of each month and invokes him in sentiments like these:

> In the northwest of the land of Urgyen
> On a blooming lotus-flower
> You attained supreme wondrous perfection.
> You are called the Lotus-born
> And are surrounded by a retinue of *dakinis*.
> I follow your example –
> Approach and grant me your blessing.

(The *dakini* was a female spirit who accompanied the gods at the highest levels. In Tibet she was seen as naked, symbolic of unveiled truth.)

Padmasambhava may be described as an early syncretist. In Tibet he encountered two indigenous traditions: nature worship and **Bon**, a generic term originally associated with priestly functions, such as divination and burial rites for the protection of the living and the dead. Over the centuries there has sometimes been conflict between Buddhism and native traditions, but the main outcome is that in Tibet it has assimilated certain of the earlier features, a process of syncretism that gives Tibetan Buddhism a distinctive stamp.

This distinctiveness is reflected in the fact that, while we are exploring Tibetan Buddhism as part of the Mahayana tradition, it strictly belongs to a third tradition, the *Vajrayana*, or 'diamond vehicle'. The diamond, *vajra*, also known to Tibetans as *dorje*, is unchangeable reality: the emptiness or void (*shunyata*), described by Nagarjuna (see pages 58–9). It is referred to in Zen in a famous saying that, despite the virtually limitless number of phenomena that we encounter as objects of the five *skandhas*, '*there is not a thing there*'. The *vajra*, or *dorje*, which coexists with the world of phenomena, can be known and understood only in enlightenment; but, once understood, it is as adamantine as a diamond: hence the name of this third vehicle. Padmasambhava describes it in these words:

> The secret mind of all the Buddhas,
> Omniscient wisdom
> Transmitted by the symbol of eternal strength and firmness,
> Clarity and emptiness, the *dorje* essence,
> Like heavenly space –
> It is wonderful to see the true face of reality.

If the 'true face of reality' is, then, the void, how real are the phenomena that we encounter? There is a difference of opinion about this, depending on how one is to interpret the faculty described as *chitta* (or *citta*). We saw on page 57 that it can be used as a synonym for *manas* (the thinking mind) or *vijnana* (consciousness), or for mental energy generally. However, in the teaching of a school that greatly influenced Tibetan thinking, the **Yogachara**, *chitta* has a different connotation. This school was founded in the fourth century CE by a convert from Hinduism to Buddhism, **Asanga** (meaning 'Unbound'). He propounded the concept of *alaya-vijnana*, meaning literally 'storehouse consciousness'. The standpoint here is that *chitta* is the only true reality: all the world's phenomena, the objects of human perception, together with the faculty that perceives them, are contained within it. Only the *karma* inherited from past errors blinds us to this truth, causing us to believe that the objects of empirical enquiry are 'real': ultimately, the true nature of things is *tathata*, or '*suchness*' (a word similar in meaning to 'Buddha-nature'). This belief is a step beyond that even of the philosopher Berkeley, who stated that nothing exists independently of minds that perceive them: 'to be is to be perceived'. Here, even that which is perceived by human minds is viewed as ultimately illusory, not least because the minds themselves are illusory.

This teaching is epitomised in the pursuit of what Tibetan Buddhists term *dzogchen*, or 'great perfection', also known as *ati-yoga*, 'extraordinary yoga'. Tradition has it that Padmasambhava received it from the *dakinis* and buried it in one of a number of places where he left the so-called *termas*, or 'treasures':

religious writings that were hidden away, pending the arrival of one who would understand and be able to expound them. (The most famous *terma* is *The Tibetan Book of the Dead* – see below.)

The basic teaching of *dzogchen* in the Yogachara School evolves from the above-mentioned concept of *alaya-vijnana* (storehouse consciousness), described by Padmasambhava as the 'naked' mind that underlies our surface, or day-to-day consciousness. Sadly, most people are blinded to *alaya-vijnana* because of their attachment to *samsara*, the cycle of birth and rebirth; but when, in periods of prolonged meditation, they enter this deep state, they experience union with *shunyata*, the void, sometimes described as the realisation of the 'rainbow body'. This is the sense of the dissolution of the physical body into light, a state of meditation that, it hardly needs to be added, few actually attain, although over the centuries many have testified to its reality.

The Tibetan Book of the Dead (*Bardo Thodol*) develops these ideas along lines indicated by the literal meaning of those Tibetan words: 'liberation through hearing in the in-between state'. The in-between state referred to (*bardo*) is the one between one cycle of experience and the next. There are three of these, all associated, in some way, with light. The first is the moment of death (*dharmakaya*), when a dazzling white light appears; the second is the *bardo* of supreme reality (*sambogakaya*), when the five colours appear that are associated with the five *buddhakulas* (literally 'Buddha families', to be described below); the light in the third *bardo* is less bright, but the phenomena relate to the six modes of existence (*bhava-chakra*) that were outlined on page 67, and in Tibetan Buddhism are known as the **Wheel of Life**.

The depiction of this Wheel is probably the most familiar of all Eastern iconography. It is a representation of *samsara* and mostly contains scenes that illustrate the six modes of existence already described – those at the higher, and those at the lower levels. Because death is common to all of them, the Wheel is held in the claws of Yama, God of the Underworld. The causes of *samsara* are depicted at the centre of the Wheel: the cock, symbolising desire; the pig, symbolising ignorance; and the snake, symbolising hatred and aggression. The Wheel is surrounded by scenes that depict the twelve factors of *pratitya-samutpada* (conditioned arising): ignorance, power of formation (creativity), consciousness, mind and body, the six senses, contact, sensation, craving, grasping or attachment, becoming, birth, and death. The whole of the *bhava-chakra* illustrates how profound philosophical ideas can be imparted through iconography, although it can also be interpreted at a populist level.

The *Bardo Thodol* aims to instruct its readers on how to bring about their rebirth in the higher, rather than the lower, realms, and this, perhaps more than any other feature of non-Theravada Buddhism, illustrates the difference in emphasis from the more stringent approach of that tradition, where the inexorable consequences of *karma* are accepted without qualification. These words by HH The Dalai Lama in his foreword to one edition of the *Bardo Thodol* illustrate this point:

> Although how or where we are reborn is generally dependent on karmic forces, our state of mind at the time of death can influence the quality of our next rebirth.

How then do Tibetan Buddhists pursue *dzogchen*? In their tradition, three processes are viewed as enabling to any seeker after that state of perfection; Buddhists of other schools would no doubt also use some, if not all, of them. The first is the recital of a *mantra*, a series of syllables that are believed to contain cosmic powers. The function of the *mantra* is to enable the meditator to concentrate, either on the written form of the syllables or on their sound. The advice is:

> At the time of reciting:
> Neither too fast nor too slow,
> Neither too loud nor too soft.
> It should be neither speaking
> Nor distraction.

The recitation should be accompanied by a form of visualisation known as *sadhana*, from the root *sadhu*, meaning 'reaching perfection'. The one who practises it (known, when he/she achieves success, as a *sadhaka*) brings to mind the image of a divine being with whom he/she seeks ultimately to be identified. This should not be interpreted as a form of magic but rather as self-identification with a particular energy principle that is believed to be present. Direction in this activity is provided by the 'Buddhakulas', or 'Buddha family', mentioned on page 80. These are five different aspects of wisdom, each symbolised by a family whose head (*tathagata*) has gained supreme enlightenment, *samyak-sambuddha*. By visualising one of these lords of the five families (Vairochana, Akshobhya, Tanasambhva, Amitabha – of the 'Pure Land' school – and Amoghasiddhi), it is believed that the follower can gain some of his *punya* (merit) through the energy that is present.

The oldest and most important mantra of Tibetan Buddhism is *OM MANI PADME HUM*, literally 'OM, jewel in the lotus, hum', and is associated with the *bodhisattva* Avaloki-teshvara. The two middle words probably mean the 'jewel' of the 'naked' or 'enlightened' mind, *bodhi-citta* (described above), which arises in the 'lotus' of human consciousness. The words express a basic feeling of compassion, the longing to reach *nirvana* for the sake of all sentient beings. The six syllables are also associated with the six levels of being in *bhava-chakra*, the Wheel of Life.

A second aid in seeking *dzogchen* is the *mandala*. Anyone who has studied Tibetan iconography will be familiar with these intricate designs, which are used as a focal point for a particular visualisation. The meaning of the word is, roughly, 'centre and periphery'; at the centre is a particular deity, for whom the *mandala* is his environment. He is normally surrounded by a palace with four gates facing the four directions; at the outer rim are usually circles of flame in the five colours that represent the five Buddha families. The *mandala* may be painted, drawn with coloured sand (often destroyed on completion to symbolise *anicca*, impermanence), represented by heaps of rice, or be three-dimensional.

The third aid is the *mudra*, literally 'seal' or 'sign', referring to a symbolic gesture of the hands. *Mudras* are used during the recital of *mantras*, or while contemplating *mandalas*, and during the performance of the public liturgy. It is believed that they help to bring about a connection between the meditator or worshipper and the Buddha visualised in the *sadhana*. There are ten main *madras*, all having a distinct significance. The most famous is the *anjali mudra*, the *mudra* of greeting: here, the palms are pressed together, fingers raised upright, and held at the level of the chest. This is a customary gesture of greeting in India and symbolises *tathata*, 'suchness'. In meditation it is customary to use the *dhyana mudra*, with the back of the right hand resting on the palm of the left so that the thumbs touch; the hands are then placed in the lap. The right hand represents the state of enlightenment, the left, the world of appearance; the combined gesture symbolises the state in which the one has been overcome by the other.

As in all Buddhist traditions, the *sangha* as a monastic order is prominent in Tibetan Buddhism. A unique feature in this school is the *lama*, literally 'none above', who is both an expert in the *dharma* and a spiritual guide to those who have 'entered the stream'. Because of the prominence of the *lamas*, Tibetan Buddhism is sometimes described in the West as 'Lamaism'; but this is to characterise the whole by a single feature, and Tibetans reject the inference as much as Roman Catholics object to the designation 'Papists'.

To become a *lama* and head a monastery (or more than one) requires many years of study and meditation, including at least three years in retreat. No Tibetan monk can pursue his own way without the constant direction of a *lama*, to whom absolute obedience is due. The *lama* will also lead public rituals for monks and laity alike, and usually has political influence alongside the spiritual. The chief *lama* is called the **Dalai Lama**, which literally means 'teacher whose wisdom is as great as the ocean'. It is believed that every one of the fourteen Dalai Lamas has been a reincarnation of his predecessor, a line of succession that goes back to the *bodhisattva* Avalokiteshvara. His deputy is the **Panchen Lama**, who assumes the role of leader during the interregnum between the death of one Dalai Lama and the 'emergence' of the next.

The great pillars of Tibetan Buddhism are the strong discipline, and the profound teaching, based, as we have seen, on Nagarjuna's concept of the void (*shunyata*) and Asanga's concept of 'mind only' (*yogachara*). These two pillars have produced a distinctive form of **Tantra**, the Hindu version of which was discussed on page 23. Many of the Hindu features are retained in this school of Buddhism, particularly the recognition of the seven *chakras*. *Chakra* literally means wheel, or circle, but in Tantrism it refers specifically to the subtle centres from which energy is channelled through the body. These are located in six places:

1 between the genitals and the anus (Muladhara-chakra);
2 at the base of the genitals (Svadishthana-chakra);
3 at the abdomen (Manipura-chakra);
4 near the heart (Anahata-chakra);
5 at the throat (Vishuddha-chakra);
6 between the eyes (Ajna-chakra).

Hindu Tantrism teaches that there is a serpent, *kundalini*, coiled around the base of the spine, which, once awakened (as it can be in Tantric meditation) rises through the *chakras* to express itself in forms of spiritual knowledge and mystical visions. In Tibet, it is believed that, by concentrating on any one of the *chakras* during meditation, spiritual qualities associated with that particular centre of energy can be achieved.

The final step is to awaken Sahasrara-chakra, the seventh *chakra*, located over the crown of the head. In Hindu Tantrism it is believed that to meditate on this *chakra* brings about union with the god Shiva, leading ultimately to cosmic consciousness. In Tibet the imagery is different, with no reference either to Shiva or to any other god; instead, the emphasis is on taking the meditator into the void, or state of 'suchness'.

There are three categories of the way to spiritual fulfilment: ground, path and fruition. The *ground* is the one who meditates; the *path* is the way of meditation, which purifies the ground; the *fruition* is the attainment of the 'great perfection' of *ati-yoga*, or *dzogchen*. As mentioned on page 73, Tibetan Buddhists recognise the twin polarities of male and female, representing, on the one hand, rationality and skill, and, on the other, intuitive wisdom and compassion. The highest experience involves the union of both – a belief that, as we shall see in Chapter 11, is pivotal in the Chinese teaching of *yin* and *yang*.

It has been possible in this chapter to give an account of only a selection of expressions of Mahayana Buddhism, and some significant schools, such as Japanese Nichiren Buddhism, have had to be left unexplored. Enough should have been presented, however, to indicate that, while it is possible to study the basics of Buddhist teaching at an elementary level, Buddhist philosophy attains a level of profundity that, to be understood, calls for mental resources as strictly as does any school of Western philosophy or theology. This may explain why Buddhism, more than Hinduism or, indeed, any other school of Eastern philosophy, has made major inroads in the West.

THE BUDDHIST DIASPORA

Alongside the phenomenon of Buddhist expansion stands the paradox that it is virtually non-existent in India, the country of its birth, and it may be helpful to end this chapter by indicating why this diaspora, or dispersion, occurred.

The first, and most important, reason was the Muslim invasion, motivated by the Islamic justification of *jihad*, or 'holy war' as a valid means of gaining converts to their faith. Buddhists, with their dedication to *ahimsa*, non-violence, were more at risk in this situation than were the Hindus with their warrior caste, the *kshatriya*. Moreover, Buddhists were more dependent on the *sangha* than were the Hindus, and these orders of monks were easily identifiable and therefore vulnerable to the Muslims, who, in addition, by depriving the laity of much of their property, forced them to reduce drastically the material support that they could offer to any *sangha* that survived.

The second reason was the antipathy of much of Hinduism. There were two palpable grounds for their opposition: Buddha's refusal to accept the Vedas as supremely authoritative where beliefs were concerned (hence his being listed among the *nastika*); and his rejection of the caste system. The first angered the scholars because Buddha claimed to have received a revelation beyond the guidelines that others found sufficient for their needs; and Hindus generally saw his social ideas as dangerous because they undermined the entire structure of their society. The universalism of Buddhism was thus at war with the nationalism of Hinduism, to the extent that even the saintly scholar Shankara declared Buddha an enemy of the people.

The third reason, noted by Peter Harvey in his *Introduction to Buddhism* (p.140), is more subtle. It was what Harvey terms 'the dilution of the distinctiveness of Buddhism relative to the rising power of Hinduism'. This dilution intensified with the advent of Mahayana Buddhism, many features of which seemed, to the laity, similar to those they encountered in their native religion. Many of the devotional exercises, especially those used in Tantrism, did not seem to need two discrete expressions; Shankara established religious orders not dissimilar to the *sangha*; and in their shared belief in the 'two levels of truth' (*samvriti-satya* and *paramartha-satya* – see page 59), it seemed that even on philosophical matters there was a possible rapprochement between the two. The weakening of the caste system in some Hindu quarters, and growing vegetarianism in others, helped to blur differences on social and ethical matters. The Hindu recognition of Buddha, in the sixth century, as an incarnation of Vishnu, served to intensify the impression that India did not need a second major religion (if that is how Buddhism should be described). The consequence is that, while Hinduism remains the national religion of India, Buddhism has become a worldwide phenomenon, no longer looking to India for spiritual inspiration (although, of course, pilgrimages are made to some of the historic places of significance in the Buddhist chronicles). Although not in every respect similar, there is a further parallel here (see page 71) with Judaism and Christianity.

9 Chinese philosophy I: Taoism

INTRODUCTION

We have seen that one of the three major religions/philosophies of China over the past two millennia has been Buddhism. While not many Chinese today would describe themselves as Theravada Buddhists, many have, without feeling compelled to surrender their own traditions, accommodated themselves to a Mahayana school, such as Pure Land and Ch'an (Zen) Buddhism. In fact, until the nineteenth century, the only foreigners whom the Chinese did not view as barbarians were the Indians, who were respected because of their Buddhist teachings.

However, Buddhism arrived in China only in the first century CE; for many centuries prior to that, the Chinese had had schools of philosophy of their own, which continued to coexist, and sometimes to blend, with this new form of expression. The most significant of these native traditions came to the fore around the middle of the Chou (Zhou) dynasty in the sixth/fifth centuries BCE, a period generally accepted as the golden age of Chinese philosophy (see my comment about this age universally on page 152). It is often claimed that, during this period, there were 'a hundred schools of thought', but this is a misrepresentation of the situation, since the majority of these so-called schools were in fact variations on one another. Careful analysis suggests that there were six major schools:

1 **Taoism**, based on the *Tao Te Ching*.
2 The **Yin–Yang School** (Yin–Yang Chia).
3 **Confucianism** (Confucius, Mencius, Hsun Tzu).
4 **Mohism** (Mo Tzu, Mo Ti or Mo Chia).
5 The **Legalist School** (Pa Chia).
6 The **School of Names** (Ming Chia).

Our concern will be with only the first three of these schools, with a brief reference to the fourth. The Legalist School was primarily concerned with the question of effective government and indicated, as its name suggests, how this may best be achieved through the effective use of the law as an instrument to control the people. The School of Names (a literal translation of its title) refers to a group of philosophers who have been compared to the Sophists of ancient Greece. Their interest lay in the analysis of words and their meaning, with the aim of avoiding logical errors in language. They are mentioned, usually in critical terms, mainly by representatives of the first four schools. All but one of their writings (and that survives only in part) have been lost, which, as one commentator, Laurence Wu (*Fundamentals of Chinese Philosophy*, p.183), has remarked, 'is highly indicative of the general Chinese attitude toward this school'.

In the chapters on Hinduism and Buddhism, the matter of whether it was philosophy or religion that we were discussing was left unresolved. With Chinese thought it is possible to be less ambivalent. While there is a supernatural, even magical, element in some of the teachings (particularly Taoism), the schools in the main fall into the arena of philosophy rather than religion (although this will be further explored in later chapters). The Chinese word for philosophy is *zhe-chue*, or *zhe-xue*, which means much the same as the word in English (via the Greek): love of wisdom. It is important to be aware from the start, however, that this does not mean the pursuit of knowledge for its own sake. Chinese scholars point out that the character *zhe* (wisdom) depicts both a hand and a mouth, indicating that ideas and behaviour, theory and practice, should be consistent with each other: a person should not be just 'philosophically minded' but should see to it that the creation of beautiful ideas goes hand in hand with the leading of a happy and fulfilled life. If the ideal Indian is a *guru*, the ideal Chinese is more likely to be a cook. It has to be stressed – and this will become clearer as we proceed to examine the schools in detail – that, while the concepts of *maya* and *duhkha* are not absent from Chinese thought, they play nothing like the central role that they have in India. Thus it is important to be careful when using the generic term 'Eastern philosophy' or 'Eastern thought': the differences between Indian and Chinese approaches to many of the issues that we are exploring is, as A. Bahm has indicated in his book *Comparative Religion*, sometimes as great as those between Western and Eastern thought.

In much of Chinese literature in this field there is a strong element of what Westerners would characterise as humanism: that is, the assertion of the intrinsic value of life on Earth. However, unlike the humanism of the Western Renaissance, which emphasised individual freedom and personal fulfilment, Chinese humanism sets greater store on the relationship between individuals and their fellows: social empathy rather than personal development is their overriding aim. Two central features of Chinese thought follow from this emphasis. The first is that philosophy, far from being the somewhat esoteric pursuit that it is sometimes held to be in the West (particularly the English-speaking West), is accepted as a natural facet of life, relevant to even the most mundane activities, such as preparing a meal, choosing one's clothes or planning a home. The second feature follows from this: since philosophy permeates the whole of life, the question of whether the values under discussion are human or religious does not arise. Behaviour is both a human and a spiritual matter, and the search for 'truth' both a human and spiritual enterprise.

Because of this fundamental concept, Chinese thought tends to approach areas of conflict from a 'both–and' rather than an 'either–or' perspective. This synthetic approach leads to tolerance between different schools of thought that followers of certain Western traditions – particularly those who shudder at the very mention of the word 'relativism' – are liable to criticise as suggestive of a lack of firm conviction. Lin Yutang, who has popularised Chinese philosophy in *The Importance of Living* and other works, drolly illustrates the lack of absolutism in his country's thought-processes with the observation that every Chinese is a Confucian when successful, a Taoist in times of failure (one might add that they may also be Buddhists when meditating). We shall return to this key issue in Chapter 18.

A further point to note when reading Chinese philosophy is that it emerges from a rural, rather than a Western-style urban, context. Most of the examples, and much of the imagery, reflect this background: mountains, streams, plants, animals and clouds, rather than machines, buildings, roads, computers and mechanical means of transport. It may be, consequently, that, if we are to give Chinese thought a Western application, some adjustment of the contextual element will be needed. However, the need to view the world ecologically rather than mechanically will remain paramount, whatever visual examples are used.

Before proceeding to a study of the schools, one final point must be made about the classical Chinese style of writing. It has often been described as one of *creative ambiguity*. Because it is expressed in pictorial form, it has a different grammatical and syntactical structure to that with which we are familiar in the West, thus denying the writings the kind of intricate analysis that is facilitated only by the use of an alphabet (or a script that includes characters that have gained 'alphabetical' qualities, as in modern Chinese). Consequently, it is incapable of presenting anything but the simplest form of a logically developed argument; it has to operate through suggestion and imagery, appealing to the intuition as much as to the rational faculty. This creates a situation of both weakness and strength: the weakness lies in the inability of classical Chinese to sustain a lengthy argument along the lines of, say, the Cartesian Meditations or Kant's *Critique of Pure Reason* (or even the writings of Nagarjuna): its strength lies in its ability to spark off ideas, often subconsciously, which readers can either follow up directly or allow to surface at will. It is significant, for instance, that, in the scores of English translations of the greatest of the Chinese classics, the *Tao Te Ching*, the expressions of the ideas abstracted from the original text vary enormously. The fact is that the classical Chinese language is, as Laurence Wu acknowledges, 'an excellent tool for poetry but not for systematic or scientific thought: one finds . . . profound insights, brilliant aphorisms, interesting metaphors, but few elaborate arguments' (*op. cit.* p.11). Students of Chinese texts, turning, perhaps, from Calvin's *Institutes of the Christian Religion*, or

Aquinas's *Summa Theologica*, must judge for themselves not only which of the two styles is the more instructive, but also which is able to reach more deeply into the hearts and minds of readers.

TAOISM

The Taoist school was not the earliest of the Chinese schools, but its central concept is found throughout most Chinese writings, whether as a key element in the philosophy concerned or, at the very least, as one that must be taken into consideration. Even Confucius, who, as we shall see in Chapter 12, expressed certain views that Taoists held to be the reverse of their own, claimed to be sympathetic to Taoism, attempting to express its values in areas left largely undeveloped in their writings.

We need to be clear from the outset that Taoism has two quite distinct – and, in many ways, totally opposing – expressions. These are **tao-chia** and **tao-chiao**: philosophical Taoism and religious (or magical) Taoism, respectively. Our main concern lies with the former, since it is this expression that relates to other schools of thought under survey in this book and has made an increasing impact on Western thinking over recent decades. In China itself, however, *tao-chiao* has probably influenced far more people over the centuries than has *tao-chia*, and this will be acknowledged by outlining its main characteristics in the next chapter.

The *Tao Te Ching*

The book known as the *Tao Te Ching* is, along with the *I Ching* and the *Analects* of Confucius (both of which will be considered in later chapters), one of a triumvirate that reach the highest peaks of classical Chinese creative writings. The word *ching* is an honorary title, given only to works of the highest eminence: the straightforward translation is, simply, 'classic'. The meaning of the word *Tao* is discussed at length on pages 90–6, but it may be defined here as 'the unknowable source of all things'; it is the 'way' that brings into being, by various stages, the whole of creation, physical, mental and spiritual. Very loosely, it may be equated with the Hindu concept of *brahman*, the ground of being: but that ground is, according to the Vedanta tradition, not only definable but also recognisable as the same spirit that is manifested in the *atman* of each individual; the *Tao*, on the contrary, remains mysterious, the origin of all things rather than the manifestation of them.

This manifestation is the *Te*; it is the power of the *Tao* revealed in the world of phenomena, together with the 'virtue' that this power brings about in anyone, or anything, that follows the way. By 'virtue' is meant genuineness, in the sense of being true to one's own nature: avoiding artificiality and pretence. Taoism has, as we shall see, much to say about what we should today term ecological issues: the lotus blooms, the tiger roars, the eddy whirls: all these, by following their own natures, bear witness to the *Tao* by expressing the *Te*. Similarly, the human being who toils, and loves, and reflects according to his or her basic needs and drives and intuitions, thereby reveals the virtue of the *Te*.

The *Tao Te Ching* is a short book, consisting of just five thousand pictograms, and is therefore often referred to by the Chinese as the 'Text of the Five Thousand Signs'. It has eighty-one short chapters and can easily be read at a single sitting. This would be a misuse of the book, however, since each chapter presents a particular idea for meditation or reflection; it is typical of the non-analytical style of classical Chinese writing described earlier, calling for an intuitive, at least as much as a reasoned, response from the reader. Like all the great spiritual and contemplative classics, such as the *Bhagavad-Gita*, A Kempis's *The Imitation of Christ*, or Marcus Aurelius's *Meditations*, it is to be pondered over slowly rather than read as a formal treatise on a theme.

According to tradition, it was written by **Lao Tzu** in the sixth century BCE, but its genesis is now held by Chinese scholars to have been some two centuries later: the earliest existing copy dates from around 200 BCE. 'Lao Tzu' means 'great master', a title rather than a name, and there is no certainty that it refers to a single historical person. More likely, the *Tao Te Ching* brings together the accumulation of ideas about *Tao* and *Te* over some centuries prior to their final editing and presentation as a single work (rather like the Gospels). Yet the legend persists that there was a Lao Tzu, that he actually met Confucius, and that Confucius was so bedazzled by him that he conferred on him the highest possible accolade: 'He is like a dragon.' There is a persistent further legend, based on the 'Historical Records' (*Shih-chi*), which date from around the second century BCE, that he was born in what is now Honan Province, was archivist to its king, Chou, fell out with the king and resigned his post, and travelled west, never to be heard of again. At the mountain pass of Hsien-ku, through which he left, he was met by Yin Hsi, the Guardian of the Pass, who recognised him as a man of insight and asked him to write down his deepest thoughts before he left. These thoughts, so the legend goes, are the *Tao Te Ching*; having read them, Yin Hsi became a recluse and was eventually admitted to the Taoist pantheon as an immortal (*hsien*, see pages 103–4). He is said to be the author of the *Kuan yin tzu*, describing certain Taoist methods of meditation. Then he too travelled west and disappeared for ever.

Whatever its origins, and whoever its author or authors, the *Tao Te Ching* speaks across the centuries and cultures. The translation used here (unless otherwise stated) is by Man-ho Kwok, Martin Palmer and Jay Ramsay, published by Element in 1993. Martin Palmer writes in the preface:

> Whoever it was who edited the collection of wisdom sayings and teachings ... was a genius. Although unknown to us, his work continues to speak to us and to challenge us to re-examine our thoughts and ways. It ... is one of the few religious texts that can be read and enjoyed by people of many different faiths as well as by those of no specific faith. It has no creator

God. It has no deities. It has no spirits or religious dogmas. What it has is the notion of the Way – a Way which we each need to make our own, but which flows through time and cultures, just as the river, so often pictured in the text, flows naturally down to the sea, bringing everything with it.

The *Tao*

Taoism, as the name suggests, centres itself on the concept of the *Tao*, a difficult idea to express in words, as is affirmed from the start by the *Tao Te Ching*. Its famous opening lines highlight the problem:

> The Tao that can be talked about is not the true Tao. The name that can be named is not the eternal Name.

If we were to take the author here at his word, the discussion would presumably cease at this point; but, since the *Tao Te Ching* itself continues with its five thousand pictograms, we may be emboldened to proceed. The word *Tao* literally means 'Way'. In many traditions this denotes the way of man, an outline of moral behaviour; and it is in this sense that numerous Western philosophical and religious traditions use the word. In Taoist thought, however, it has a distinctive metaphysical meaning.

The Tao is the all-embracing origin of all things, the first principle from which all appearances arise; it is the ground of being, the underlying reality that sustains the universe and makes possible its ongoing existence and activity. We cannot see the *Tao*; it is not manifest to the senses, but without the *Tao* there could be no consciousness of anything. All things and all creatures have their being only because of the *Tao*, the source of all that exists. Chapter 25 begins with a straightforward declaration of this mystery:

> Before the world was
> And the sky was filled with stars . . .
> There was
>   a strange unfathomable Body.
> This Being, this Body is silent
>   and beyond all substance and sensing.
> It stretches beyond everything
>   spanning the empyrean.
> It has always been here, and it always will be.
> Everything comes from it, and then
>   it is the Mother of Everything.
> I do not know its name. So I call it *Tao*.

The nearest that Western philosophy approaches to this concept is in the Greek expression of the *logos*, the underlying principle in all things. In Hindu thought we have seen the idea expressed through the doctrine of *brahman*; in Buddhism, there is the concept of the *dharmakaya*, meaning 'the body of the great order': the true nature of Buddha which is at one with all that exists, the transcendental reality and the essence of the universe. In these other Eastern schools, however, the ultimate is given a name that reflects its nature; and it is affirmed that a follower can experience that nature within his or her own being. In Taoism, the ultimate remains mysterious and unknowable, so that its very being can be divined only because of the forces, and their consequences, to which it gives rise. The *Tao* is not even describable as the Origin of the universe; that Origin is *Ch'i*, or primeval breath: and the *Tao* is the source of *Ch'i*, the origin of the Origin.

This complex notion is expressed in chapter 42 of the *Tao Te Ching*:

> The Tao
> gives birth to the One;
> The One
> gives birth to the two;
> The Two
> give birth to the three;
> The Three give birth to every living thing.
> All things are held in *yin*, and carry *yang*:
> And they are held together in the *Ch'i*
> of teeming energy.

The One, then, is *ch'i*, literally vapour or, as translated above, breath; it also means energy, or spirit, and is similar in connotation to the Hebrew word *Ruach*, which can refer to either the breath or the Spirit, whether of God or of human beings. It is the life-force that pervades and vitalises all things, the cosmic energy that brought the universe into being and continues to sustain it. It can therefore be identified with *yuan-ch'i*, the primordial energy in which what Taoist thought describes as 'the Two' are still intermingled.

The Two are the twin forces of *yin* and *yang*. We shall consider these more fully in Chapter 11, but it may be mentioned here that they represent the polar opposites that underlie all that is and all that occurs in the universe. Their substantial manifestations are Earth and Heaven, which are two of the 'three legs of the tripod'. The third 'leg' is humanity, and together they are designated simply as 'The Three'. From these Three springs 'every living thing'. The Chinese phrase for this is *wan-wu*, which literally means 'ten thousand things, or beings', and many English translations retain the quaintness of the original phrase. Effectively it means 'things too numerous to count': everything, in fact, that the universe contains.

Inherent in Taoism is the concept of *fu*, meaning to return, or to recur. The law that underlies all appearances, everything that comes into being, is that they will return to their origin. Since all things originate in the *Tao*, it is to the *Tao* that they must ultimately return. Chapter 40 of the *Tao Te Ching* states that 'returning (or recurrence) is the motion of the Tao', while chapter 25 states, 'And being greater, it infuses all things, moving far out and returning to the source.'

There are a number of ways in which a disciple of Taoism may interpret this concept of returning. As we shall see later, it is closely linked with the twin forces of *yin* and *yang*: when anything reaches one extreme it reverses from it and moves towards the other extreme, and so on continuously. One can therefore view the process of returning as one of living a harmonious, balanced life: partly active, partly quiescent; partly social, partly solo. And the Taoist ideal, with which Confucius, despite differences of emphasis in his teaching, would not have disagreeed, is to experience life as a state of constant movement from one extreme to the other, recognising that (to take just one example of the extremes that most people encounter in their lives) action is enhanced by quiescence, and passivity enriched by activity. There are frequent references throughout most classical Chinese writings to the value of returning to one's roots between spells of activity away from them; and the image of the mother, or of the homeland, establishes itself firmly in these writings.

In other passages, the return is described as recovering one's original simplicity, or *p'u*. Literally, this means rough timber, an unhewn block: symbolic, therefore, of plainness or innocence. The ideal it envisages in a human being is one who has put aside both pretentiousness and pretence, and seeks to live like a newborn child, untouched by the cynicism of the world. But there is a difference: unlike a newborn child, such a person achieves simplicity against the backcloth of experience. Not out of ignorance but with, and despite, full awareness of the human condition, the goal of simplicity can be reached.

There are two main characteristics of the state of *p'u*. The first, and basic, of these is *wu wei*. This phrase tends to be translated negatively, in the sense of doing nothing, or 'include me out' (*ohne mich* – 'without me' – as the German phrase has it). From the writings of Chuang Tzu (see pages 97–103), this may sometimes appear to be a justifiable interpretation of the phrase, which can certainly be translated as 'non-doing': but there is a positive connotation to this characterisation. It is non-doing in the sense of doing nothing when there is nothing positive that can be done; acting, in other words, only when the time is ripe and the occasion demands it. Otherwise, as Chuang Tzu remarked, we are simply flaying the air, engaging ourselves in action that may temporarily improve our tempers but will not improve the situation a whit. A more accurate translation of *wu wei* would therefore be 'spontaneous action', not far removed from Zen's idea of hitting the target without taking aim. It means behaving intuitively, even unintentionally: expressing one's real feelings based on the real self, rather than on any kind of projected image that one may create of oneself. It is thus akin to Sartre's idea of 'good faith' and Buber's teaching about the 'I–Thou' relationship between persons. It is childlikeness without being childish, and it brings to mind Jesus's words, 'You must become as little children.' This kind of spontaneous action, devoid of any kind of premeditation, is a mark of a Taoist saint: one who speaks without reflecting on possible personal consequences of his remarks. (Chuang Tzu was, as we shall see, one such person; Buddha is acknowledged by Taoists to be another; it would be no exaggeration to describe Confucius as a third.)

The expression *wu wei* is, then, a supreme mark of returning to the *Tao*, of being in tune with, and faithful to, the source of being. The irony is that, despite apparent non-action, the *Tao Te Ching* affirms that 'nothing is left undone': a gentle touch, even an inflection of the voice, at the right place and time may be infinitely more effective than the most frenetic activity. Sometimes even the gentlest activity is superfluous to requirements, as Confucius illustrated in his comments (*Analects* 421) about the legendary Chinese emperor, Shun:

> He achieved order without taking any action ... There was nothing for him to do but to hold himself in a respectful posture and face due south.

This is to apply *wu wei* in the world of human affairs; at heart, however, it is a mystical experience, a sense of oneness with the source of being. The word *wu* on its own suggests the second characteristic of *p'u*: 'emptiness', or, as noted above, 'non-being'. It describes anyone so imbued with the power and virtue of the *Tao*, the *Te*, that he/she has become free from all passions and desires, and thus is 'empty'. (It is unsurprising that Taoists welcomed Buddhists from India, with their teaching of a void, and a 'state beyond desire'.) Such a person will be free from all attachments, unconcerned with worldly ambition or rewards, and victorious over envy and hatred, because he/she has lost the desire for wealth and fame. But herein lies a great mystery, a paradox, which can be known only to followers of the Way: by seeking nothing, so the *Tao Te Ching* affirms, everything comes one's way. Chapter 32 expresses this paradox; it refers to 'rulers', but it applies to all who seek Taoist wisdom:

> The Tao has no name
> > it is a cloud that has no shape.
> If a ruler
> follows it faithfully,
> then every living thing under heaven will say yes to him ...
> A ruler who walks the Way
> Is like a river reaching the sea
> Gathering the waters of the streams
> > into himself
> as he goes.

As we shall see in Chapter 10, religious Taoism (*tao-chiao*) encouraged followers to believe that, beyond, and perhaps above, these spiritual benefits, material rewards such as health and longevity might also accrue. Philosophical Taoism, however, viewed these worldly benefits as totally irrelevant to the main quest, which is to be in spiritual harmony with the *Tao*, as manifested in the *Te*; and this brings us back to the concept of *fu*, discussed earlier. To understand its mystery and recognise that all things not only originate in but return to the *Tao*, is to become enlightened, to achieve *ming*, or 'luminosity', a state beyond all material considerations. It is to recognise that the *Tao* is not only the source of all human endeavour, in the sense that without it no endeavour would be possible in the first place, but also its goal, since all things must ultimately return to their origin. This is a universal law, which the Chinese define as *ch'ang*, meaning the permanent, as opposed to the changeable. *Ch'ang* was defined by one philosopher, Han Fei-tzu, in the third century BC in these words:

> Things which now exist and then perish; which suddenly come into being and as suddenly die; which first bloom and then fade – such things are not *ch'ang*. Only that which was created simultaneously with the separation of Heaven and Earth, and will not perish before Heaven and Earth, can be called *ch'ang*.

To understand this is to achieve a mystical harmony with the *Tao*. Even the word 'understand' here may be misleading, since it suggests that the harmony can be achieved by striving to realise the *Tao* through intellectual processes. This is impossible: the *Tao* certainly manifests itself in human and worldly activities and qualities through the *Te*, as we have seen, but in itself the *Tao* is unknowable, since its essence is non-being, or nothingness.

This state of nothingness is known as *tzu-jan*, meaning 'being such of itself'. That is, it is something that is in total harmony with itself, needing nothing from outside or beyond itself in order to attain completion. The *Tao* is absolutely loyal to itself: it denotes the highest expression of being, which is a state of changelessness, of non-becoming: and therefore (and here lies the supreme mystery), of emptiness or non-being. It is a state of total spontaneity, and those who wish to be at one with it must also live spontaneously, laying aside their human intentions and becoming oblivious to external pressures or motivations. Chapter 25 of the *Tao Te Ching* ends with these words:

> Humanity is schooled by the Earth;
> Earth is taught by Heaven,
> And Heaven is guided by the Tao.
> And the Tao
>   goes with what is absolutely natural.

That final phrase can be translated simply as 'suchness', the spontaneous and intuitive state of *tzu-jan*. What Lao Tzu is saying is that oneness with the *Tao* can be experienced only when all self-conscious striving, whether marked by scholarly research, rigorous self-denial or devoted attendance at religious rituals, is recognised as being incapable of leading a person to *ming*, enlightenment. Like the Fourth State in Advaita Vedanta, *tzu-jan* takes us beyond the pairs of opposites, beyond all structuring and categorising, to a free-flowing state in which boundaries are blurred and the individual and nature are one. (Postmodernism, perhaps, two-and-a-half millennia before the word was invented.) It has been well said by numerous commentators that the surest expressions of Taoism by human beings are to be found not in their writings but in abstract art, and much Taoist literature uses this form to represent and interpret the elusive nature of the *Tao*.

In the writings of Lao Tzu's successor, Chuang Tzu, this concept of 'blurredness' was given clear expression:

> Tao may be known by no thoughts, no reflections. It may be approached by resting in nothingness, by following nothing, pursuing nothing ... The Sage teaches a doctrine which does not find expression in words.

What is being acknowledged here is that the mystical experience cannot be described verbally, nor can it be spoken of accurately in metaphorical terms, since there is no other experience or circumstance in the world with which it can be compared without risking either an over-simplification of the experience or, paradoxically, an over-complication. The fact is that to be at one with the *Tao* is too natural, ironically, for many to achieve, especially in the technology-dominated world of the West, where logic and hard work are twin gods and 'being natural' is usually interpreted derogatorily as 'doing your own thing'. This thought is expressed with awesome clarity in chapter 14 of the *Tao Te Ching*:

> When you gaze at something
> > but see – nothing;
> When you listen for a sound
> > but cannot hear it;
> When you try to grasp it
> > and find it has no substance
>
> – then these three things
> That go beyond your mind
> Are moulded together in the One.
>
> Its surface doesn't shine, but nor is its base dull.
> Given this, it is only knowable as no-thing.
> Confront it – it has no head;
> Come behind it, and it has no tail ...
>
> If people could follow the ancient way,
> then they would be masters of the moment.
>
> And if you know this way
> then you have seen the timeless way of the Tao.

The natural way of Taoism is illustrated by its acceptance of nature as complete in itself; to try and improve it will lead only to disaster, since any change in what is perfect can only be towards a less-than-perfect state (a truth that is as necessary for God as for the natural world, interestingly enough). This idea, which should evoke a sympathetic response in anyone whose philosophy is the slightest shade of Green, was expressed forthrightly by the second of the major Taoist philosophers, Chuang Tzu, whom some have described as effectively a halfway house between philosophical and religious Taoism. We now turn to a discussion of his views, along with those of *tao-chiao*.

10 Later developments in Taoism

CHUANG TZU

There is somewhat more historical evidence for the life and writings of Chuang Tzu, the second major Taoist figure, than there is for Lao Tzu; but this is not saying a lot. We know that he lived in what is now Honan province from 369–286 BCE; that he was married; and that he held a minor administrative post in Ch'i-yuan (the minor aspect reflecting his own choice, since he refused to follow the normal route to the higher positions, which was to serve under a prince or ruler). Private details of his life and character emerge from his book, the classic *Chuang-Tzu*. This contains thirty-three chapters, but only the first seven, known as the 'inner' chapters, were actually written by him; the fifteen so-called 'outer' chapters and the eleven 'mixed' chapters were almost certainly written by his disciples.

Chuang Tzu's philosophy is closely in tune with Lao Tzu's, and his writings are both a continuation and an extension of the ideas contained in the *Tao Te Ching*. They contain a good deal of wit and subtlety, not unmixed with asperity, and sometimes the humour is so dry that any unwary reader could easily miss it. There is in fact an acerbic, even abrasive, side to the *Chuang Tzu* that is not found in the earlier Taoist classic. It was not translated into English until 1881, and one reviewer who greeted it with enthusiasm was Oscar Wilde. Writing in the *Speaker* in 1890, he characterised it as 'the most caustic description of modern life I have met with for some time'. He continued:

> Chuang-tzu ... is a very dangerous writer and the location of his book in English, two thousand years after his death, is obviously premature and may cause a good deal of pain to many thoroughly respectable and industrious people ... It seems to me that if once we admitted the force of any one of Chuang-tzu's destructive criticisms we would have to put some check on our national habit of self-glorification.

Even discounting Wilde's delight in irony, this comment suggests that in studying Chuang Tzu we are doing more than peruse a set of ancient chronicles from an antiquarian's perspective. So what is it that gives him a contemporary significance, and, in particular, how might his ideas be seen as potentially dangerous for a nation or a government?

It is important not to approach Chuang Tzu without being well versed in the *Tao Te Ching*, because the teaching contained in the earlier book permeates the later one. Fundamental to it is the acceptance of the underlying creative and sustaining energy of the universe emanating from the *Tao*, and manifested in each creature and entity through the *Te*. These two forces are the catalyst of Chuang Tzu's philosophy, even where it involves itself in issues that the *Tao Te Ching* left unexplored or undeveloped.

A central feature is, again, the concept of *wu wei*. We saw in the previous chapter that this should be translated not as 'inaction', as we often find, but as 'action that is appropriate to the situation', or 'going with the flow'. To act inappropriately will do harm rather than good, like a farmer who tries to help wheat to grow by giving it a tug (an apt example for Chuang Tzu's teaching, but actually used by his contemporary, Mencius – see Chapter 12). In many circumstances, there is effectively nothing that can be done except to wait: anything else is, as we saw in Chapter 9, simply 'flaying the air', improving the situation not a whit. This 'flaying' includes much of the talking in which human beings engage themselves: they spend hours telling one another how they would deal with problematic situations but their talk, in most cases, is no more, and no more effective, than hot air (a quintessentially Chuang Tzu concept). So quiescence and silence are, according to Chuang Tzu, not only effective ways of coming to terms with situations, they are often the only realistic course open to us. (The British prime minister in 1926, Stanley Baldwin, was unwittingly expressing this Taoist philosophy when, at 9.30 p.m. on the evening before the General Strike, he went to bed.)

For Chuang Tzu, *wu wei* was the key to successful living, and his delineation of it gives him a unique slot in the history of the world's ideas. To live according to *wu wei*, as we saw earlier, means that one's behaviour, whether expressed in words or in actions, becomes intuitive and spontaneous. That is to say, one does not spend time always looking for alternatives in any situation and giving reasons why one way is preferable to another. As A.C. Graham puts it in his introduction to *Chuang-Tzu – the Inner Chapters*:

> People who really know what they are doing ... spread attention over the whole situation, let its focus roam freely, forget themselves in their total absorption in the object, and then the trained hand reacts spontaneously with a confidence and precision impossible to anyone who is applying rules and thinking out moves.
>
> (*op. cit.* p.6)

In his third chapter, Chuang Tzu spoke of a butcher whose knife had remained as sharp as ever for nineteen years because, by carving the animal as he did, he never cut a ligament, a tendon or a bone. Similarly, a carpenter knows how to chisel a wheel in such a way that he neither glides pointlessly over the surface of the wood nor makes indentations in it. The art of skiing is to forget about technique and become one with the slopes of the mountain; and the same principle applies to whatever we undertake: the aim is to lose self-consciousness, to stop thinking about what we are doing, and commit ourselves to it. Thus, through the simplicity of spontaneity, anyone may the more effectively play a musical instrument, act a role in a play or perform to his or her highest potential in a sport. This is close to Zen, the philosophy that envisages the archer's hitting the target without taking aim. Followers of both schools openly accept the view of the *Tao Te Ching*, quoted earlier: 'Tao invariably does nothing, yet there is nothing that is not done' (chapter 37). Overdoing is in fact not only unnecessary but also destructive, like gilding a lily, or painting feet on a snake.

Relativism

So far, there is little to be found in Chuang Tzu's teaching that would cause palpitations in the establishment, as forecast by Oscar Wilde. Two extensions of *wu wei* may indicate what Wilde had in mind. The first is the emphasis that Chuang Tzu laid on what we would today call relativism. One clear example of facing life in terms of alternatives is moral decision-making, a process by which people feel called upon to select, from a variety of choices that seem to be present, the 'right' way to behave towards other people. They are likely to extol the use of reason in this process, together with the wisdom received from 'on high' – the sanctions and rules formulated by those who, whether through politics or religion, have come to be viewed as having spoken authoritatively on moral matters. Chuang Tzu would have none of this. For him, the need to be both intuitive and spontaneous applied in this field just as much as in the field of personal skills. Consequently, the assertion that a particular form of moral behaviour was to be observed *only* because it was the received rule or because it stood out as the most logically consistent way to behave meant a denial of the naturalness of *wu wei*, which in this context may be translated as 'unmotivated action'. To act out of fear of the consequences, or in order to gain some kind of reward (whether earthly or heavenly) or even so as not to be out of step with one's neighbours, was to introduce an external motive to one's behaviour, which thereby deprived it of its authenticity.

It is, said Chuang Tzu, unnatural to categorise moral actions as either universally 'good' or 'bad', because this means forcing into some kind of straitjacket what should be spontaneous, a free expression of the basic self. On this issue, he crossed swords with Confucius (or, to be more accurate, with his successors), who expected people to practise certain virtues as 'the will of heaven', whether or not they were in accord with the will of the person so attempting to practise them. For Chuang Tzu, the essential factor in moral behaviour was to act in accordance with one's own nature. If this meant, as with Chuang Tzu it sometimes did, that one treats other people rudely, then so be it: better that than to express artificially the virtue of *li*, or propriety, which, as we shall see in Chapter 12, was one of the cardinal virtues in Confucianism. The practice of *li* may make people civil to one another on the surface, but this is hypocritical if it masks underlying differences or hatred between them: like resolving never to call another person a fool except when standing to attention.

Chuang Tzu argued that the received wisdom concerning right and wrong (dominated by the Confucianist thinking to be discussed in Chapter 12) was in any case distorted: those who stole vast territories became monarchs or rulers and had still to be treated with respect, while ordinary people, often forced by hunger to steal not a country but merely a loaf of bread, were treated as criminals. He would have approved of the old English ditty:

The law imprisons man or woman
Who steals a goose from off the common;
But then it lets the villain loose
Who steals the common from the goose.

In any case, Chuang Tzu argued, did not a thief often show more virtue than those who punished him? Chapter 29 tells of robber Chi, debating with Confucius the virtues of bravery, righteousness, wisdom and justice. When entering a house to burgle it, Chi said:

To know where the valuables are hidden indicates high intelligence. To enter into a house first shows bravery. To leave it last is an act of righteousness. To know whether to enter a house or not is wisdom, and to divide spoils according to merits is justice. It is impossible to become a great robber without possessing all of these five virtues.

Perhaps it is because they acknowledge the presence of these virtues that people tend to sympathise with Robin Hood, Dick Turpin, and even the Great Train Robbers.

We shall discuss this issue of relativism more broadly in Chapter 15. Chuang Tzu's approach is similar to that of those Hindus who seek the state 'beyond good and evil'. Of course, he would have acknowledged that, just as a piano player has to learn the technique of playing before he/she can enter into the spirit of it, so a child must learn about moral rules before reaching the state of *wu wei*. But the ultimate aim is to advance beyond behaving according to a set of received rules and regulations to a state of naturalness, simplicity and spontaneity: to behave otherwise as an adult would be, in Chuang Tzu's view, not to have achieved moral maturity.

In a famous passage in the second chapter of *Chuang Tzu*, we find a clear-cut denial of the concept of ethical absolutism, with its acceptance of the view that forms of behaviour, independently of circumstances and persons involved, can be categorised as right or wrong, good or bad.

Suppose you and I argue. If you beat me instead of my beating you, are you really right and am I really wrong? If I beat you instead of your beating me, am I really right and are you really wrong? Or are we both partly right and partly wrong? Or are we both wholly right and wholly wrong? Since between us neither you nor I know which is right, others are naturally in the dark. Whom shall we ask to arbitrate? If we ask someone who agrees with you, since he has already agreed with you, how can he arbitrate? If we ask someone who agrees with me, since he agrees with me, how can he arbitrate? If we ask someone who disagrees with both you and me to arbitrate, since he has already disagreed with you and me, how can he arbitrate? If we ask someone who agrees with you and me, since he has already agreed with you and me, how can he arbitrate? Thus among you, me, and others, none knows which is right. Shall we wait for still others?

This is what is known in Western moral philosophy circles as thorough-going sceptical relativism. It springs from the Taoist emphasis, illustrated copiously by both Lao Tzu and Chuang Tzu, on being natural: living harmoniously not only with the natural world around us (with all the ecological implications that follow) but also with oneself. This, said Chuang Tzu, is the secret of happiness: it is knowledge of the *Tao*.

Of course, there are problems with this attitude, some of which Chuang Tzu discusses. In the light of modern explorations into the concept of self, can we ever be as certain about what it means to be natural as Chuang Tzu seems to suggest? More pertinently, how should we react to one for whom being natural is to engage in what others regard as unacceptable behaviour, such as the urge to behave violently towards other people, or being sexually attracted to children? Chuang Tzu's *laisser-faire* philosophy, applied today, would have to take account of these undesirable expressions of 'nature', as John Stuart Mill, high priest of liberalism, conceded by stating that, even in a world where every individual had a right to his or her viewpoint, their behaviour towards others must be restrained if it becomes 'a nuisance'. An important consideration to be borne in mind is that those with socially unacceptable drives are a tiny minority of the population as a whole. In the post-Darwin age it can be added that human nature has its own way of dealing with those who commit 'nuisances', just like nature itself: by one means or another, it denies them the freedom to express their 'unnatural' tendencies. For the rest, which is the vast majority of the human race, these words from chapter 2 remain Chuang Tzu's counsel:

Forget the passage of time, and forget the distinction of right and wrong. Relax in the realm of the infinite and thus abide in the realm of the infinite.

The more we can view life *sub specie aeternitatis*, the less we shall suffer unhappiness, which Chuang Tzu believed to spring mainly from ignorance, short-sightedness (metaphorically speaking) and the immaturity that leads people to seek the immediate gratification of desires, instant solutions to problems and the removal of what Heidegger was to call 'anxiety'. The one issue that, more than any other, causes people to behave in this way is the fear of death, and Chuang Tzu discussed this with typical frankness and idiosyncrasy. Both life and death, he said, should be understood as relative phases of the process of *Tao*. For the survivor of a loving relationship that has been ended by death – for Chuang Tzu, the death of his wife – there will of course be a deep sense of loss: but it is the survivor, not the deceased, who is the loser, and he/she must come to terms with the changes that this loss must mean. The sorrow of death is the sorrow of the living, not of the dead, who are at rest and in peace in the eternal harmony of the *Tao*. In the same chapter Chuang Tzu pose the poignant question:

> How do I know that loving life is not a delusion? How do I know that in hating death, I am not like a man who, having left home in his youth, has forgotten the way back?

This is the heart of the Taoist philosophy: to lose the sense of ego in union with the *Tao*; to transcend both the usual distinctions expressed in the world around us and the distinction between 'me' and 'not-me'. It is a theme that recurs in a variety of ways throughout virtually the whole of Eastern philosophy, but it is expressed in a particularly unambiguous way in the writings of Chuang Tzu. Worldly concerns he laid aside by refusing a high position in the government of his province (arguing that he preferred to go fishing); and his expression of the need to lose the ego led him to profess a form of anti-anthropomorphism, a refusal to view *Homo sapiens* as uniquely the crown of creation. This is illustrated in his famous dream that he was a butterfly. 'I do not know', he said, 'whether I was then a man dreaming I was a butterfly, or whether I am now a butterfly dreaming I am a man.' Like any other Taoist, Chuang Tzu would have found offensive the headlines in the British press when Everest was first climbed in 1953: 'Everest Conquered', they proclaimed. A more fitting announcement, according to Taoist thinking, would have been to the effect that the climbers had experienced a few moments of rapport with the mountain before scurrying down to safer levels.

There is in Chuang Tzu's writings an anarchic element that was viewed with suspicion by the civil authorities of his day, and encouraged Wilde to comment as he did. Chuang Tzu believed that the best government was no government, since the process ran counter to the naturalness he advocated. He even recommended that one should proceed through life pretending to be useless, so as to avoid being imposed on by those in authority. It is significant that, while Confucianism has been reintroduced into Chinese school syllabuses, no mention has been made of Chuang Tzu. In fact, for some 1,500 years, no great scholar has advanced his views.

This does not, however, mean that he has not been influential, as this assessment by Chan Wing-Tsit (*A Source-Book in Chinese Philosophy*, p.179) indicates:

His impact on Buddhism has been tremendous, especially in the development of the Zen School. He has been a main source of inspiration in Chinese landscape painting and poetry. As part of Taoism, his philosophy helped to transform ancient and medieval Confucianism into Neo-Confucianism ... His revolt against traditionalism and conventional standards, his poetic mysticism, his subtle individualism, his insight into human nature, his profound interest in how to live and how to respond to all things, and his broad view of things, remained inexhaustible sources of inspiration for the Chinese.

And may, perhaps, become so for the West.

RELIGIOUS TAOISM (*TAO-CHIAO*)

As mentioned in chapter 9, alongside the so-called philosophical Taoism of Lao Tzu and Chuang Tzu (*tao-chia*), another form developed over the centuries: *tao-chiao*, generally translated as 'religious Taoism'. One wonders whether this is in fact the most apposite translation, since, as we have seen, in Chinese (as in much Indian) thought the distinction between religion and philosophy is unclear. Some commentators consequently suggest that we should translate *tao-chiao* as 'Taoist magic', and that will be the emphasis in this brief summary.

Philosophical Taoism found its response among the more laterally-minded Chinese: those with sensitivity, perception, and an inner sense of security that enabled them to appreciate the somewhat cryptic suggestions of Lao Tzu and Chuang Tzu. For the ordinary people, however, their comments were either not delineated clearly enough to be comprehensible, or, worse, were expressed so subtly that the point was misinterpreted. Many of them, for example, took Chuang Tzu's recommendations not to worry about death to mean that death could be conquered – quite literally; and the quest for immortality became a central feature of *tao-chiao*. Numerous commentators have described the *Chuang Tzu* as a halfway house between *tao-chia* and *tao chiao*, and some of its suggestions about how to experience a long life no doubt lend force to this interpretation. Basically, however, there is such a gulf between Chuang Tzu and Taoist magic that to hold the one responsible for the other seems as illogical as blaming Luther for the Peasants' Revolt. It is an example of the problem that often occurs when a laterally-minded writer meets a literally minded reader. The authors of the Old and New Testaments would no doubt have sympathised.

The main difference between *tao-chiao* and *tao-chia* lies in the former's literalistic interpretation of the quest for immortality (*ch'ang-sheng pu-ssu*), which in the *Tao Te Ching* and *Chuang Tzu* had been described in spiritual terms as union with the *Tao*. The aim, according to practitioners of *tao-chiao*, is to become an immortal, or *hsien* (mentioned on page 89): one who is no longer subject to 'the world of dust' and is master of a variety of magical skills such as ascending into Heaven, overcoming demons or wild animals, making himself invisible, riding the clouds, and transmitting long-forgotten knowledge. These 'immortals' have played a prominent part in Chinese literature, legend and art, and one cannot appreciate the full significance of Taoism if they are ignored. Some of them are held to have left the terrestrial plane behind and become celestial, and have been described by one writer (*EPR* 137) in these colourful terms:

> Some immortals ascend to the clouds, their body upright, and they fly among the clouds without the beating of wings; some glide across the cloudy vapour by harnessing a dragon and ascend up to the very steps of Heaven ... Their kind has attained an eternal life, free from death; but before they reach their goal they have to shed all human emotions and all ambitions about fame and glory.

Many commentators on Taoism suggest that its central feature is to be found in this quest for immortality. This would be a false judgment with reference to *tao-chia*, but it is worth examining in this second context. It is certainly the case that, in the pursuit of this goal, there emerged over the centuries following the death of Chuang Tzu numerous schools of *tao-chiao*, some to be short-lived, others to endure for centuries, well into the Middle Ages. We may mention a few that, historically, are the most important because of the superabundance of their followers. The **Inner Deity Hygiene School** allocated deities to various parts of the body and called on its followers to keep a special diet while at the same time visualising the deities. Normally the diet called for abstinence from meat and wine (because the deities disliked the smell of these) and from eating grain (*pi-ku*), which is said to nourish worms, the enemies of the deities. This was the negative aspect of fasting: the positive side was that it enabled the practitioner to prolong his or her life. Communal fasting (*chai*) was a central feature of this and many other Taoist schools; fasts often lasted for several days as part of a complex ritual that included collective repentance. In the sixth century CE, this school was displaced by the **School of the Magic Jewel**, which placed greater emphasis on the salvific powers of the deities.

A school that remained active until the fifteenth century was the **Five-Pecks-of-Rice School** (*wu-tou-mi tao*), so called from the price of admission paid to the priest, or *tao-shih*. In addition to mass confessions and ritual fasts, this school made use of talismans (*fu-lu*). These were strips of paper, metal or bamboo, inscribed with lines similar to Chinese writing, and believed to be able to ward off illnesses, ill fortune and demons. *Fu-lu* is also a central feature of a school that survives, in Taiwan and Hong Kong, to the present day: the **Way of Right Unity** (*Cheng-i tao*).

The Five-Pecks-of-Rice School also encouraged its followers to engage in *ho ch'i*, a practice that normally causes raised eyebrows among students when first encountering *tao-chiao*. It is a form of communal sex and is one expression of *fang-chung shu*, literally 'arts of the inner chamber'. This is a collective term for all kinds of sexual techniques that, it was affirmed, could lead to the realisation of the *Tao* and the attaining of immortality (*ch'ang-sheng pu-ssu*).

The belief propounded was that, since the male *yang* can be nourished only by the female *yin* and vice versa, the way to immortality lay in frequent practice of the sex act with as many partners as possible. However, it was also believed that the expenditure of semen, one of the essential bodily fluids, lay counter to the achievement of immortality; hence the aim for the male was frequent penetration without emission. Clearly, like the Tantric rites, this practice lay open to abuse, and it was condemned by the school of *ch'uan-chen tao*, mentioned below, mainly because, as a simple matter of fact, female partners were exploited. It remains the case, however, that Chinese art is replete with sexual symbolism, with various objects unambiguously representing male and female genitalia. A sympathetic exposition of the issue has been made by Jolan Chang in *The Tao of Love and Sex*.

A school that was very similar to Five-Pecks-of-Rice Taoism was the **Way of Supreme Peace** (*T'ai p'ing tao*), although it also contained the distinctive feature of healing by magic. The latest school to emerge, and, alongside *cheng-i tao* (the Way of Right Unity), one of the two central streams of religious Taoism, was the **Way of Realisation of Truth** (*ch'uan-chen tao*). This was founded in the twelfth century CE and effectively combined elements of Taoism, Confucianism and Buddhism. It maintained the emphasis of another school, that of *nei-tan*, or inner elexir (inner alchemy) as the supreme means of achieving immortality. In this, *nei-tan* opposed the school of *wei-tan*, or outer elixir, which advocated the use of certain chemical substances (gold and cinnabar, mercury ore) as alchemical substances that would lead to immortality. *Nei-tan* taught that the immortal soul can be developed from the three life-preserving energies of *ching* (essence), *ch'i* (vital energy) and *shen* (spirit).

The Way of Realisation of Truth made the practices that followed from this belief famous in the history of Taoism. Practitioners engaged in a variety of meditative breathing techniques, the most famous of which is *embryonic breathing* (*t'ai-hsi*). Basically, this is a combination of holding the breath and then allowing it to circulate through the body, from the soles of the feet to the brain. It is the attempt to breathe as practitioners imagine an infant in the womb would breathe (hence the name). It was believed that the breath is the physical expression of vital energy (*ch'i*), so the retaining of it played a key role in achieving long life and, ultimately, immortality. (In its simplest form, this school taught that human beings have a certain number of breaths to make, so the slower one breathes the longer one lives.) Eventually, the idea of retaining the physical breath came to be recognised as a misunderstanding of the belief that the spirit is to be found within, but to this day there are practitioners of embryonic breathing wherever Taoism manifests itself. Since a slow pulse-rate, alongside slow and deep breathing, are universally acknowledged as indicative of fitness and health, embryonic breathing may be worth some reflection; its practice may be linked with Yoga where, as we have seen, correct breathing is viewed as one of the key steps to spiritual enlightenment.

It remains a moot point how far one can be said to be able to understand Taoism through *tao-chia* alone. Martin Palmer, for instance, in *The Elements of Taoism*, argues that this is impossible, and spends as much time on *tao-chiao* as on *tao-chia*. If the title of this present book is to be interpreted comprehensively, then we must presumably understand popular forms of any religion or philosophy alongside their more erudite expressions. Since a full analysis of these forms would demand much more space than is available, and – more to the point – virtually a lifetime of personal experience, this cannot be achieved here. Let it suffice that these popular expressions are acknowledged, as any student of Christian doctrine may acknowledge those of the charismatic persuasion who are either unable or unwilling to accept the discipline involved in deeper study. Meanwhile, it is worth affirming that to be a Taoist need not mean practising embryonic breathing.

One physical expression of Taoism that can be, and is, observed by followers of both *Tao-chia* and *Tao-chiao* is *T'ai ch'i (ch'uan)*, literally 'the fist (-fighting method) of the supreme ultimate'. This is a form of meditation based on physical movements, coordinating mind and body in slow, flowing movements, which produce a harmonisation of the energies of *yin* and *yang* in the body (see Chapter 11). Laurence Wu (*op. cit.* p.85) describes it as

> a graceful, rhythmic exercise, consisting of a sequence of choreographed movements which is executed slowly with breath control and mental concentration. It has aptly been described as 'meditation in motion'. One can learn to execute the whole sequence of 108 movements so smoothly and effortlessly that one experiences *wu-wei*.

Those who have practised this form of meditation testify to its ability to ease tensions in both the mind and the body, unblock the energy meridians, and thus enhance both physical and spiritual health. It originated only in the fourteenth century, but Lao Tzu and Chuang Tzu would surely have recognised both its physical and spiritual value.

11 Chinese philosophy II: The Yin–Yang School

On page 91, there is a quotation from chapter 42 of the *Tao Te Ching*. Here it is in a different translation (D.C. Lau, Penguin Classics):

> The way begets one; one begets two; two begets three; three begets the myriad creatures.
> The myriad creatures carry on their backs the *yin* and embrace in their arms the *yang* and are the blending of the generative forces of the two.

Thomas Cleary (*The Essential Tao*) translates that second sentence as:

> . . . all things bear yin and embrace yang,
> with a mellowing energy for harmony.
> And they are held together in the *ch'i* of teeming energy.

As already mentioned, it is impossible to give a 'definitive' translation of any piece of classical Chinese writing, and the variations quoted here illustrate how differently a few words can be expressed, although without losing track of the basic message. We have noted that the 'One' is *T'ai-chi*, literally a 'ridge beam', signifying the 'supreme ultimate', and often translated as 'primordial breath'. In the *I Ching*, to which we shall turn on page 114, it refers unambiguously to the ultimate reality, the ground of being from which all else arises. It is the primal manifestation of the *Tao*, which cannot be named.

T'ai-chi in its turn produces the two original energies of *yin* and *yang*: the philosophical perspective that arises from these two concepts (or, more accurately, this single concept, since neither can be considered without reference to the other) is fundamental, not only for the school that bears its name, but also for the Taoist and Confucian schools. It is in fact a *sine qua non* for the understanding of Chinese philosophy as a whole.

The names *yin* and *yang* have a prosaic origin, being respectively the northern and southern faces of a mountain – the slope facing away from the sun, therefore mainly in the shade, and the slope facing the sun, therefore mainly lit up. Any mountain has these two faces, and three necessary truths follow from this simple statement. The first is that neither aspect can exist without the other; it may be a pleasant reverie to imagine a mountain with all its slopes perpetually lit and warmed by the sun, but that would require a transformation of the whole cosmology. It follows, second, that both aspects are necessary if the picture is to be complete. This obviously applies to a description of a mountain, but the philosophy of *yin* and *yang* is based on the view that nothing and nobody can be characterised without reference to both their *yin* and *yang* aspects. Third, it is therefore impossible or, at any rate, unreal and unnatural, to look on either the *yin* or the *yang* aspect of anything or anybody as more important or more necessary than the other.

All this is illustrated in yet another translation of chapter 42, that of Arthur Waley in *The Way and its Power*. His second sentence is:

> These ten thousand creatures [i.e. everything that exists] cannot turn their backs to the shade without having the sun on their bellies, and it is on this blending of the breaths that their harmony depends.

In a footnote to the word 'breaths', Waley states that he means the warm 'breath' of the sun and the cold 'breath' of the shade. 'Hence,' he adds, '"breath" comes to mean a "state of the atmosphere" in a wider sense.'

The first known mention of *yin–yang* in a philosophical context is made in the commentary on the *I Ching* (the Book of Changes), the *Shih-i*, or 'Ten Wings', in its most important section known as *Hsi-tz'u*. There it states: 'One yin, one yang, that is the Tao.' The *Tao*, it states, arises from the interaction of *yin* and *yang*: so the unknowable, unnameable is manifested through these twin agents. The *Shih-i* is variously dated, traditionally as early as Confucius in the sixth century BCE, but modern scholars are inclined to place it some two to three centuries later. Another early account of *yin* and *yang* is found in a work that almost certainly dates from the third century BC, the *Lu-shih ch'un ch'iu*, literally 'Spring and Autumn Annals'. This work develops the idea that all things have their origin in the *yin* and the *yang*, the darkness and the light, in these words:

> The Great One produces the two poles (i.e. Heaven and Earth), which in turn give rise to the energies of the dark (yin) and the light (yang). These two energies then transform themselves, one rising upwards and the other descending downwards; they merge again and give rise to forms. They separate and merge again. When they are separate, they merge; when they are merged, they separate. That is the never-ending course of Heaven and Earth. Each end is followed by a beginning; each extreme by a transformation into its opposite. All things are attuned to each other. That from which all beings arise and from which they have their origin is known as the Great One; that which gives them form and perfection is the duality of light and darkness.

(EPR 429)

The duality of *yin* and *yang* is, then, held to be integral to the universe in all its manifestations, both as a simple matter of fact and as the clue to its unfathomable mysteries. For example, as Fritjof Capra explains in *The Tao of Physics*, from studying the physical world we learn that all matter contains positive and negative charges, protons and neutrons; and this dichotomy epitomises the *yang* and the *yin*. Devolving from the basic nature of matter is its universal expression in dual form: north and south, darkness and light, cold and heat, wetness and dryness, softness and hardness, and so on; our experience of life on Earth is one of duality, a pendulum moving back and forth between two extremes; day yields to night and night to day, the darkness and coldness and appparent death of winter move inexorably and perhaps unnoticed into the light and warmth and budding life of spring. Each extreme returns eternally to the other: neither can be without the other, since wholeness is contained in duality: the one is in fact two, and this is the *yin* and the *yang*, in which the completeness of the *Tao* is made manifest.

This duality applies to the characteristics of living entities. People display *yang* assertiveness and *yin* receptiveness, *yang* dominance and *yin* submissiveness, *yang* leadership and *yin* discipleship, *yang* hardness and *yin* softness, the active *yang* and the passive *yin*, creative *yang* and fertile *yin*, all seen, in the perceptions of the *yin–yang* school, as reflections of the natural contrast between Heaven and Earth, or between fire and water. Some of the delineations made by the Chinese may seem artificial, such as *yang* dragon alongside *yin* tiger, or *yang* odd numbers alongside *yin* even numbers, but the distinction as it relates to human characteristics and values is one that many people find to grow in significance the more they reflect on it.

Two of its applications are particularly illuminating. The first, which we have already encountered in Indian philosophy, is the balance between reason and intuition. Chinese thought generally, whether the mystical Taoism or the more practical Confucianism, lays emphasis on this balance as an essential ingredient of a comprehensive life. Anyone who lives their life under the sole direction of the cognitive or the rational side of their natures will be, quite literally, one-sided: to ignore the emotive and intuitive facets is likely to produce human beings who may be respected by their peers for their intelligence, but will be, as Kierkegaard famously remarked in his *Concluding Unscientific Postscript*, of little use to anyone outside the world of academia because of their lack of humanity and common sense. Intelligence has its place: but so, too, has reflective wisdom.

As we have seen, Chuang Tzu unambiguously advocated the need to 'be natural': to act according to intuition rather than by deliberately taking thought and working out pros and cons; in other words, to follow *yin* rather than *yang*. In Western philosophy, as in Western culture generally, this side of human nature has, on the whole, been neglected, and, in some schools (such as Logical Positivism), even been judged to be non-philosophical because unverifiable. Yet most of the important decisions made by human beings spring from intuition rather than reason: relationships, interests, loves, jobs, even putting flowers in vases. Western religions, too, are *yang*- rather than *yin*-dominated: their God is paternal, as opposed to the maternal nature of the *Tao*.

The second application of the *yin–yang* perspective relates to the fact that the *yang* is masculine and the *yin* feminine, and the implications that follow for the union (or disunion) of the sexes. As we saw earlier, the *yin–yang* emphasis is that there cannot be one without the other, that each needs the other in order to be complete, so that neither can be adjudged to be more important, or more necessary, than the other. At the most basic of levels, of course, there would be no life at all without these twin elements. However much either may sometimes wish that the other would disappear, there is no alternative to the coexistence of the sexes. The *yin–yang* philosophy enters into the matter more deeply than this, however, and gives expression to a reality that the Western world is slowly beginning to appreciate: no human being is entirely *yang* or entirely *yin*, as no mountain is entirely *yang* or *yin*. Normally men have more *yang* than *yin* and women more *yin* than *yang* (although there are enough exceptions to this generalisation to encourage caution against speaking in absolutist terms), but every man has some feminine (which is not to say female) qualities, and every women some male qualities (with the same cautionary concession). The so-called battle of the sexes arises primarily because of the tendency among both sexes to value the *yang* over the *yin*: to extol the extrovert rather than the introvert, to encourage assertiveness rather than meekness, with the consequent ambition to be dominant rather than submissive. At the very least, this tendency reflects profound ignorance (if that is not an oxymoron) concerning the true nature of the universe, and how things really get done. As Lao Tzu never ceased saying: when it comes to real strength, what can compare with water, the essence of the *yin*? So, as his 28th chapter states:

> Know the male
> But keep to the role of the female. (Lao)

or, in another translation:

> Know the strength of man, but keep a woman's care. (F'eng)

or, in yet another:

> Understand the thrust of the yang –
> But be more like the yin in your being. (Palmer)

Alan Watts (*op. cit.* p.22) gives this laconic comment on the sexual application of *yin* and *yang*:

> Obviously, the male has the convex penis and the female the concave vagina; and though people have regarded the former as a possession and the latter as a deprivation (Freud's 'penis envy'), any fool should be able to recognise that one cannot have the outstanding without the instanding, and that a rampant *membrum virile* is no good without somewhere to put it, and vice versa.

Apart from the area of male and female sex and sexuality, where men are naturally male and women female, the main consideration of *yin–yang* for men and women is that, no man being exclusively *yang* or woman *yin*, the happiest relationships between partners are those where this is intuitively recognised. The man will be the *yang* to the woman's *yin* in some areas, while the woman will take the *yang* role in others. For both to seek the *yang* role in every respect is likely to make the relationship into a battlefield (and the converse, a graveyard). What is needed in 'balance in imbalance', otherwise we reach the *reductio ad absurdum* (which is a polite phrase for total folly) expressed by certain American feminists, who demanded the removal of the betrousered male and beskirted female symbols from public lavatory doors on the grounds that women are as likely to wear trousers as men. The only remedy for this tunnel vision would be a display of the respective genitalia.

The key to the relationship between *yang* and *yin* is in fact not competition but recognition of inseparability: what the Chinese call **hseng sheng**, or 'mutual arising' (not to be confused, of course, with the Buddhist concept of *pratitya samutapada*, conditioned arising, as taught by Nagarjuna and discussed in Chapter 6). *Hseng sheng* means not just that one cannot exist without the other, but that one is constantly moving towards, and taking the nature of, the other. It can be expressed even more pungently: within the *yang* is the kernel of the *yin*, and vice versa. This truth can be exemplified in nature: as winter moves into the darkness of *yin*, simultaneously the *yang* forces are preparing for the summer. The dead leaf falls from the tree, but the seed of next year's leaf remains. Flowers decay, but the force that produced them merely retreats beneath the surface of the ground, sustaining the life that is as real underground as it is in its summer glory. In all life is the certain seed of death, and in death the seed of life; the joy of any relationship is tinged with the inevitability of sorrow. There is no such thing as 'happy ever after', even if children demand such endings to their fairy-tales. There is no universal panacea for pleasure: everything has its up- and down-side, and it is an

Diagram of the Supreme Ultimate (*T'ai-ch'i-tu*)

expression of immaturity, or shallowness, to expect otherwise. Without the down-side, how could we know we were on the up-side?

This profound truth is illustrated by the classic symbol of *yin* and *yang*, the *T'ai-chi-t'u*, or 'diagram of the supreme ultimate' (p. 111), where the dark portions represent *yin*, and the light, *yang*. Wherever a diameter is drawn, each semicircle will contain a mixture of the two in varying proportions; and, it should be noted, in the heart of each is the seed of the other.

This diagram, and the philosophy it depicts, gives us a consummate expression of relativeness as the key to the universe. It confronts those who believe that values, whether relating to human behaviour (morals or politics), religious beliefs or aesthetics, can be classified as simply 'good' or 'bad', 'right' or 'wrong', or, to use the diagram directly, 'black' or 'white'. Apart from the obvious fact that no epithet would have any meaning without its opposite (could we understand what 'hot' means if it could not be contrasted with 'cold', 'honest' with 'dishonest', 'creative' with 'humdrum'?) it affirms what we have seen in Chuang Tzu's teaching (page 100): no villain is without virtue and no saint without sin. More: we cannot discuss what virtue is until we know its opposite; and, more still, within the virtue itself is the seed, or essence, of its opposite. Bernard Shaw said of a certain person, perhaps of the Mother Teresa vintage: 'She lived for others; you could tell the others by their haunted expression.' As there is an up-side to criminality (as illustrated by Chuang Tzu), so there is a down-side to altruism.

This is expressed unambiguously in the *Tao Te Ching* (chapter 2, Feng and English translation):

> Under heaven all can see beauty as beauty only because there is ugliness.
> All can know good as good only because there is evil.
>
> Therefore having and not having arise together.
> Difficult and easy complement each other.
> Long and short contrast each other;
> High and low rest upon each other;
> Voice and sound harmonise each other;
> Front and back follow one another.

We shall discuss in Chapter 15 the implications of this relativistic teaching for ethical norms. From the religious perspective, its most important point of reference is to life and death, and it is interesting that Watts translates the third line of the above quotation as:

> 'To be' and 'not to be' arise mutually.

Just as we know what we mean when we talk of a fat person only because there are thin people (if everyone were shaped like Billy Bunter the words 'fat' and 'thin', in this context at least, would not exist), so we know what living means only because we have encountered death. So: no death, no life; *we know we are alive only because we have once been dead*. In fact, if all creatures were eternal, there would be no verb 'to live'. Put another way, if, with the god Krishna in the *Bhagavad-Gita*, we could affirm, 'There never was a time when I was not, and there never will be a time when I shall not be', then the joy of living would cease. To exult in being alive is possible only within the cycle of life and death. (In the phenomenological sense, of course, Krishna's words hold true for everyone: each of us will experience the act of dying, although not death itself. In this sense, the universe came into being only with my birth and will cease to be at my death; and I am eternal.)

The point made in the *yin–yang* philosophy may be difficult to grasp but is central to the teaching of the school: as sound comes out of silence, and light from space, so does being come from non-being. In other words, the void is creative: it is the *yin* to the *yang* of the 'ten thousand things' that the universe contains. Nothings are needed to give meaning to somethings, spaces to solids: they are in fact as mutually necessary as sleeping is to waking and as front is to back. Watts (*op. cit.*) asks, 'How can one speak of reality or is-ness except in the context of the polar application of void?'

Apart from this metaphysical context, the *yin–yang* principle is, or can be, applied by the Chinese to every area of life. The organs of the body are categorised as either *yang* or *yin*, and the remedies when they malfunction must be of the same category: the principles of homoeopathy, treating like with like, are *yin–yang* principles. Food is similarly categorised: most flesh is *yang*, for instance, and vegetables *yin*; and the healthiest diet will have both in balanced proportions. (Nobody conversant with the *yin* and the *yang* will express surprise at the violence in the USA after witnessing the enormous steaks consumed there on a daily basis; nor the general insipidity of people anywhere who, by choice or of necessity, live only on Pythagorean fare.)

The *Yin–Yang* School (*Yin–Yang Chia*), while acknowledging all that has been said, also stresses that the central feature of the philosophy lies in its acknowledgement that there is no point where things are static. In a way, its position is akin to that of Buddha's doctrine of *anicca*: nothing stays the same from one micro-second to the next. *Yin–yang* does not offer Buddha's concept of discontinuity, however: the now and the not-yet belong to, and are part of, each other, along with the used-to-be. Even this comment is not fully in tune with the Chinese view of time, which is, as the *T'ai-ch'i-tu* indicates, cyclical rather than linear. Eternity is a circle, having neither beginning nor end. Within it, the *yin* is constantly moving and changing into the *yang*, and the *yang* into the *yin*. Joseph Needham expressed this idea in these words:

> The Yang having reached its climax retreats in favour of the Yin; the Yin having reached its climax retreats in favour of the Yang.
>
> (Quoted in *East of Existentialism*, p.199)

The essence of the universe is, then, in a word, *change*: and the full expression of this idea is given in the book which takes that word as its title: the Book of Changes, or *I Ching*.

THE *I CHING*

No book, not even the *Tao Te Ching*, has played as great a part in Chinese thought as the *I Ching*. The word *ching* means, as we have seen, 'classic' or 'manual'; the word *i* means 'change' or 'transformation', and the book provides guidance to the reader about how to accept change, adapt to it, live with it, and benefit fully from it. It may be described as a manual of instruction about how to swim with the tide or go with the flow. The process of change is brought about, as we have seen by the interaction of the *yin* and the *yang*, the manifestation of the *Tao*. The Book of Change(s) can therefore be described as redolent with Taoist ideas; but, as we shall see in Chapter 12, there are close ties also with the Confucianist philosophy.

The basic structure of the Book of Change(s) is formed by eight trigrams (*pa-kua*), each of which consist of three broken and/or unbroken horizontal lines. The broken lines are *yin*; the unbroken, *yang*. There are eight possible combinations of these lines, ranging from all-*yang* (*Ch'ien*, or Heaven) to all-*yin* (*K'un*, or Earth). The six in between are formed from an intermingling of *Ch'ien* and *K'un*, and all are named after a particular natural phenomenon. The eight trigrams are:

Heaven *Ch'ien*	Thunder *Chen*	Water *K'an*	Mountain *Ken*
─────	── ──	── ──	─────
─────	── ──	─────	── ──
─────	─────	── ──	── ──

Earth *K'un*	Wind *Sun*	Fire *Li*	Lake *Tui*
── ──	─────	─────	── ──
── ──	─────	── ──	─────
── ──	── ──	─────	─────

To gain a trigram, use is made either of yarrow stalks or coins, whereby a particular number is achieved; even numbers are *yin*, odd numbers *yang*; three throwings will yield a trigram; the process is then repeated in order to yield a hexagram, of which there are, of mathematical necessity, a possible sixty-four.

The original use of the *I Ching* was probably as a manual of prophecy, with the answer 'Yes' to the inquirer's question being provided by the unbroken *yang* line, the answer 'No' by the broken *yin* line. The trigrams were also widely used in the context of the alchemical teachings of the inner and outer elixir (*nei-tan* and *wai-tan*, see page 105). The later philosophical interpretation of the hexagrams came about through a deeper understanding of the *yin–yang* philosophy of change as the prime factor in all that exists. The *yin* is continuously moving into the *yang* and vice versa, hence any interpretation of the readings, made as though the situation were static, must inevitably be shallow and – more to the point – unnatural. C. Marshall, in his *I Ching* (p.21) states:

> The concept behind any augury is that each moment in time has its own particular quality and that the history of the past and the unfolding story of the future are constantly held in an ever-shifting present. If you throw the coins, or lay out the Tarot cards, or cast a horoscope, you can see the essential dynamics of the current moment in time. The influences of the past have created the present situation, which contains the seeds of the future unfolding of events.

So, under the influence of Confucius and his successors, commentaries were written that interpret the readings (or auguries) in relation to change: so if a *yin* line emerges from the throwing of a six, which is the lowest (that is, most extreme) expression of *yin* (*yin* moving into *yang*), or a *yang* line accrues from a nine, the extreme of *yang* (*yang* moving into *yin*), there are two commentaries to be read: the one accompanying the original throwing, and the one accompanying the change(s). The most famous English translations of the original Chinese text of the *I Ching* are by Wilhelm and Blofeld.

Any reading of the text will indicate immediately that the *I Ching* is considerably more than an almanac. It is cryptic in style, cannot be read quickly, and, like the *Tao Te Ching*, more for use in meditation than for study. Many Westerners use it in this way on a daily basis, reflecting on the passages that relate to whatever hexagram they throw. Others use it when facing a dilemma to which there is no cut-and-dried answer, but which needs calm contemplation, allowing the intuition, as well as the reason, to come into play. Such a dilemma faced a group of my students one May: with exams approaching, they wondered how they should prepare for what in prospect seemed daunting. With one student acting on behalf of the group, they threw number 41 in the hexagrams, which is, on top, the trigram *Ken*, or Mountain, known as 'keeping still', and below, *Tui*, or Lake, known as 'the joyous'.

The reading in the chapter is too long to quote, and in any case the inquirer needs to consult the section relating to the change from *yang* to *yin* that is identified as occurring in this hexagram. The basic 'Judgment', however, is brief:

Decrease combined with sincerity
Brings about supreme good fortune
Without blame.
One may be persevering in this.
It furthers one to undertake something.
How is this to be carried out?
One may use two small bowls for the sacrifice.
(Wilhelm/Baynes translation)

Interpretations of these cryptic remarks will vary according to the person(s) involved. The group concerned saw the first three lines as an indication that life would not have lost its *raison d'être* if they performed badly in the exams; the next two lines seemed to suggest that the exercise had intrinsic value; and from the final mysterious statement they garnered the viewpoint that one did not need to be prominent in order to be eminent (my phrase, but the gist of their interpretation).

The *I Ching* is effectively a response to the universal desire (and, for many, the need) to make sense of life and understand why things happen, representing a rejection of the view that everything is simply a matter of chance. Just as the highest achievement of Heaven is perfect harmony, reflecting the *Tao*, and manifested in the union of *yin* and *yang*, so the greatest harmony that any human being can achieve is the balance that arises from understanding the flow of *yin* and *yang* in his or her life. The *I Ching* was written in the belief that by meditating on the hexagrams, anyone could be facilitated along the way to this goal. As Appendix I of the *I Ching* states enthusiastically:

How vast is the originating power of the chian [hexagram] ... unitedly to protect the Supreme Harmony: this is indeed profitable and auspicious.

The theory of the Five Agents (Wu-hsing)

Wu-hsing literally means 'five movers' and is also known as *wu-te*, the five virtues. We may think of them as five elements, and they have played a many-faceted role in Chinese history and thought. It was originally an independent school, but around the first century BCE it combined with the *Yin–Yang* School, to which it has since been considered to belong.

The five elements are water, fire, wood, metal and earth. In one sense these may seem to be an elementary description of the world as we encounter it, but in Chinese thinking they stand for abstract forces and symbols that characterise the basic nature of matter. It is in the basic nature of water to moisten and flow downward; of fire to heat and to rise; of wood to bend and straighten again; of metal to be shaped into a variety of forms; of earth to be fertile. Alternatively, the five can be viewed as a continuous cycle, in which each both masters and is mastered by another. Thus, on the one hand: wood gives rise to fire, fire to earth, earth to metal, metal to water (through the distillation of dew), and water to wood; conversely, water will conquer fire, fire melts metal, metal can destroy wood, wood can conquer earth, and earth overcomes water.

The five elements have had many applications throughout Chinese history: dynasties are associated with one or another; they are linked with the seasons, the directions of the compass, colours, flavours, numbers, the planets and the internal organs. These last are of great importance in Chinese medicine. Since each organ is associated with one of the elements, the cure when that organ is malfunctioning is to treat it with a remedy associated with its natural conqueror. A simple example of this approach is that hot ginger soup is prescribed for chills or colds, and watermelons for fevers; and to the present day the medicinal properties of herbs are classified in terms of the five agents. It is a common-sense approach typical of the Chinese, and we shall see how Confucius used it to strengthen his advocacy of the five relationships that he believed should characterise human society. (The reader is referred to the Bibliography for further reading about the Five Agents, which play so conspicuous a role in Chinese life and thought.)

The *Yin–Yang* School has been described as 'naturalistic', and this seems a fair assessment. There is no attempt in this school to do other than interpret and align oneself with the forces we encounter in the world around us. God and the supernatural are absent from its considerations, except in metaphorical terms such as 'Heaven'. Whatever decision we may reach, then, regarding the status of any other Chinese school as a religion, this one must be excluded from that categorisation. One can belong to any kind of religion or to no religion at all and still live one's life according to the principles of *yin* and *yang*. The application of these principles to the world of social problems and political affairs would probably be more effective than any other factor in ridding the world of its imbalance and bringing about a state of harmony, health and cooperation.

12 Chinese philosophy III: Confucianism

As we saw earlier, in philosophical and religious terms there have been three major influences in China. One is Taoism, in both its *tao-chia* and *tao-chiao* expressions; the second is Buddhism, which, while not native to China, was to establish so firm a hold there in its Mahayana mode that the Chinese could be forgiven for looking on it as native to themselves; the third, and the most typically Chinese of all, is Confucianism. This philosophy – and we shall see that, of all the schools discussed in this book, it has least claim to be termed a religion – has made such an indelible mark on Chinese personal and socio-political life that Confucianism and China are almost as ineradicably linked as Hinduism and India.

The great name in this school is of course Confucius himself, but there have been a host of Confucian scholars and philosophers over the centuries. We shall look at two of these who, by the pure originality of their thinking, have made distinctive contributions relevant to the theme of this book: Mencius, living two centuries later than Confucius, and his direct ideological descendant (he could be described as the Huxley to Confucius's Darwin); and, in the twelfth century CE, Chu Hsi, the outstanding mentor of Neo-Confucianism, which was effectively a synthesis of Taoism, Buddhism and Confucianism. Other teachers will be mentioned in passing, in relation to particular debates in which the major protagonists were engaged.

CONFUCIUS

This name, with which even children in the West are familiar, is the Latinised form of **K'ung Tzu** (sometimes transcribed as K'ung Fu-tzu), or Master K'ung. He lived from 551 to 479 BCE, during the so-called Spring and Autumn Period (722–481) of the Chou Dynasty (1111–249). Tradition had it that during its founding era this dynasty had been ruled by men who were highly principled, in particular the kings Wen and Wu. By K'ung's time, however, Chou had fallen prey to internal conflicts and attacks from beyond, and his own state of Lu (now Shantung) was in fact ruled by usurpers. This may help to explain why it was that he experienced frustration in his chosen calling as a civil servant, and why at the age of fifty he resigned to become a peripatetic teacher, a role that many other learned Chinese, including Mencius, also assumed. He gathered a large number of students around him, amounting eventually to some three thousand.

According to tradition, Master K'ung spent his final years writing a number of books, including the *Shi Ching* (Book of Songs), the *Shu Ching* (Book of Writings), and the *Ch'un Ch'iu* (Spring and Autumn Annals). All we can say for sure is that these books are among the Confucian classics and reflect K'ung's teaching. His philosophy is expressed most directly, however, in the work that, along with the *Tao Te Ching*, is at the peak of Chinese philosophical writing, the *Analects*. It is generally held that K'ung did not write this work, but that it was compiled by his disciples after his death. Here is the essence of Confucianism, and it is significant that Chan Wing-Tsit, in his comprehensive compilation *A Source Book in Chinese Philosophy*, uses only this work to illustrate K'ung's teaching. It was, along with Mencius and two other Confucian classics, the *Ta Hsueh* and the *Chung Yung*, one of the so-called 'Four Books' (*ssu-chu*), which were used as the basis of Chinese civil service examinations from 1313 CE until as recently as 1905.

Almost any extract from the *Analects* will illustrate why it is that the name of Confucius has become synonymous with sound common sense (reflected in the phrase, 'Confucius, he say . . .'). In Book II,15–17, we read:

> The Master said, He who learns but does not think is lost. He who thinks but does not learn is in great danger . . . Shall I teach you what knowledge is? When you know a thing, to recognise that you know it; and when you do not know a thing, to recognise that you do not know it. That is knowledge.

(Perhaps even more basic is his laconic statement in IX,17 that he had 'never seen anyone whose desire to build up his moral power was as strong as sexual desire'.)

Master K'ung's prime consideration, and the central theme of the Analects, was how people might live harmoniously together. He was therefore concerned with ethics rather than metaphysics, although Mencius and other successors were to develop this strand in their teaching. From K'ung's point of view, it was a difficult enough task to cope with other people here and now without introducing speculation (for he viewed it as no more than that) about a future life, or a divine being who might influence events in this world from some invisible world beyond. He frequently referred to 'the Way of Heaven' (*t'ien*) and even referred to the emperor as 'Son of Heaven' (*t'ien-tzu*), but the word is normally used with an ethical connotation, signifying the highest pinnacle of human behaviour. Any ruler, as we shall see, was held by K'ung to be uniquely placed both to practise the virtues himself and to set an example for others. K'ung was questioned about *t'ien* apropos of 'God in heaven' but was at best agnostic and generally sceptical on the matter. It seemed to him absurd to believe that the 'will of heaven' could be modified as a direct consequence of prayers sent 'up' by people on Earth: so the sensible procedure was to forget about praying and tackle the problems of living as they stared one in the face. In this, to be sure, all people have the examples of their ancestors to inspire them; but K'ung refused to speculate about any influence that the spirits of the dead might have on the human situation. *Analects* XI,11 states:

> Tzu-lu asked how one should serve ghosts and spirits.
> The Master said, How can there be any proper service of spirits until living men have been properly served?
> Tzu-lu then ventured upon a question about the dead (whether they are conscious).
> The Master said, Until a man knows about the living, how can he know about the dead?

This perspective is reminiscent of the New Testament words: 'He who does not love his brother whom he has seen, cannot love God whom he has not seen' (I John 4:21); but K'ung's philosophy is totally humanistic in its suggestion that relationships with others should be based on secular, rather than spiritual, considerations. To make the love of God one's ultimate aim in human encounters, rather than to have regard for others for their own sakes, would have seemed to him an unrealistic diversion from the clearly defined, self-disciplined way that he was offering to his followers.

The way of Confucius is based on two definable and unambiguous human qualities, which have given Confucianism its distinctive stamp. They may be described as the *yin* and the *yang* of relationships, in the sense that each, while apparently poles apart (like justice and mercy), needs to be tempered by the other. They are *jen*, or loving kindness, and *li*, or propriety.

The Chinese pictogram for *jen* gives a clear indication of its meaning. It shows the sign for a human being, together with the sign for 'two'. Thus *jen* embraces all the qualities that enable one human being to express ideal behaviour towards another. It is the equivalent of the Greek word *agape*, for which, as for *jen*, the word 'love' is too general and too vague a translation. It is based on sympathy for others, an empathy with them, and a desire for them to achieve their best good. It is mirrored in Kant's description of goodwill, which to him was the ideal basis of all human intercourse. It meant that no other person was to be treated as a means to an end (that is, one's own selfish end) but rather should be treated as at all times an end in him or herself. 'Respect for persons' would be a not inapposite translation of this quality, fostered by a sense of mutuality (*shu*) and loyalty (*chung*) in any relationship. Master K'ung himself, when asked if there was a single saying that one could act on all day and every day, gave the simple and straightforward guideline already quoted on page 5: 'Never do to others what you would not like them to do to you' (XV,23). This expression of the Golden Rule in negative form is probably easier to follow than its converse, especially if it is the case that human beings are more united in what they dislike than in what they like. On the other hand, he also said (VI,28): 'To apply one's own wishes and desires as a yardstick by which to judge one's behaviour toward others is the true way of jen.'

The roots of *jen*, he affirmed, were piety (*hsiao*) and obedience (*ti*). These were the qualities that characterised the ideal man, or **chun-tzu**, literally 'duke's son', one whose nobility of title is reflected in his behaviour. The piety called for is the veneration of parents by children, and the obedience that of the younger brother to the older, whether within a family or in the community generally; thus respect for the old became a central feature of the Chinese cultural tradition. This does not always mean yielding to them whatever the issue, but treating them in the way to which, by their years, they have become entitled. Confucius (IV,18) was typically practical:

In serving his father and mother a man may gently remonstrate with them. But if he sees that he has failed to change their opinion, he should resume an attitude of deference and not thwart them. He may feel discouraged, but not resentful.

Mencius, Confucius's natural heir, later (*Mencius* IV,19) linked respect for parents with self-respect:

Which is the greatest service? The service of parents is the greatest. Which is the greatest of charges? The charge of oneself is the greatest. I have heard of keeping oneself, and thus being able to serve one's parents. But I have not heard of failing to keep oneself, and yet being able to serve one's parents.

The expression of *jen* in relationships is an ideal that Confucius shared with, or in which he was to be joined by, representatives and leaders of most of the major world religions. The second of the two pivots of Confucian ethics is, however, more idiosyncratically K'ung Tzu's emphasis. *Li* is normally translated as 'propriety'; it was originally (that is, in pre-Confucian times) related to the correct conduct of rites and ceremonies, that everything should be done, in St Paul's words, 'decently and in order'. It was extended to embrace the customs and traditions of the community, with the implication that these should be faithfully preserved. Master K'ung went a step further and applied it to inter-human relationships, giving a structure to the ideal of *jen*. Just as mercy without justice is likely to encourage crime, so *jen* without *li*, he suggested, could easily degenerate into a simplistic expression of mawkish sentimentality. K'ung Tzu could no more have joined the Beatles in singing 'All you need is love' (the idea is in fact hilarious) than he could have deliberately deceived a neighbour over a commercial transaction. The combination of *li* and *jen* makes it possible to win an argument without losing a friend; to accept one's superiority over another without making him or her feel belittled (and inferiority without feeling humiliated); or – quint-essentially Chinese – allowing a defeated opponent to 'save face'. The emphasis of *li* is that some arguments must be won, some people are superior to others, and some opponents have to be defeated.

Master K'ung indicates the significance of *li* with great clarity in the Analects (VIII,2, Wilhelm translation):

Deference ['courtesy', in Waley's translation] that lacks propriety (form, li) becomes servility ['tiresome'], caution without propriety becomes timidity, courage without propriety becomes rebelliousness, honesty without propriety beomes rudeness [or 'inflexibility becomes harshness' in Waley].

The distinction here is subtle, and an insensitive person may well be incapable of appreciating it. In order to learn what *li* means in practice, any person will need to acquire *chih*, or wisdom, the ability to discriminate between the nicely differing modes of behaviour that are in tune with the forces of *yin* and *yang*. To express propriety in one's dealing with others, therefore, means that nothing is done in excess, whether in words or in actions. In the harmony of *yin* and *yang*, one is never too strident, never too muted; happy doing ordinary things well rather than constantly attempting the extraordinary or the impossible; living well, but living well within oneself. 'Nothing in excess' could be a Confucian catchword, reminiscent of the ideal of the mean as taught by Aristotle, with whom Master K'ung is sometimes compared.

A key element in the practice of *li* is the fulfilling of one's duty, for which the Chinese word is *i*. This quality can be translated as righteousness, honesty, uprightness; people who observe *i* observe the requirements demanded of them by their roles and stations in life, and the care shown in making this observance must inevitably give direction to any expression of *jen* toward others. This may sound a bland statement, but in fact it is highly pertinent. Master K'ung considered that loving kindness can manifest itself only in ever-widening circles, with the inevitable consequence that the *jen* that is expressed abates in its intensity as the circle widens: this, for K'ung, was a natural state of affairs, an unalterable condition of humanity. An individual's first duty is filial piety, *xiao*, followed by duty to his clan; and although, as we shall see, K'ung laid great significance on the subject's duty to the state, he viewed this as secondary to the primary duties. He would probably have agreed with E.M. Forster, who remarked that, given a choice between betraying a friend or betraying his country, 'I hope I should have the courage to betray my country.'

This concept of circles of relationships is in direct conflict with a philosophy that was to be expressed a century later by the founder of the Mohist School, Mo Tzu, or Mo Ti (Master Mo, *c.* 468–376 BCE). He taught that loving kindness (*jen*) should be shown to others without distinction or favouritism: the needs of distant strangers or local enemies should rank as highly in any person's consciousness as those of his family or clan. Mo was in fact expressing an early form of utilitarianism as was to be taught in the nineteenth century by John Stuart Mill, whose argument was that any moral decision should have as its end the increase in human happiness. With that

K'ung would have agreed; where they would have parted company was in Mill's assertion that, when decisions are required about how best to achieve this end in any given circumstance, 'everyone [is] to count as one, nobody to count as more than one'.

To Confucius, and even more to his successor, Mencius, this aim would have seemed both unnatural and against the ground rules of propriety. Each of them had more than his share of common sense, based on calm observation of people. From this they concluded that most people find it difficult enough expressing goodwill to those around them without multiplying the problem by introducing the whole of the human race into the equation. On the other hand, they were also aware that some people find it is easier to express love for people they are never likely to meet than for those with whom they share the frustrations of daily living.

K'ung therefore had no truck either with the ideal of loving one's enemies, which was to receive superb expression in the New Testament, or with the utilitarian ideal of having neither favourites nor 'also-rans' in one's relationships. If love were to be shown as much to one's enemies as to one's friends, what advantage lay in being a friend? And what wife could cheerfully accept that, while her husband loved her no less than all the other women in the world, he loved her no more than them? What was needed, according to Confucius, was the quality of conscientiousness to others (*zhong*); this means that, while one may make a diligent effort to practise *jen*, one is not called upon to repay evil with good.

Master K'ung taught that there are five relationships (*wu-lun*), which together form the basis of human interaction (*wu-ch'ang*, or 'five constants'). The constants are *jen*, *li*, *i*, *chih* (wisdom or insight) and *hsin* (trust); by observing *wu-lun* meticulously (that is, by living according to the implications of the relationships) people may achieve order in their personal lives and, by extension, the community as a whole may coexist harmoniously. In each of the *wu-lun*, the first named should have the dominant, *yang* role, and the second the submissive *yin*. The five are:

- father and son;
- husband and wife;
- older brother and younger brother;
- (older) friend and (younger) friend;
- ruler and subject.

Thus a man can expect to show both *yin* and *yang* qualities in his relationships. A father, for example, will be *yang* in relation to his wife or his children, and *yin* in relation to the ruler (or older friend). A son will be *yin* in relation to his father and *yang* in relation to any younger brother or friend. K'ung does not discuss the problems that may arise in a family if number two son (to use a Chinese phrase) has more innately dominant qualities than his older brother; nor – and this is a considerably larger sticking-point – does he allow women anything but a *yin* position *vis-à-vis* any male. The *Analects* hint that he was married, with a son and a daughter, but there are no domestic details. We may conclude that, like two other pioneer visionaries of the ideal society, Plato and St Paul, there is a lacuna at this point in his thinking, so that effectively he has nothing to teach us on the subject. K'ung himself seems to have been aware of this omission, suggested by his comment in the *Analects* (XVII,25):

> Women and people of low birth are very hard to deal with. If you are friendly with them, they get out of hand, and if you keep your distance, they resent it.

Some interpreters soften the saying by making it apply to 'maids and valets'.

Master K'ung's main public concern was with the selection of rulers, and the style in which they should govern. His view was that a 'trickle-down effect' operated between ruler and subjects, whereby if he showed virtue in his dealings, they would follow his example. To one ruler he said (XII,19):

> If you desire what is good, the people will be good. The character of a ruler is like wind and that of the people is like grass. In whatever direction the wind blows, the grass always bends.

He accepted in general that rulers reached their position 'with the mandate of heaven', but he argued that this situation was not irreversible. If ever, by despotism or greed, they betrayed the trust thus conferred upon them, it was right that they should be overthrown and replaced. Where this occurred, the qualities to look for were integrity and strength of character, fostered by a love of education. These qualities would enable them to overcome the pettiness that leads to the mistreatment of subjects, causing them in their turn to become rebellious. Mencius was later to give unambiguous expression to this admonition:

> If a ruler regards his ministers as his hands and feet, then his ministers will regard him as their heart and mind. If a ruler regards his ministers as dogs and horses, his ministers will regard him as any other man. If a ruler regards his ministers as dirt and grass, his ministers will regard him as a bandit and an enemy.
>
> (IV,B,3)

A particular concern of Kung Tzu's was what he termed 'the rectification of names', meaning that there should be a correspondence between a person's title and his behaviour. 'Let the ruler *be* a ruler,' he said (XII,11), 'the minister *be* a minister, the father *be* a father, and the son *be* a son.' A ruler who is too lazy to tackle the problems in his region, a minister who is too greedy to serve others, a father who ignores his paternal obligations and a son who is indifferent to his filial responsibilities: all are, in their different ways, catalysts of disorder and dissension. Get the names right, suggested K'ung, and there arises the possibility of justice and order in the land; ignore the names, and the door is open to contention, disharmony and strife. Every name contains qualities that correspond to the essence of whatever or whoever is referred to by that name. If ruler, minister, father or son follows the *Tao* of his role by living up to the ideal that the name indicates, there will be harmony between the name and the expression of it in practice. 'A noble person [*chun-tzu*] will not tolerate disorder in his words. That is what matters', he said (*Analects* XIII,3).

The School of Names was later to become an autonomous school, but without Master K'ung's wise, non-obsessional and, above all, comprehensively human perspective it came to represent a somewhat narrow, even pedantic, form of what Western philosophy might describe as linguistic analysis.

We may summarise Confucius's views on government in the following statements:

1 The purpose of government is to provide for the welfare and happiness of all its people.
2 The right to govern is not sustained by heavenly decree, but by the ability to make its people happy and secure, with equal justice before the law.
3 In the selection of leaders, no role should be played by wealth or breeding, but by integrity and virtue, arising from a love of education.
4 Excessive taxation, barbarous punishments and aggression towards people within the state and beyond should be outlawed.
5 The best government is that which governs least, dedicating itself to the development of the character and culture of the people.

This last statement is a reflection of Taoist thought, especially about *wu-wei*. I quoted on page 93 Confucius's commendation of the legendary ruler, Shun, who seems to have been content to let things be and not to intervene in his subjects' affairs (XV,4):

> To have taken no [unnatural] action [*wu-wei*] and yet have the empire well governed, Shun was the man.

Confucius constantly emphasised education as the key to happy and successful living, 'to go on learning so that you do not notice yourself growing old', as he stated in the *Analects*, and this emphasis puts him among the foremost of the world's humanists. He was one of the first people in history, and certainly the first in China, to take up teaching as a full-time occupation, and to suggest that the educational process was life-long. He thus stands among the protagonists of *educere*, rather than *educare*, as the essence of education: to go on growing, humbly aware that, however learned one is, there is infinitely more to know, rather than viewing education simply as the gateway to a qualification that offers economic opportunities to its owner. L.C. Wu closes his study of Confucius (*op. cit.*, p. 31) with these words:

> Confucius's ethic is a rational approach to human happiness and good society without any supernatural grounding. Confucius taught the Chinese

that happiness and virtue are correlatives which are complementary to each other . . . This spirit of happiness can be readily found among the Chinese regardless of their educational level, social or financial status. This is Confucius's contribution. It is the noblest of human achievements.

This may explain why it is that, after some years of neglect, Master K'ung has returned as a compulsory subject of study in Chinese schools. Even Mao Tse-tung acknowledged that he ranked worthy to be studied alongside Marx, Engels and Lenin. How far he would have been happy in their company is, however, a matter of some speculation. Independently of their political views, one suspects that, like any other claimants to possession of the 'truth', their self-assuredness, a corruption of self-assurance, would have made it difficult for him to relate to them at any more than a surface level. To be a *chun-tzu* (gentleman), he knew, a key virtue was the humility to accept that one may be wrong on any issue, however firmly that belief be held.

MENCIUS (MENG-TZU)

Second only to K'ung Tzu in the Confucian hierarchy is Mencius (*c.* 372–289 BCE). In many respects both his life and his teachings were remarkably similar to those of his mentor. He was born in the same province, followed in his earlier years the same profession, experienced similar frustrations because of the political and moral chaos brought about primarily through selfish and ineffectual government, eventually became a roaming teacher and counsellor, offering advice to rulers, and disputing with those whom he believed to be the authors of 'perversive doctrines'; and, like Confucius, he felt at the end of his life a sense of disappointment and failure.

The philosophy of Mencius is often described as 'idealistic Confucianism', an expression based partly on his optimistic view of human nature, partly on his greater emphasis on the spiritual dimension in following the Confucian virtues. If Confucius was China's Aristotle, Mencius was more akin to its Plato, of whom he was a contemporary, and with whom he is often compared. He was also a contemporary of Chuang Tzu, but there is no record of their ever having met each other – an encounter that would surely have been beneficial not only to both of them but also to all whose lives have been enriched by their teaching.

Like the Analects, the book *Mencius* was probably edited by disciples, although under closer supervision by their mentor than was the earlier book. It is structured more carefully than the Analects, and from it we can infer that Mencius was a sharp debater, uncompromising in his views, and not so ready as Confucius to admit that he might be wrong on any matter. He seems to have spent considerable time in arguing his case with rival philosophers, who were more numerous in his time than two centuries earlier.

Mencius accepted Confucius's emphasis on the twin virtues of *jen* and *li*: how they embrace *chung* and *shu*, express themselves in *xiao* (*hsiao*) and *chun-*

tzu, and are directed by a sense of righteousness, or *i*. So far as guidelines for successful living are concerned, therefore, Mencius offered no radical departures from the Confucianist canon. Where he differed was on a matter that has been the subject of continual debate over the millennia, to which he offered an unambiguous standpoint: human nature, and his view, for which he remains one of the key historical protagonists, that it is inherently good.

Confucius had held the belief that human nature cannot be characterised as inherently either 'good' or 'bad' (the reason for putting those words in quotations will emerge later). In a sense, he took an existentialist view, arguing that each person's nature (what Sartre called 'essence') developed as a direct consequence of the path they followed through life: the choices they made, the priorities they established, the extent to which they observed the five relationships, and so on. Above all, he held that the most certain route to goodness lay along the path of education. The broadening of the mind that this would ensure would enable a person more comprehensively to show loving kindness, observe the proprieties and express righteousness in his or her dealings. In other words, goodness was a product of the *educere* process (see page 125), and, while many were prevented from following this way because of factors beyond their control, nobody was inherently incapable of achieving it. Confucius could, therefore, well have been the first to declare, 'Existence precedes essence.'

Mencius disagreed with this neutral position. His view was that people were born with their natures intact, and that the natural human instinct is towards goodness. 'Which of you,' he asked his audience during one debate on the subject, 'seeing a child playing on the edge of a well and stumbling, would not instinctively spring to its aid, lest it fall to its death?' To Mencius, this – what we should today call reflex – reaction proved that people are predisposed to be altruistic. He observed the generations of people throughout history who had willingly accepted personal inconvenience, sacrifice, suffering and even death for the sake of others: was this to be described as unnatural behaviour? This seemed to him to be necessarily the case if the opposite position were taken.

There is a close similarity here between Mencius's view and that of Plato and, two millennia later, Jean-Jacques Rousseau, although without the Platonic concept of reincarnation after a period in heaven, the world of forms, or ideals, which was an integral feature of their philosophy. Mencius did not discuss *why* people were altruistic from birth; he simply affirmed that this was the case, based on empirical evidence.

His critics wanted to know why, in that case, many people in a host of situations – as observation would continually confirm – behaved selfishly, showing indifference towards others' needs, and even going to the extent of causing them deliberate harm. Mencius's reply was that evil was the result of unnatural behaviour. Because of circumstances, people's natural goodness could be distorted or suppressed; what was needed, therefore, was a community that allowed free rein to their natural constituents: loving kindness, righteousness, respect for others, piety. In a famous passage, he compared human nature to the way water behaves:

> Man's nature is naturally good just as water naturally flows downward. There is no man without this good nature; neither is there water that does not flow downward. Now, you can splash water and cause it to splash upward over your forehead; and by damming it and leading it, you can force it uphill. Is this the nature of water? It is the forced circumstance that makes it so. Man can be made to do evil, for his nature can be treated in the same way.
>
> (VI,1,6)

Mencius lived, of course, 2,000 years before Newton's discovery of gravity, otherwise he would at the very least have needed to find a different analogy. More important philosophically is the question, which relates to Plato's and Rousseau's theories also, of how, if all people are born with perfect natures, imperfections arise at all. Logically it seems the case that, if they are naturally altruistic individually, they will be so collectively; the only escape-route from this logic would be to assert that the natural life is one of isolation, so that all social intercourse is unnatural: which would leave a question mark over the need for altruism in any case.

The fact is that Mencius's whole position is tautological, since by the word 'good' he means whatever is fully in tune with human nature, and by human nature he means whatever may be described as 'good'. This is a circular argument: if, on the one hand, whatever is inborn is defined as human nature, and, on the other, human nature is characterised as 'good', then Mercius's conclusion that 'bad' behaviour must be characterised as 'unnatural', may follow, but only by a monumental process of question-begging. It is as if a person were to argue that Christians live good lives and, on being told of a practising Christian who treats others shabbily, replies, 'In that case I would not describe him as a Christian at all.' (We leave unexplored the vexed questions of how far 'goodness' and 'badness' are absolute terms, and whether the words have any definable meaning at all. Mencius lived not only before Newton, but before the age of postmodernist relativism cf. p.100.)

Independently of these considerations, Mencius made the following statements, which encapsulate the logical consequences of accepting his basic proposition:

1 The ability possessed by men without their having to acquire it is innate ability, and the knowledge possessed by them without deliberation is innate knowledge . . . These feelings are universal in the world.

(VII,A,15)

2 He who exerts his mind to the uttermost knows his nature. He who knows his nature knows Heaven. To preserve one's mind and to nourish one's nature is the way to serve Heaven.

(VII,A,1)

3 When there is repeated disturbance, the restorative influence of the night will not be sufficient to preserve [the proper goodness of the mind] ... People see that he acts like an animal, and think that he never had the original endowment [for goodness].

(VI,A,8)

4 Pity the man who abandons the path and does not follow it, and has lost his heart and does not know how to recover it.

(VI,A,11)

5 Confucius said, 'Hold it fast and you preserve it. Let it go and you lose it.' He was talking about the human mind ... *The way of learning is none other than finding the lost mind.*

(VI,A,11,8)

Those italicised words perfectly express the humanist approach to education, and they are reflected in Pope's famous couplet in his *Essay on Man*:

> Men must be taught as if you taught them not,
> And things unknown proposed as things forgot.

One practical expression of Mencius's idealism was his proposal for the 'well-field system' in agriculture. Each square (*li*) of land (about one-third of a mile squared) is divided into nine equal squares in the shape of a noughts-and-crosses chart. Eight farmers each own one of the outside squares, leaving the central square to be farmed by all of them on a rota basis. Each keeps the proceeds from his own patch, but the proceeds from the central square provide the taxes for all eight of them. (This square can of course be expanded or contracted according to the rate of taxation.) Mencius proposed this as a middle way between totally individualised and completely communalised farming; he believed that it would leave the way open for people both to cooperate with one another and to have the personal satisfaction of reaping the fruits of their own labour.

It is interesting to speculate whether this system would work in practice. Would each farmer work as hard on the central square as he did on his own patch? It would need only one backslider to upset both the system as a whole, and the feelings of the other seven at the same time. One wonders how many of them would find themselves feeling unwell on the eighth day when it was their turn in the middle. Who would be held to blame if the tax authorities felt underpaid? The resolution of this conundrum depends on whether one is an idealist or a cynic: it would certainly be a test of Mencius's theory.

One Confucianist who would have scorned the well-field system on the grounds that it would lead to controversy brought about by self-interest was **Hsun Tzu** (*c.* 298–238 BCE), generally revered as the 'third sage' in the Confucian hierarchy. While in essential aspects he agreed with Confucian teaching, he disagreed with Mencius about human nature. In fact, if Mencius was the Rousseau of Confucianism, Hsun Tzu was its Hobbes. Two of his disciples became leading figures in the Legalistic School, and he has (wrongly, according to many modern sinologists), been characterised as the midway figure between it and Confucianism. The *Hsun-Tzu* consists of thirty-two chapters, which are effectively a series of essays on a range of subjects. They indicate that, if on some issues he was more legalistic than Confucius, in others, such as his view of *T'ien* (Heaven), he was more Taoist. His writings are not included among the Chinese classics, but his critical and analytical approach to philosophy makes him a particularly attractive subject of study in modern China.

Chapter 23 of the *Hsun-Tzu*, probably the best-known essay in the book, is entitled, 'The Nature of Man is Evil'. Its first two paragraphs give the gist of his beliefs on the subject, and because of their simplicity of expression they need no further elucidation:

> The nature of man is evil; whatever is good in him is the result of acquired training. Men are born with the love of gain; if this natural tendency is followed they are contentious and greedy, utterly lacking in courtesy and consideration for others. They are filled from birth with envy and hatred of others; if these passions are given rein they are violent and villainous, wholly devoid of integrity and good faith. At birth man is endowed with the desires of the ear and the eye, the love of sound and colour; if he acts as they dictate he is licentious and disorderly, and has no desire for *li* or justice or moderation.
>
> Clearly, then, to accord with man's original nature and act as instinct dictates must lead to contention, rapacity, and disorder, and cause humanity to revert to a state of violence. For this reason it is essential that men be transformed by teachers and laws, and guided by *li* and justice; only then will they be courteous and cooperative, only then is good order possible. In the light of these facts it is clear that man's original nature is evil, and that he becomes good only through acquired training.

Hsun Tzu's theory is in some respects a reflection of Aristotle's contention, expressed a century earlier, that the law exists to spur people on in the pursuit of 'the good'.

One other emphasis in Mencius's teaching distinguishes him from Confucius and links him somewhat more closely with the Taoist and *Yin–Yang* schools. This is his philosophical mysticism, in accordance with which he speaks not only of cultivating order in the community, but also of achieving order within oneself by cultivating *ch'i*: vital breath, or energy. We have seen earlier (page 91) how important is the concept of *ch'i* in Taoism, both as a focal point of meditation and as a means of achieving physical harmony, both within oneself and in relation to the universe as a whole. *T'ai-ch'i* is the term used for the supreme ultimate, and *T'ai-Ch'i Ch'uan*, as we saw on page 106, is a form of physical exercise designed to create a sense of personal harmony with it.

Mencius wrote (II,A,2 and VII,A,1,1):

When I cultivate this great *ch'i* within me, all things are then complete within me ... [therefore] he who completely knows his nature, knows Heaven.

By 'Heaven', he was referring to the cosmic order, which for him was a moral one: his view was that moral principles both reflect and devolve from the metaphysical principles of the universe (there is a nuance of Kantianism in this perception). All people are at the same time citizens of society and of Heaven. With this emphasis he went further in the direction of mysticism than had Confucius. The Master had certainly introduced the concept of Heaven into his teaching, but more as an indication of the source of the values he taught than as a goal for people to attain. Mencius stressed that, in the process of cultivating the great *ch'i*, we need not only human principles such as duty and righteousness, which Confucius had unambiguously outlined, but also both an understanding of, and sense of harmony with, the *Tao*.

Mencius thus combines two of the disciplines of Hinduism: Jnana Yoga, or spiritual understanding, and Karma Yoga, the discipline of action and work. This balance gives his teaching the completeness found in the harmony of *yin* and *yang*, which may well be seen as the aim of all religious philosophies and their practitioners (see Chapter 18).

NEO-CONFUCIANISM

During the centuries immediately following Mencius's death, the mystical element in his teaching was given little prominence among students of Confucianism, who preferred to concentrate on the school's practical emphases. Advocates of other philosophical schools and perspectives were viewed, on the whole, as rivals rather than exponents of alternative facets of the truth they were all seeking. There were in fact numerous disputations, not all of them harmonious, between adherents of the different philosophies.

Between the third and eighth centuries CE, however, a process of synthesis took place that brought about a modification of the Confucianism taught by the Master. The main schools that were involved in this process were the two which, alongside Confucianism, still constitute the main streams in Chinese philosophy/religion: Taoism and Buddhism. Through the influence of these two schools, Confucian thought underwent a transformation, with the result that it began to acknowledge more directly the role of the mystical when interpreting both the universe in general and human life in particular. It was during this period that the *I Ching* gained its significance as a guide to a spiritual interpretation of the world; and the concept of the *Tao* as the primordial principle of the universe was seen to connect with the practical guidelines of Confucius, so that (for instance) the five relationships taught by the Master could be described as 'the *Tao* of relationships'. This synthesising process is known as Neo-Confucianism and has great significance for any modern discussion of the subject. It was during this period that the so-called

Four Books, which were, as mentioned earlier (page 119) used in Chinese Civil Service examinations, assumed their authority.

The most important contribution of Neo-Confucianism, however, was its extension of Mencius's view of the metaphysical rationale for traditional ethics. The person most closely associated with this teaching, and generally regarded as the greatest of the Neo-Confucians, was the twelfth-century philosopher **Chu Hsi** (1130–1200), a prolific writer, and lecturer at the Confucian College of Bai Lu Dong (White Deer Grotto) near Shanghai. In his earlier years he was a student of Buddhism but turned from this philosophy because of its teaching of *anatta*; Chu Hsi held that there is a basic self, and his philosophy is built around this belief.

The two fundamental components of his teaching are *li* and *ch'i*. We have met both these words already, but his interpretation of them, particularly his combination of them, is distinctive. In traditional Confucian teaching, *li* means propriety; but Chu Hsi used it in its second (although not secondary) sense of the absolute, the cosmic order: in fact, as he interprets the word, it becomes highly reminiscent of the *Tao*. *Li* is the principle, the formal aspect of a thing (the thing-in-itself); *ch'i*, as used by Chu Hsi, is its material representation in any specific instance. *Ch'i* cannot exist without *li*, and *li* cannot be known without *ch'i*. Things are thus the instruments by which *li* finds expression; everything has its *li*, which alone establishes that thing's nature. Furthermore, the *li* of a thing pre-exists the actual coming into being of that thing (as opposed to Confucius's more existentialist perspective): the essence of anyone or anything precedes their actual coming into existence. One is reminded of Plato's theory of forms in this teaching, although the emphasis in Chu Hsi is on what Christians would term 'realised eschatology', described by Dietrich Bonhoeffer as 'the beyond in the midst'. For Plato, the forms remain in Heaven, either dimly remembered by the philosophers who have escaped from the shadows of the cave, or encountered in moments of revelation by those who 'can suddenly perceive a nature of wondrous beauty' (*Symposium*, 211).

For Chu Hsi, the form of a thing (or person), and its actual expression in a particular instance, are potentially one, and he summarised this idea with the words, 'Everything has an ultimate *ch'i*, which is the ultimate *li*' (*Recorded Sayings*, chapter 94). In the same passage, however, he added words that link his teaching more closely with *tao-chia* and, although not quite so directly, with the Hindu idea of *brahman* and the ground of being:

> That which unites and embraces the *li* of heaven, earth, and all things is the Supreme Ultimate [*T'ai-Ch'i*].

In the *Complete Works of the Master Chu*, chapter 49, he adds:

> The Supreme Ultimate is what is highest of all, beyond which nothing can be. It is the most high, most mystical, and most abstruse, surpassing everything.

Thus *T'ai-Ch'i* is, as Chu expresses it (p.244), 'the *li* of all *li*, the *li* of the universe as a whole'. Every individual therefore has not only his or her own *li* within his or her *ch'i*, but also partakes of the ultimate *li*. Chu Hsi states:

> This one Supreme Ultimate is received by each individual in its entirety and undivided. It is like the moon shining in the heavens, of which, though it is reflected in rivers and lakes and thus is everywhere visible, we would not therefore say that it is divided.
>
> (*Recorded Sayings*, chapter 94)

If we accept the findings, such as they are, of Chapter 2, this must be judged to be a highly religious statement. Chu Hsi adds to this perspective a cosmological consideration. He taught that the universe's existence is a consequence of the continually alternating phases of *ch'i*, which he held to oscillate between rest and motion. It is at rest in *yin* and in movement in *yang*, and from the oscillation arise *wu-hsing*, the five elements of earth, fire, metal, wood and water (discussed on pages 116–7), which, by their infinite combinations, give rise to the material world, There are some reflections here of the alternating appearance and disappearance of the universe (evolution and involution) taught in the Hindu school of Sankya Yoga (see page 26).

Laurence Wu comments on this teaching with these words (*op. cit.* p.245):

> All creation was an evolutionary process from simple to complex life, through a continuous succession of birth, decay, death, and re-creation. In view of the role played by *li* and *ch'i* in the production of things, Joseph Needham's translation of *li* as 'principle of organisation' and *ch'i* as 'matter-energy' in *Science and Civilisation in China* are quite apt.

Whether religious or otherwise, these ideas have played a formative part in creating one feature of the Chinese mind.

In the final chapters of this book, we shall consider the similarities and differences between the various Eastern schools on which we have reflected, together with their Western counterparts. The *modus operandi* will be by a process of extrapolation of the key issues, as they seem to the writer, raised in the foregoing chapters.

13 Metaphysics without theology I: The ground of being

Most of what has so far been presented has been an account of the main Eastern emphases over a broad spectrum of thought. There is much, of course, that could be added to make the picture comprehensive, but it seems reasonable enough to hope that the preceding chapters will have served to dispel some of the misconceptions that tend to arise when Westerners first decide to taste the flavour of the East. A *little* knowledge may not always be, as Pope suggested, a dangerous thing, but the assumption of only vague generalities about Eastern philosophy can easily leave people floundering in a world of make-believe.

In these final chapters, as indicated at the end of Chapter 12, I shall therefore identify some of the key Eastern ideas as I perceive them, discuss any major differences in emphasis between them, and, where apposite, compare and contrast them with their Western counterparts. This exercise will inevitably bear a more personalised stamp than was called for in the previous chapters; but, since the issues to be discussed are all matters of current debate, these chapters may well be treated as pointers for discussion among those who share an interest in the subject. Living philosophy means not only studying what others have believed and taught, but also asking where *we* go from here.

The central feature of religion, if the argument presented in the opening chapter is accepted, is belief in the numinous: the acknowledgement that the universe contains two essences, the material and the spiritual. This, and this alone, gives meaning to the other ideas and practices normally associated with a religion. There has been some debate over the most apposite word to describe this dimension, but one writer (William Johnston) has opted for the word *mystical*. He states:

> All authentic religion originates with mystical experience, be it the experience of Jesus, of the Buddha, of Mohammed, of the seers and prophets or of the Upanishads.
>
> (*The Inner Eye of Love*)

On the face of it, this seems a fair statement; but it is important for those who accept it to be aware of what it is to which they are committing themselves and, more to the point, what they may be discarding. A century ago, William James offered his own definition of mysticism in his Gifford Lectures of 1901–2, still being reprinted as his *Varieties of Religious Experience*. He writes of the reality which he perceives:

> It is that our normal waking consciousness, rational consciousness as we call it, is but one special type of consciousness, whilst all about it, parted from it by the filmiest of screens, there lie potential forms of consciousness entirely different. We may go through life without suspecting their existence; but apply the requisite stimulus, and at a touch they are there in all their completeness ... No account of the universe in its totality can be final which leaves these other forms of consciousness quite disregarded.
>
> (*op. cit.* p.374)

James suggests that these experiences can be described only in the field of the metaphysical and proceeds to attempt the impossible by describing the kind of effect they have on him:

> The keynote of it is invariably a reconciliation. It is as if the opposites of the world, whose contradictoriness and conflict make all our difficulties and troubles, were melted into unity. Not only do they, as contrasted species, belong to one and the same genus, but *one of the species*, the nobler and better one, *is itself the genus, and so soaks up and absorbs its opposite into itself*.
>
> (*ibid.*, his itals.)

He acknowledges that this is 'a dark saying' but suggests that 'those who have ears to hear' will understand.

It is impossible, reading those lines, not to be reminded of a number of features of Eastern philosophy. Shankara's image of the snake and the rope to illustrate the experience of *moksha* is a vivid expression of the condition of enlightenment: he may not have spoken of having 'ears to hear', but his having 'eyes to see' means the same. His philosophy is strictly that of Advaita Vedanta, but the mysticism to which it gives expression can be found in all schools of Hinduism, whether at the 'higher' or 'lower' (that is, popular) level. *Moksha*, the aim of all Hindus, is a state in which eyes are opened to an immanent reality that needs only a moment to be recognised, and is separated from us, as James puts it, by 'the filmiest of screens'.

This concept is central to the Hindu teaching about *samadhi* as the highest peak of Yoga, and, in particular, the emphasis in Advaita Vedanta on the Fourth State, *turiya*. Both Yoga and *turiya* bear witness to the loss of dualistic awareness that occurs in this condition of 'suchness': the surrendering of self-consciousness, the ego, into a universal whole, so that there is no longer 'me' as subject and the world of the senses as object. As the water-drop enters the ocean, from which it can in no respect be distinguished, so the individual self unites with the Self, with the same provision: and, while this state cannot possibly be communicated to others (because the very act of doing so is to resort to the tools of the dualistic state that has been left behind), those who know this, know this, as will be further considered when we discuss the question of *authority* (Chapter 16). Vivekananda, the teacher of Advaita Vedanta who took the first World Parliament of Religions in Chicago by storm in 1893, expressed the matter in these words in his *Raja Yoga*:

> All the different steps in yoga are intended to bring us scientifically to the superconscious state or Samadhi . . . Just as unconscious work is beneath consciousness, so there is another work which is above consciousness, and which, also, is not accompanied with the feeling of egoism . . . There is no feeling of I, and yet the mind works, desireless, free from restlessness, objectless, bodiless. Then the Truth shines in its full effulgence, and we know ourselves – for Samadhi lies potential in us all – for what we truly are, free, immortal, omnipotent, loosed from the finite, and its contrasts of good and evil altogether, and identical with the Atman or Universal Soul.

It is tempting to characterise Buddhism as effectively presenting the same message as Hinduism, but Buddha's teaching of *anatman* – no soul – and his indifference to God, or *brahman*, means that we cannot band Buddhism and Hinduism together as variations on a theme. What we can say, whichever branch of Buddhism we may have in mind, is that the state of *nirvana*, to which all Buddhists aspire, is, like *samadhi*, a non-dual state. The drop of water in the ocean metaphor would certainly be a misleading description of this state from a Buddhist perspective, since that assumes the presence of a universal ground of being; but the Buddhist concept of the enlightened mind – **bodhichitta** – refers to a state beyond desire (*duhkha*) whereby the one who seeks *nirvana* has achieved **shunyata**, the emptiness or void described on pages 58–9. Thus, to refer back to Nagarjuna's teaching about levels of truth, while at one level one can but acknowledge the existence of the world identified through the senses, at a deeper level one passes beyond this world into the void, the world of 'suchness': in other words, one is either on the way to, or has actually entered, *nirvana*.

How far the phenomenon of experiencing the void is similar to that of the Fourth State, and in what respects they differ, is beyond the power of any mortal being to describe. What seems certain is that both are descriptions of the mystical state; and if we were to concentrate in particular on the mysteries of the Tantric rites, which bear the stamp of both Hinduism and Mahayana Buddhism, we should probably conclude that they are united in more respects than they are divided.

If we turn to Taoism, it is immediately apparent that the loss of the sense of ego, which seems to characterise all mystical experiences, is its *sine qua non*. The imagery of going with the flow, and the drop of water entering the river and thence joining the all-embracing sea, seem to be expressions of what James is describing. Perhaps most pertinent of all is his expression of the genus soaking up its opposite into itself, which perfectly exemplifies the activity of *yin* and *yang* (see the quotation on page 108).

Again, however, one must take care not to rush into making simplistic comparisons, this time between Indian and Chinese thought. The Hindu doctrine of *brahman* may be compared with that of the *Tao*, and, in the sense that union with either of these calls for a surrender of wilfulness on the part of any individual, there is, I suppose, a parallel. But there the similarity ends: union with *brahman* means absorption into that which can be known, if only intuitively; union with the *Tao* is not immediately possible, since the *Tao* is unknown and unknowable, experienced only through its twin forces of *yin* and *yang*. It is only by surrendering oneself to these forces and living harmoniously with them that any person can experience the *Te* and begin to understand the mystery of the Way. Only the first half of Job's confession to Yahweh (42:6) could be said of the *Tao*: 'I had heard of thee by the hearing of the ear, but now mine eye seeth thee.'

The mystical element in Taoism, which is its central feature, has a different form from that found in either Hinduism or Buddhism. Both these Indian philosophies discount the natural and material world around us; Taoism, while of course rejecting any hint of materialism in its teaching, expresses the view that the loss of ego that is required from any seeker after the Way is typically experienced through a sense of oneness with, rather than in-difference to, the natural world, amounting virtually to a state of personal surrender to it. Taoist art, even more than Taoist literature, expresses this desire to eradicate the 'me-me' syndrome in human existence, a process that calls for self-emptying and humility. Any rural scene painted along Taoist lines shows people and property blending into the landscape, sometimes to the point of being virtually invisible: self-effacement indeed.

Taoism, at least in its *tao-chia* expression, is ambivalent about the future life (of which more in the next chapter) and agnostic, if not atheistic, about God, although George Chryssides has argued that it is possible to equate God with the *Tao* (see Bibliography). The mysticism of the *Tao Te Ching* is more Wordsworthian than religious, a sense of awe brought about by the natural world around us, rather than by the presence of an almighty being. In his 'Lines Composed above Tintern Abbey', Wordsworth wrote:

> ... And I have felt
> A presence that disturbs me with the joy
> Of elevated thoughts; a sense sublime
> Of something far more deeply interfused,
> Whose dwelling is the light of setting suns,
> And the round ocean, and the living air,
> And the blue sky, and in the mind of man.

Chuang Tzu might have penned those words, or something like them, but not Buddha or Shankara. Taoism in fact gives expression to the belief that there are around us unseen forces which are not beyond the reach of scientific exploration and with which we can, with patience, and in the right frame of mind, align ourselves. Fritjof Capra has discussed this alignment in *The Tao of Physics*, and his disquisition indicates that, while the Taoist approach to living may sometimes be *combined* with that of an Indian or Western school, it cannot be *equated* with any other. Insofar as philosophical Taoism blends a sense of the numinous with, on the one hand, a rejection of materialistic values and, on the other, a recognition of the importance of the natural world, it may well emerge as the way whereby future Western civilisations, disillusioned with both materialistic values and theological niceties, may embrace and pursue the spiritual dimension. To neglect this dimension can cause a fair amount of religious aberration, as we see often enough in Western civilisation today.

How does this Eastern experience relate to the theistic religions? The rock on which Judaism, Christianity and Islam stand is acknowledgment of and loyalty to the One Supreme God. How far this relationship must be categorised as dualistic, rather than the monistic or non-dual experience of mysticism, is a matter for lengthier discussion than can be afforded here. There have of course been mystics in the theistic traditions, whether Jewish (Buber's 'I and Thou' contains hints of both Hindu and Taoist beliefs), Islamic (of whom the Sufis are a supreme example) and Christians such as Meister Eckhart, Julian of Norwich, St Teresa, St John of the Cross, George Fox and William Law. One major difference between all these and their Eastern counterparts, however, is that, while the latter express their mysticism as a natural feature of their beliefs (so that the Hindu *guru*, for example, is revered and emulated by the people even if he/she is not always fully understood by them), mystics of the theistic traditions have generally had to contend with orthodox believers who have not been averse to accusing them of virtual or actual heresies. These include the claim to have received divine revelation outside the normal channels (Holy Scripture and Tradition); pantheism; indifference to the historical revelations of their respective faiths; and disregard of moral and social problems reflected in the world around them. G. K. Chesterton, a convert to Roman Catholicism, went so far as to describe mysticism as 'beginning in mist, centred round "I", and ending in schism'.

Perhaps the suspicions of theistic commentators can be said to be reactions to statements of mystics such as Martin Buber, who affirmed in his *I and Thou*: 'When you get to the Thou, God is no more.' And Meister Eckhart certainly did not endear himself to his orthodox colleagues with his affirmation:

> When a person has true spiritual experience, he may boldly drop external disciplines, even those to which he is bound by vows.
>
> (*Sermons*, 3)

He was writing in the Middle Ages ('The Age of Faith'), and was unwittingly giving expression to Shankara's concept of living 'beyond good and evil', which we shall discuss in Chapter 15. The general question of how far the personalised God of the theistic traditions can survive as the talisman of the spiritual dimension is a vexed one, which has, over the past century or so, heated up a cauldron of contention. Nietzsche, although raised in a strict Lutheran culture, came to view any belief in divine providence as a sign of human fallibility and weakness, an abdication, on the believer's part, of responsibility either for him/herself or for the world in which he/she was placed. God was dead, Nietzsche asserted: but, in the words of the old music-hall song, 'He's dead but he won't lie down.' Nietzsche appreciated full well that so long as people tried to avoid anxiety, the bed-mate of responsibility, by seeking solace in God's grace; so long as their eyes were fixed on Heaven and the reward they would receive for loyalty to Him on Earth; so long as heads remained bowed and knees bent in His Name: thus long the idea of God as the object of worship and the source of authority would survive.

The problem which Nietzsche compellingly propounds is that this God, pithily characterised by John Robinson in his *Honest to God* (1963) as 'the God of the gaps', cannot survive in our scientific, technological, computerised age unless people, consciously or unconsciously, pretend that nothing has changed over the centuries, and that we can still go on believing in Creationism, the Fall, and the infallibility of Holy Writ, based on the allegedly pious, but effectively buck-passing view of St Paul that 'the foolishness of God is wiser than men, the weakness of God is stronger than men' (I Corinthians 1:25).

The folly of this viewpoint lies in its thoroughgoing spiritual dualism. We are presented on the one hand with an almighty, omniscient, omnipresent (etc.) God, whose essence is spirit. On the other hand stand those multitudes of followers whose spirituality consists in being His obedient servants. Their purpose in life is identified as seeking His will and following it, in the belief that knowledge of what He commands is gleaned primarily from either sacred writings handed down over the centuries, or from the utterances of his hierarchical representatives here on Earth. The dualism arises because the sense of the spiritual is not viewed as a universally intuitive feature of human beings, but as an 'act of grace', a gift bestowed by God, for reasons that are not immediately obvious to any objective observer, on only a small proportion of His creatures. The theistic religions may well protest that the spiritual rewards of their respective faiths are available to all, but effectively the route to these rewards is circumscribed by God's acts of revelation: and He seems to be arbitrary in the choice of those to whom He wills to reveal Himself.

To enter the metaphysical world as it is comprehended in Eastern thought is a phenomenological experience of a different kind. For a start, in both Indian and Chinese philosophy, the way – whether to *samadhi, nirvana,* or union with the *Tao* – is not only open to all but, in Indian philosophy at least, will eventually be found by all. In Hinduism, this universalist perception springs naturally from the belief that we are all divine, even if in this cycle of experience we are not yet aware of it. Consequently, it falls to each individual to find his or her way to enlightenment. There are many gods at popular levels of Hinduism, of course, and most Indians turn to one or other of them from time to time to help them with some spiritual or practical problem. This does not, however, mean that they are thereby casting aside their personal responsibility for finding the ultimate goal. The path that any Hindu takes in the quest for this goal is the path that he or she chooses. It may be a well-worn path, pioneered by a *rishi*, or *guru*, or seer, and followed by millions; it may be a lesser-known path, followed by a smaller number who find that the spiritual exercises it involves accord with their particular propensities and inclinations; it may even be a fresh path, with the individual seeker himself or herself the pioneer of new expressions of the spiritual life (and perhaps the developer of new spiritual exercises). The goal, however, remains the same for all; and nobody can fail to achieve it, even though it may take many cycles of experience (reincarnations) before *samadhi* is entered for all eternity.

The crucial feature of this quest is that, since it is a journey of discovery of one's own divinity, there is no God 'out there' dictating the terms. Essentially this is also the case with Buddhism, since this is, to all intents and purposes, an atheistic philosophy (in the strict sense of being one that rejects the theistic standpoint). Those who hold that it is impossible to accept the metaphysical dimension without also believing in a personal God are therefore quite prepared to exclude Buddhism from any discussion of religion; at best, they accord it a low level in the religious hierarchy.

Those who have participated in Buddhist forms of meditation will be able to judge if this is a fair comment on their activity: there are, after all, enough Western meeting-places for Buddhists of various kinds to discount any plea of ignorance on the matter. What seems undeniable is, first, that these acts of meditation have as their aim the encouragement of the intuitive side of human nature rather than, as in so much of Western theistic liturgy, appealing to the senses, if not to the reason; second, that this process of awakening is a manifestation of the metaphysical dimension; and, third, that there is therefore in Buddhist, as in Hindu, meditation an expression of metaphysics without theology, an experience of the numinous without God. It may be argued by those who accept this situation but who are not deeply impressed by it that the same experience can, and does, occur during the performance of music, a play, or even a walk in the countryside. The Buddhist reply might well be: quite.

That would certainly have been Chuang Tzu's comment, or indeed that of any dedicated Taoist, who would be in accord with both Hindus and Buddhists in their affirmation that to seek the spiritual (or divine, if that word is preferred) in human experience is to look no further than at what that experience naturally has on offer. If Hindus can fairly be characterised as seeking the divine not by prostrating themselves before an omnipotent creator and law-giver but in the tranquillity of their inner selves; and Buddhists as seeking the detachment and harmony that comes not in some temple erected to the glory of the supreme life-giving deity but through the *chitta*-consciousness of the inner void; then Taoism may be judged to be even more representative of this naturalism, since its call is for followers of the Way to find it amid their daily surroundings, to unite with the principles of *yin* and *yang* that govern these surroundings, and to live in such harmony with them that, as we have seen, the experience becomes one of absorption.

There is in the Shenxi Province of modern China the remote hermitage of Lei Gu Tail It is situated on top of a mountain and can be reached only by an arduous three-hour climb (a process known locally as 'walking the dragon's back'). The hermitage itself is part of the mountain, and below it is a small, open-sided, square-shaped building that serves as a Taoist temple. Trees grow in its rooms and courtyards; in its gardens is grown all the food needed to sustain the Taoist masters who live there (one is over 100 years old and has not left it since before the Communists took over the country in 1949); and the whole building can easily be missed with a cursory glance since it is formed from the materials found in the local rocks and soil. It commemorates the story and the site where, centuries ago, a Taoist hermit played a game of chess with the emperor to decide who should own the sacred mountain of Hua Shan. The Taoist won, and Hua Shan remains a centre for Taoists, its sacredness arising from its naturalness, which imparts to any visitor a sense of mystery and the ineffable. It could almost be described as a centre of 'realised Taoism' – 'the beyond in the midst' quoted on page 132: words which, to be fair, were used by the Christian Dietrich Bonhoeffer to describe the immanence of God.

It is significant of the Taoist experience of the numinous that it depends less on the concept of a personal God than Hinduism or even Buddhism. It is encountered in the natural flow of universal forces, and while the rural setting that gave it birth remains its native theatre, there are many Taoists who have moved into centres of urban life and found that the ideas enunciated by Lao Tzu are relevant even amid the essential artificiality of much that occurs in that setting. This is right and proper: after all, if it were possible to experience that to which Lao Tzu testified only in a particular environment, Taoism would have little to do in the modern world except give guidance on how to get away from it all. What the modern world surely needs is how to find tranquillity amid the mental and physical stress of living: Taoism seems ideally suited to provide that, and the appearance, after some millennia, of tentative Taoist shoots in the West may be viewed as a sign of hope in our time.

14 Metaphysics without theology II: Human nature and destiny

We saw in the previous chapter that it is feasible to reject a materialist philosophy of the universe without necessarily accepting a theological interpretation: one can, as Eastern philosophy illustrates, accept the numinous without thereby being obliged, whether by the processes of logic or the forces of tradition, to believe in the personal God of monistic theism. We turn now to another central issue in religious thought that has also hinged on theistic belief in the idea of a God with a will and purpose for His creatures: what we are, and what is to become of us.

HUMAN NATURE

The debate about what a human being is can at one level be reduced to a simple conflict of opinion between monists and dualists. On the one hand are those who hold that we are composed of only a single, material, substance, so that we can all be categorised in terms of the laws of matter to which every part of every human being is subject. These 'parts' include not only our physical processes but also our mental activities and so-called spiritual experiences, since neither of these can occur without the brain. So it is that the highest reaches of human invention, the profoundest insights, the most blinding visions, the mystic absorption of a St Teresa or a Vivekananda, and the white-hot creativity of a Shakespeare or a Beethoven can all be viewed as simply matter in motion, the consequence, in Bertrand Russell's words, of 'a collocation of atoms which had no preview of the end they were achieving' (*The Independent Review*, December 1903). Followers of the Charvaka teaching in India (see pages 43–5) would have no difficulty with this affirmation.

In the opposite camp are the dualists, who contend that it does not make sense to identify our processes of thinking, feeling, willing, believing and, in particular, the sense of awe and mystery experienced in a variety of contexts, religious and otherwise, as a series of physically induced (and therefore physically induceable) conditions. To explain away the 'visionary gleam' as simply an example of matter in motion does not *seem* to do justice to human aspirations over the ages. The archetypal dualist in Western philosophy was of course Plato, who unambiguously described human beings as comprising both the tangible and identifiable body and the intangible but equally irrefutable soul. He characterised the human condition as one of constant ambivalence, with everyone torn between the demands made by their two conflicting natures. Those who let their bodies dictate their lives would inevitably become a prey not only to sensual desires but also, much worse, to the prejudice and bigotry that are born of ignorance. To follow the leadings of the soul, on the other hand, meant escaping from the artificiality and shadowy existence of the cave (his famous metaphor) and discovering the pure light of Heaven, which brings wisdom and understanding. In the *Timaeus* (34c), he wrote:

> God made the soul in origin and excellence prior to and older than the body, to be the ruler and mistress, of whom the body was to be the subject.

I guess that, if we could poll everyone who has ever lived on what exactly they mean by a 'human being', Plato's delineation, in its essentials at any rate, would top it.

I have suggested, however, that it would be simplistic to assume that the problem of human nature could be settled as a plain choice between the two opposing philosophies of materialism and dualism. We need only to reflect on some of the main contributions of Eastern philosophy in this field, and then take a closer look at the scriptures of the theistic religions, to become aware that there are many shades of opinion between these two extremes.

The closest to the Platonic view among the schools we have studied is to be found in Hinduism, in the Upanishads and the *Bhagavad Gita*. For example, the Chandogya-Upanishad states:

> This soul of mine within the heart is smaller than a grain of rice, or a barley-corn, or a mustard-seed, or a grain of millet, or the kernel of a grain of millet. This soul of mine within the heart is greater than the earth, greater than the atmosphere, greater than the sky, greater than these worlds.
>
> (III,14,3)

Ramanuja, an eleventh-century commentator on the *Bhagavad-Gita*, made this affirmation:

> The soul cannot be understood as an aggregate of many parts, for everywhere it is apprehended as being other than the body, being that which measures and of one form. It is that which says in the body, 'I know this.'
>
> (II.18)

This is the Hindu philosophy of *atman*, the essential self that Hindus of all schools believe must be discovered if they are not to spend their lives beguiled by *maya*, the illusion that whatever appeals to either the body or the mind has any lasting worth. All Hindu forms of meditation, from Yoga to

Tantra, have as their aim the enlightenment, *moksha*, which begins with the recognition that everything that we encounter in the world is, in the word of the Jewish book of Ecclesiastes, vanity. Once this has been firmly accepted, the way is open for the exploration of the spiritual reality to which the *atman* testifies, leading ultimately, as we have seen, to the recognition that *atman* and the ground of being, *brahman*, are one.

So far as Hinduism is concerned, we can safely say that the dichotomy between materialism and dualism holds. Hinduism is dualistic as Platonism is dualistic, though with different emphases. Plato taught that the cultivation of the soul would best be achieved by the pursuit of learning (the Greek word *psyche* can, after all, be translated as 'mind' as well as 'soul'); Hinduism, on the other hand, offers the pursuit of *samadhi* and the experience of the Fourth State, *turiya*, as the natural habitat of the soul (or basic self, as I have suggested should be the translation of *atman*). Both schools agree, however, not only that we have a soul, but that it should also be the navigator, or pilot, of our lives (the Greek word is *kybernetes*, literally steersman, used figuratively by Plato, Philo and others in this context: Hindus would not disapprove of the term).

When we turn to Buddhism, however, the issue becomes a good deal more complicated, as must be evident to anyone who has reflected on one of the three basic marks of existence identified by Buddha: *anatman*, literally non-self or, in the terminology we have been using, no-soul. We have already identified what is to all intents and purposes an atheistic philosophy in Buddhism: are we now to include it among the monistic materialists?

So far as Mahayana Buddhism is concerned, the answer to this must be unambiguously in the negative. The interpretation of *anatman* (which is, after all, a straightforward enough word) made in these schools relates to morals rather than to metaphysics. The 'no-soul' translation of the Sanskrit word is laid aside in favour of 'non-self'. This could of course still be understood as a metaphysical concept, meaning that human beings possess no fundamental essence; but the Mahayana interpretation relates to the state beyond the demands of self, in which the flames of desire have been eliminated and the frustrations of *duhkha* overcome. By this interpretation of *anatman*, it is not the self that is dead (or non-existent from the start): *the enlightened person, having achieved Buddhahood, is dead to self.*

As a feature of the 'good life', this is of course a thoroughly viable point of view, which affiliates of numerous other schools can easily understand and with which, whether religious or secular, they might well agree (morality in Eastern thought is discussed in the next chapter). The question is whether this interpretation accurately reflects what Buddha meant by *anatman*, and it is difficult to avoid the conclusion that on this issue Mahayana Buddhism blurs the boundaries. To the extent that Buddhism in, for example, China, Japan and Tibet (to say nothing of most of its Western manifestations) assumes that there is an eternal essence in people, there seems little to choose, in this respect, between its philosophy and that of Hinduism. Commentators have in fact suggested that, in the process of dispersion, Mahayana Buddhism has assumed elements both of its Hindu origins and of the religions indigenous to the lands where it has established itself. Because the elements borrowed have varied from country to country, it is impossible to generalise about these syncretistic processes, except to say that all of them, whether consciously or otherwise, reject the literal translation and interpretation of *anatman* and effectively place themselves in the dualist camp.

The Theravada tradition is more loyal to Buddha's teaching: there is no immortal essence in human beings. Its emphasis is on the void, which can be entered into only by practising non-attachment, not just to sensual pleasures and other worldly pursuits but also to intellectual activities and aesthetic delights. All Buddha's key emphases, epitomised in the Noble Eightfold Path, have as their aim the discovery of this void (if that is not an oxymoron): the experience of nothingness; the lasting peace of silence; the bliss of annihilation. I know that many Buddhist scholars do not accept this stark interpretation of Buddha's teaching. Edward Conze, for instance, in *Buddhist Thought in India* (1962), states categorically, 'The Buddha never taught that the self "is not", but only that "it cannot be apprehended".' Conze clearly perceives a difference between these two positions, but it is difficult to recognise how, phenomenologically speaking, this perception is valid. If it is the case that I can never 'apprehend' myself, then, effectively, I have no self. It is like a room that is kept permanently locked in a house: while its existence is not denied, it plays no part in the daily activities of the house's occupants, offering them not a whit of extra space, light or comfort. Such is the self that is occasionally thought of, perhaps, but never encountered.

The question of human destiny is discussed later, even though, as the last paragraph illustrates, it cannot strictly be divorced from the concept of human nature. The chief consideration at this stage is, assuming the above account of the Theravada view of human nature to be a fair one, whether this school should be seen as representative of the materialist or the dualist philosophy. It is difficult to categorise it under either. It is not dualistic, because it denies the existence of the soul. It would be absurd to try and make the case that, in this context, 'the void' is the equivalent of *atman*. The void is, by a process of linguistic and logical necessity, empty: it is nothing, a state of non-being (if that is not another oxymoron); therefore it cannot counterbalance another entity, such as matter.

Yet we can hardly designate Theravada Buddhism as a materialistic philosophy: not, at any rate, in the sense described above. Its teaching about *duhkha*, and the need to overcome the cravings of the body, put it in a separate category from, say *Charvaka* (or, in the West, the philosophy of Hobbes). We seem to have here an example of a philosophy of human nature that is monistic without being materialistic; and if this interpretation is accepted, it demonstrates again how misconceived it is to subsume the issue within the simple dichotomy outlined earlier.

With Taoism we encounter similar problems if we are looking for an easy classification. The stillness in which Taoists are enjoined to abide, arising from their harmony with the *Tao*, can be realised only by achieving its unity, its simplicity and its emptiness. There is a parallel here between this teaching of emptiness and that of Theravada (and, sometimes, Mahayana) Buddhism about the void, and it is not surprising that a sense of kinship has often been expressed between followers of the two schools.

For Taoists, the essential requirement is to be natural, as the phrase 'human nature' suggests. This naturalism is achieved by being at one with the world in which we are placed, itself a manifestation of *yin* and *yang*, the twin forces of the *Tao*. There is no mention of the soul, no reference to an immortal essence in human beings. Chapter 16 of the *Tao Te Ching* states:

> The sage rules from the purest motives
> Relying wholly on quiet and inner peace.
> He watches the seasons rise and fall
> And if he knows how things grow, he knows
> They are fed by their roots . . .
>
> This quiet feeding is the Way of Nature.
> If you understand *ch'ang* – this principle of nurturing,
> you can understand everything . . .
>
> Any man can become wise in this
> And he can walk the Way of Heaven . . .
>
> Life can end in pain –
> But if you live like this,
>   under the Tao
> You will fill your days with breath.

This teaching is in line with the mystical tradition referred to in the previous chapter, where the issue of 'body and soul' or 'body versus soul' does not arise. Taoism remains silent about the dualism question, but this is a silence born of agnosticism rather than scepticism: since we cannot know in this life whether we have immortal souls or not, the wise policy is to go with the flow and yield to the eternal forces around us. It would be fair to say, therefore, that, like much of Buddhist expression, Taoism is a means of coming to terms with this life rather than a study of what to do about the next. This should not be taken to imply that Taoists, any more than Buddhists, give no thought to the question of our future destiny: only that it plays a less important role in their deliberations than it does for adherents of some other religions.

I leave to Chapter 15 a discussion of the related issue, raised earlier, of whether human nature is essentially altruistic or egotistic.

HUMAN DESTINY

Any discussion of the ultimate goal of human existence is of course inextricably bound up with the question of human nature. Nobody, without being self-contradictory, can hold a monistic, materialist view of human nature and at the same time believe in some form of survival after death (except, perhaps, via genes handed on to the next generation), or indeed in any sense of purpose in life outside or beyond the challenges of this present existence. It may be argued, with Nietzsche, Sartre and others of an existentialist turn of mind, that this philosophy encourages those who hold it to take the affairs of this world more seriously than is possible if one's sights are set on the world beyond: but this is too glib an assumption on a matter about which generalisations are hardly possible. For every materialist who is motivated to 'make this world a better place' there is another who is happy to 'eat, drink and be merry, for tomorrow we die'.

As with the question of human nature, there is a kinship between the teaching of Plato and that of Hinduism about human destiny. To their common belief that the soul is immortal, both add the conviction that its natural habitat is a spiritual one: 'Heaven', or whatever other appellation it may be given. It is a state or condition about which both sides are naturally reticent, but both share the imagery of perpetual light, or bliss: that is, it is a desirable state to achieve, one not subject, in Hindu terminology, to *maya*, or, in Platonic language, to the blinkered condition of the cave. He described the body as a tomb (*soma sema*), so the final goal was, quite literally, to be rid of it. This could happen only after an indefinite number of reincarnations, when the light had finally dawned and one could enjoy Heaven for ever.

The *Bhagavad-Gita* expresses a not dissimilar view, both of the inferior condition of the body in relation to the soul, and of the soul's immortality:

> As leaving aside his worn-out garments a man takes other new ones, so leaving aside worn-out bodies the embodied soul goes to other new ones . . .
> It [*atman*] is not born, nor does it ever die, nor having come to be will it ever more come not to be. Unborn, eternal, everlasting, this ancient one is not slain when the body is slain.
>
> (II.22.20)

Differences between the two schools arise when we turn to their descriptions of how to achieve the heavenly state. Plato, as we have seen, taught that the key was to be found in enriching the mind; for Hindus it is through Yoga and the entry into *samadhi*, with the achievement of unity between the *atman* and the ground of being, *brahman*. In turn, this distinction gives a different emphasis to the condition of 'Heaven'. For Plato it was one in which the individual retained a sense of self; for Hinduism it is absorption of the self in the Self, with the consequent loss of personal identity.

This is a state that, as we have already recognised, it is impossible to describe, except, perhaps, ostensively. We can, for instance, refer to instances when we have been so absorbed in something beyond ourselves (or our selves) that we lose all awareness of time and place: these instances may certainly bear a strictly religious stamp, such as during the visions of any of the mystics;

but they may equally occur in so-called secular situations, like being 'absorbed' in a piece of music or drama or subsumed by the world of nature. In any of these situations we can lose our sense of personal identity, so that we may recall the experience only after we have, so to speak, returned to what Hindus describe as the first, dualist, state. The important thing is that we invariably recall these experiences as moments of joy: so if they are indeed a foretaste of 'Heaven', the wise person will constantly seek the experience.

Whatever path we tread through the labyrinthine ways of Buddhism, the same conclusion seems to be justified. Buddhism speak of *dhyana* rather than *samadhi*, and the implication of this state is, as we have seen (pages 65–6), that one passes gradually from concentrating on a single point, beyond intellectual activity, memory and self-consciousness, to a condition where there exists absolutely nothing: the void. Like *turiya*, the Fourth State, *dhyana* cannot be described, but those who have attained it are happy to view it as their ultimate destiny, so far as our worldly powers of apprehension make possible. The prospect of entering into *nirvana* remains as a state beyond even *dhyana*, uniquely desirable but, like the *atman*, unknowable and so indescribable.

The Jains, too, speak in rapturous terms of the highest peaks of Heaven and, even more than their Hindu and Buddhist neighbours, emphasise that anything relating to the body and its needs should be avoided in order to move more closely to it. In Taoism there is a greater agnosticism about the nature of the goal, but a firm commitment to the view that death should not be feared, or viewed in any way as undesirable, but rather recognised for what it is: the natural balance, in the sense of being the other side of the coin, to life, since, as already stated, without death we would not know that we were alive at all. Chuang Tzu, in his sixth chapter, advised his followers:

> Look upon life as a swelling tumour, a protruding goitre, and on death as the draining of a sore or the bursting of a boil.

This should be interpreted more as a positive approach to death than as a negative view of life: Taoists believe that the world, being controlled by the harmony and balance of *yin* and *yang*, the product of *ch'i*, which is the primeval breath by which the *Tao* is expressed, exists for our enrichment and happiness, so that to view it with hatred, like the Jains, or as a delusion, like the Hindus, or as the source of *duhkha*, like the Buddhists, is to belittle what should only be taken with gratitude. If anything, followers of religious Taoism, *tao-chiao*, stress this reverence for life on Earth even more than philosophical Taoists, by offering its adherents the (dubious or otherwise) means to achieve longevity. But here we are encroaching on the varied Eastern attitudes to the world and its works, which is the subject of Chapter 16.

In general, then, we can characterise Indian philosophy as one that points beyond the tangible world, to which our physical senses bear witness, to the unseen world of the spirit, which is to be found primarily through constant meditation. Chinese philosophy lays greater emphasis on human harmony with the visible world, although there is in Taoist teaching and practice a mystical element which is far from alien to that of its Indian counterparts. This emphasis on harmony is given a distinctive stamp in Confucianism, which is a philosophy of human relationships and attitudes. While Confucius's ideal was often described as living according to 'heavenly decree', his concern was with the world as it may reflect the heavenly ideal, not with any concept of Heaven that might lessen the significance of the here and now. Even Mencius, who turned more directly than his mentor to the Taoist teaching about *ch'i* (primeval breath, or spirit) in his attempt to describe the ideal life, was still concerned primarily with the ideal as it might be expressed in this world so that, like Confucius, he leaves the afterlife to take care of itself. The key question, then, is the extent to which a personal commitment to the concept of an afterlife lends meaning and purpose to this life: and there will be differences of opinion about this. Whatever conclusion is arrived at, the matter, for Confucians, is a purely pragmatic one, and it is difficult to view this as anything other than a satisfactory way of tackling the issue.

A brief comment should be made here about the theistic view on these matters, about which, in some respects, there may well be an element of dispute. All (meaning Judaism, Christianity and Islam) are agreed in rejecting the Hindu doctrine of reincarnation and the Buddhist doctrine of rebirth. There are, no doubt, adherents of all three who, secretly or otherwise, hold these views, but they are not found either in their sacred writings or in their official expressions of belief. Whatever is ultimately to become of us, this present existence is the determining factor.

The teaching of Islam is quite straightforward: fidelity to Allah will bring believers the reward of entry into Paradise, normally after a period spent in Purgatory, where the imperfections acquired on Earth will be removed; thereafter, they will enjoy eternally the delights that Allah has in store for them. Anyone unfamiliar with the Old and New Testaments may be forgiven for thinking that this scenario, or something like it, is also valid for Judaism and Christianity; and indeed, if we are to take into account only the beliefs of contemporary followers of these religions, this is a fair reflection of the case. Most Christians, for instance, if asked their views on human nature and destiny, would reply in many respects along Platonic, that is, dualistic, lines: every person is a combination of a mortal body and an immortal soul; at death, the body decays or is destroyed, and the soul of the believer proceeds to its spiritual home, which is Heaven.

About the destiny of the souls of non-believers, Christians have held continual debate. Some have argued that they will be destroyed (which denies their immortality); others, that they must undergo Purgatory before being admitted to Heaven; or that they retain their immortality, but in Hell; or, through the grace of God, they will all be forgiven and received into Heaven ('God will forgive me, that's his job', said Heinrich Heine on his death-bed); or even, more subtly, that they go to the same place as believers, but find that, for them, Heaven is Hell. Leaving aside these speculations, the question we face is whether this popular view, which has been expressed for centuries, accurately reflects original Christian thought on the matter.

Any study of the New Testament will confirm that this is not the case. In these scriptures is found teaching not about the immortality of the soul but about the resurrection of the body. St Paul in I Corinthians 15:58 describes how 'the dead shall be raised', and this teaching is embodied in the Apostles' Creed, which affirms that we believe, not in the immortality of the soul, but in 'the resurrection of the body': only then are we to experience 'the life everlasting'. Paul precedes his affirmation with the statement (*op. cit.* 57) 'we shall not all sleep', and there he was referring to his native Jewish belief, which was that at death all experience ceases. The only prospect after death, so far as classical Jewish teaching was concerned, was **Sheol**, a shadowy state that could not be described in terms that implied experience. The idea of Sheol embodies the forlorn hope that the universally witnessed evidence that the dead remain dead may somehow be false.

The same belief was held by the first Christians, with one significant addition, supplied by St Paul: when Jesus returned (as, by his teaching, they confidently expected to happen imminently), and the present Age was wound up, they would be raised in the New Jerusalem with spiritual bodies (whatever that oxymoron might mean). It was only as time went by, and Jesus's promise was not fulfilled, that they began to look elsewhere for their understanding of their destinies. They found their answer, as, later, did a section of the Jewish community, primarily in the teachings of the neo-Platonist, Plotinus (205–269), and his successors. Given a choice between immortality and resurrection at some indeterminate future date, there really was no combat.

There is of course much more that needs to be considered if the foregoing argument is to be fully substantiated, and this cannot be undertaken here. Suffice to say that, from the Eastern perspective (and here we may be forgiven for generalising), the desire for immortality, as envisaged in the theistic religions, seems misguided, since their representation of it involves the retention of individual self-consciousness, which virtually all Eastern philosophy holds to be at a lower level of being than that of absorption.

Looking at the question from a personal, phenomenological perspective, I can state that I am experiencing eternity now, and I shall never know otherwise. I know that I shall die, and others will know that I am dead; but I shall never know death, since that phrase contains yet another oxymoron. This interpretation of existence is not, I think, inconsistent with much of Eastern philosophy; but the dualistic philosophy, theistic or otherwise, seems, faced with this mode of thinking, little more than a pathetic fallacy.

15 Ethics and human behaviour

The theme of this chapter merits a book in itself. This is the case for all the previous issues, of course, but, since the question of right and wrong touches everybody, whether he or she is interested in metaphysical and ontological matters or not, there is a universality about the questions to be discussed here that is absent from the earlier areas of discussion. People may spend their lives without once reflecting on the numinous; they cannot do so without being involved in the question of right or wrong behaviour, because there is no such thing as moral neutrality. We may avoid thinking or talking about how we ought to behave, but we cannot avoid behaving: nor can we prevent our behaviour's having an affect both on our own future behaviour and on the present and subsequent behaviour of those around us (for whom moral neutrality is equally impossible). Whether we like it or not, not to hold a position, or take a stand, on a particular moral dilemma affects how that dilemma works itself out among those concerned. Not, for example, to sign a petition about an alleged injustice in a community affects the outcome of that petition, as the refusal to vote at election times affects the outcome of the election. Just as, in the words attributed to Burke, 'evil men prosper while good men do nothing', so political parties form governments on the backs of the 'don't knows' or 'include me outs' (to reintroduce the immortal Sam Goldwyn). To put the matter bluntly, there simply is no such person as a moral eunuch.

In the light of what Eastern philosophers have had to say on the subject, this affirmation may well, on the face of it, seem misguided. The Hindu reiteration that all the things of the world and all worldly events are characterised from beginning to end by *maya*, illusion, may understandably lead one to wonder whether the Hindu reaction to moral dilemmas was the inspiration of Nero with his fiddle. Similarly, the Buddhist characterisation of all that the world has to offer as the source of *duhkha*, the suffering born of frustration, can hardly, it would seem, encourage those who introduce a Buddhist presence in the community to cast more than a sideways glance at the problems that beset it. We have seen, too, how the Taoist teaching about *wu wei* has lent itself to the interpretation of doing nothing about the chaos that men in their folly create. Only Confucianism, of the philosophies studied, seems to present a set of firm moral principles as guides to life: but, supremely among these schools, this is a humanist, rather than religious, philosophy. What else are we to conclude, therefore, except that in Eastern philosophy generally there is no ethics worth discussing; or, put another way, that Eastern philosophers are apologists for the kind of fake moral neutrality identified above?

The first point to bear in mind when attempting to demonstrate that 'Eastern ethics' is not another oxymoron is that many of the speculations beloved by Western moral philosophers are ignored by their Eastern counterparts, not through ignorance about such speculations but because they do not seem important. For instance, any student of Western moral philosophy will spend time debating the source of human knowledge of right and wrong (whole books have been written on this topic). There will be discussion about whether it originates 'from above' or 'from below': whether its source is God, the law, the human conscience, or parents, society, the evolutionary process; and they will debate the respective roles of reason and feelings in reaching a decision. In the end, the likely conclusion (except, perhaps, for those with a particular axe to grind) is that there is no definitive answer to the problem.

The Eastern response to this dilemma is straightforward and down to earth. Since we cannot resolve the issue, let us concentrate on tackling the situation as it confronts us. A person hit by a poisoned arrow does not waste time trying to find out where the arrow came from: he looks for an antidote. So the basic approach to morals, exemplified in different ways by Hindus, Buddhists and Taoists alike, is to tackle the problem of how to cope with the conflicting tensions that face us daily in the world of which we are a part. Never mind how we got into the labyrinth: how do we find our way through it and, ultimately, out of it?

With this proviso in mind, we may be more positive about Eastern attitudes to moral behaviour than the earlier criticism allows. For a start, we may recognise that in Eastern teaching, 'good behaviour' is not so much an end in itself as a means of making progress towards a more important goal. In Hinduism the goal is *samadhi*; in Buddhism, *nirvana*; in Taoism, oneness with the *Tao*. The point of view of all three, therefore, is that 'bad behaviour' is not so designated because it contravenes some divine rule or law, with its built-in punishment for misdeeds, but because it is likely to make the goal more difficult to achieve. A Hindu will aim to eliminate greed because that means being deceived by *maya*, which will delay the achievement of *moksha* and condemn him or her to further cycles in the prison of *samsara*. A Buddhist will try to live by *ahimsa*, non-violence, because indifference to others' feelings creates a callousness in the perpetrator that may prevent his or her finding the tranquillity that consideration for others helps to bring about. The Taoist will avoid boastfulness because he/she realises that, every individual being part of the manifestation of the *Tao*, nobody can count him-or herself as 'more equal than others': in the eternal interchange of *yin* and *yang*, nobody, as we saw in Chapter 11, is either more, or less, dispensable than any other.

The moral injunctions of these schools are therefore to be interpreted as guidelines rather than commandments handed down from above. There is no divine rule-maker requiring obedience; no tablets of stone. Followers of these paths may be advised not to take drugs, but this is not because there is a divine decree forbidding this kind of behaviour: it is because, as a simple matter of fact, drugs alter the chemistry of the brain and are thus likely to come between the consumer and the achievement of his or her goal, whether *moksha*, *nirvana* or union with the *Tao*. The advice will be proffered in unambiguous terms, but the decision whether to take it or not is a matter of individual choice. There are, for instance, Hindus, Buddhists and Taoists who are prepared to drink alcohol in moderation, others who will not take it at all; some Buddhists eat meat, many do not; Vivekananda smoked, many Hindus do not. Each individual must, in Buddha's dying words, work out his or her own salvation; and in many respects this advice accords with Chuang Tzu's admonition to Taoists that they should be natural. With the Taoist sage, nobody needs to anguish themselves about whether they are behaving as the Jones's, let alone the Almighty, expect.

It would be wrong, of course, to characterise all representatives of the theistic religions as antipathetic to this approach to moral behaviour. Many of them would agree with the pragmatism of George Fox (1624–91), founder of the (mainly pacifist) Society of Friends (the Quakers). Asked by a soldier whether he should leave his profession, Fox replied, 'Wear thy sword as long as thou canst.' With this attitude, on a number of moral issues, many Christians would no doubt agree, but the question is how far it is representative of the religion as a whole. The Pope, head of a Church boasting 500 million members, has pronounced to be 'intrinsically evil' numerous forms of behaviour relating to sex, such as homosexuality, divorce, abortion and artificial forms of birth control; on most of these issues he is joined by Protestant fundamentalists, with support from Muslims. All of them seem more concerned to let others know where the path to salvation lies than to let them work it out for themselves. Not all theists are fundamentalists, of course; but, whatever the ratio between 'liberals' and fundamentalists may be, those who wield the authoritarian stick certainly receive the greater public attention.

The criticism that Eastern morality is too flexible is, however, only one of several that Westerners in general, and theistic Westerners in particular, make of Eastern ethics. A second one reflects what is probably an even deeper concern: the motive that underlies Eastern, more specifically (in this case) Indian, morality. We have seen how major a role the concept of *karma* plays in both Hindu and Buddhist thought. Both advocate the building up of good *karma* and eliminating the bad if enlightenment (*moksha*) is to be gained, release from *samsara* achieved, and further reincarnations avoided. This inevitably means, critics state, that good deeds like giving to the poor are not performed for their own sakes but in order to make personal progress on the path to the goal, which in turn implies that all actions, however laudable, are motivated by selfishness.

154 *Understanding Eastern philosophy*

This criticism leads to a number of issues in moral philosophy that have vexed Western philosophers over the centuries, two of which have already been discussed in this book and may be recapitulated here. The first concerns the importance of *motives* when making moral judgments (that is, in deciding how to behave). Mill and the Utilitarians argued that, while motives may tell us much about the moral agent, they have no impact on the effects of any decision: the end in view is the overall increase in the sum total of human happiness, and any deed that achieves this increase merits praise. In contrast, Kant had argued that the agent's motives were the primary determinant of the worth of the deed. Even an apparently good action lost its moral merit if performed for ulterior motives. Thus he argued that the goodness of the act of returning excess change to a shopkeeper (good, because such a deed would be universally desirable) would be undermined if performed solely with the desire of building up a personal 'feel-good' factor, or to be considered virtuous. Mill would have argued that, because the act of returning the change had the consequence that everyone concerned was happier, it was a good deed, whatever the motive behind it.

On the whole, the Christian view on this issue has been to side with Kant rather than Mill. St Paul seemed unwilling to take any praise for any of his actions, however meritorious, arguing that he was able to act as he did only because of God's grace ('it is no longer I who live, but Christ who lives in me': Galatians 2: 20). Paul's determination to eliminate any sense of pride in his own achievements set the tone for a good deal of Christian ethical teaching, which expresses a critical attitude to Eastern religions for what appears to be their unapologetic embrace of blatantly selfish motives in the pursuit of personal goals.

This leads into the second issue: can so-called selfish motives ever be totally eliminated from human behaviour, and, if not, does it matter? The English philosopher Thomas Hobbes (1588–1679) argued that it would be absurd to expect motives to be other than self-considering, since this was a true reflection of the inherent selfishness of human nature. He viewed altruism as an illusion, since the natural state of man is egotistic: even so-called saints gained pleasure from their sanctity (a startling thought, perhaps, but one about which Hobbes was undisturbed). Had he lived two centuries later, he would have seen his philosophy confirmed by Darwin, who characterised morality, throughout the whole of the human evolutionary process, as an expression of the fundamental drive to survive.

In opposition to Hobbes are those who hold Rousseau's view, or something akin to it. He held that, while all people begin their lives in a state of moral perfection, this state is altered by the social ethos, which induces people to behave deviously, dishonourably and fractiously: that is, they become selfish. Rousseau does not explain how the initial perfect state, which all people bring with them from Heaven (an idea similar to Plato's theory, discussed earlier), becomes imperfect when these perfect individuals are brought together into a group. But the idea that we enter the world 'trailing clouds of glory' (in Wordsworth's phrase) still has a strong appeal.

Realism suggests that Hobbes was nearer the mark than his opponents on this matter, and Eastern philosophers, with noteworthy exceptions such as Mencius, seem to have shared his view, if not quite so starkly (and certainly without reference to the political implications, which were his main concern). The Eastern view generally was unambiguous: it was certainly possible for people to behave in ways that could be described as altruistic, but the purpose of altruism is held to be primarily for the benefit of its agent, not that of the person to whom it is addressed. A lay Buddhist may give alms to a Theravada monk, but both parties interpret this as part of the giver's spiritual journey, not that of the receiver, who may be quite indifferent on the matter. (It may in fact be bad for his *karma* to receive this charity.) The Mahayana belief, that *boddhisattvas* remain on this mundane scene in order to help seekers to find *nirvana*, suggests an expression of altruism not found in Theravada; but this is a speculative doctrine, as unverifiable as Plato's theory of forms (Hobbes might well have argued that the *bodhisattvas* gain satisfaction from their self-sacrifice.) The Theravada tradition, with its ideal of the *arhat* who has, by his own efforts, achieved full enlightenment, is much closer both to Buddha's own thinking and to our awareness of what moral decision-making means here and now.

Christians may argue that the Hindu pursuit of good *karma* is fundamentally selfish because of its dubious motivation, but one is bound to ask how far they in their turn are rid of the idea of a heavenly reward as they tread the so-called altruistic path. Even the oft-quoted example of saintliness in our time, Mother Teresa of Calcutta, makes no attempt to hide the fact that the prime motivation in all she does on behalf of Calcutta's poor is to carve out a notch for herself in Heaven. Hobbes would not have been critical of this motive, and nor should we: does any athlete not spend years in painful training, sustained solely by the hope of winning a medal and thus achieving glory?

It seems in any case impossible for human beings deliberately to seek unhappiness, even though some of them make what appears to others to be a fairly firm attempt at it. Taoism enjoins people to be natural, and if – as seems to be the case – this state brings with it a condition of inner tranquillity, it seems to be a matter of idle debate whether this is selfish or otherwise. From my own experience, I know that I cannot be happy if those around me are unhappy, so if others judge my attempts to remove some of this unhappiness as no more than a desire for happiness on my part, so be it.

The fact is that anyone who seeks clarification of the mystery of human motivation is likely to find him or herself quickly floundering between an impasse and a dead-end. Eastern philosophers were aware of this and preferred to remain agnostic on the matter, as on the earlier one of the source of moral awareness. The general attitude on these issues seems to have been that if a problem is insuperable there is little point in spending time and energy agonising over it. Meanwhile, there is a life to be lived, decisions to be made and goals to be achieved: all these are real, identifiable and unavoidable, and time spent in speculating on what must remain unknowable seems to have little merit attached to it.

One further difficulty that Westerners have with the doctrine of *karma* is its encouragement of an indifferent, even fatalistic attitude towards those who suffer: the poor, the sick, the homeless, and so on. We saw earlier that it is a misconception to link *karma* with fatalism, since both Hinduism and Buddhism teach that whatever happens to a person, in this or any future existence, is the direct consequence of freely made choices, so that no human actions or conditions can be characterised as in any way pre-ordained, as the philosophy of fatalism implies. By the same token, however, this doctrine of personal responsibility for one's own karmic situation lends force to the view that those in distress are suffering the direct consequence of their own folly, which they alone can rectify.

At a purely practical level, any observer of the Indian scene may, not unfairly, point out that one is more likely to find missions for the down-and-outs run by Christians than by Hindus. The Christian explanation is simple: their religion lays more emphasis on caring for others than does Hinduism, whether in their sacred writings or through their traditions. Like it or not, the *apologia* concludes, Christianity is at heart both more altruistic and less fatalistic than Hinduism. This claim may be more muted when comparing Christian charity with that of Mahayana Buddhism, but comments on the paucity of charitable activity within the Theravada tradition are similar. The nub of the argument is that if a philosophy of life or a religion has as its outcome a cool indifference to others' needs, it thereby loses points in the benevolence league table, which downgrades it as a religion.

We shall look more closely in Chapter 16 at the various attitudes to society expressed by the schools under review. So far as the above suggestion is concerned, that the eradication of poverty in India is, like the removal of the caste system, stalemated by the doctrine of *karma*, there may well be a case: but those who have experienced this poverty on their doorsteps are likely to ask whether anything can really be done except tinker with the edges of the problem. Christian missions may heal, or feed, or house a few: but as one beggar disappears from the poverty line, a score take his or her place. It is consequently not indifference born of the karmic tradition that creates a negative attitude to the problem but despair that it can ever be overcome. Meanwhile, it may help if those in poverty believe that fortitude will be rewarded. If *moksha* is, as Hinduism teaches, the ultimate goal of everybody's life, then its physical circumstances – however hard it may be to accept this – are genuinely irrelevant. This argument may lend force to Marx's characterisation of religion as the opium of the masses, but the difference here is that for Hindus the reward can be won in this present existence, not in the speculative world of Heaven, which Marx heard being offered on a regular basis in Victorian England. This attitude may well be judged unsatisfactory, but one wonders if there is a realistically satisfactory solution to poverty on India's scale.

The final area to tackle is more philosophical, and represents the main challenge of Eastern philosophy to the ethical and religious values of the West. It concerns the rejection, expressed in all the schools, of moral absolutes.

We have seen how Hinduism, Buddhism and Taoism (together with Zen and Jainism) reject the theistic concept of an almighty God who, as omniscient law-giver, has manifested His will through moral injunctions that His creatures are commanded to obey. A fair proportion of modern exponents of theism may reject the primitive accounts of how these commands were delivered, arguing that, for instance, the story of Moses on Mount Sinai is just a picturesque way of responding to the question asked earlier: what is the source of our knowledge of right and wrong? They will argue that behind the picture of God's delivery of the Ten Commandments on the tablets of stone lie centuries of grappling with moral dilemmas, and that it is unremarkable that believers in an omnipotent and omniscient God like the Jews and, later, the Christians and Muslims, should attribute their moral principles to his guidance. However, even those who approach the matter in this more sophisticated way would presumably be reluctant to deny that, in the end, what is right is behaviour that is in accordance with God's will, whatever the channel by which it is made known. It is also worth keeping in mind the fact that, in any case, the vast majority of theistic believers, whether of the catholic or fundamentalist persuasion, are not so disenchanted with the primitive picture.

Eastern philosophy will have none of this. It rejects the concept of a law-giving God, and, with this rejection, the belief that there are certain moral absolutes which, on the strength of His authority, must be obeyed. We have seen how both Hinduism and Buddhism express moral injunctions not as rules that must be obeyed but as advice to the unwary. Each person's autonomy is accepted without question, so no claim is made that any leader has the right to compel a follower to behave in a particular way. The rules for monks are stricter, of course, but anyone seeking to enter an order knows what he is committing himself to, and does so freely. Although many of the remainder are likely to seek guidance from *gurus* and *rishis* on a variety of matters, they understand that, so long as their behaviour does not directly hinder another in his or her quest, they are personally responsible for the path they choose and the way they live: there is no moral straitjacket.

We have seen this attitude to morality at its starkest in Taoism, where the concept of right and wrong as a set of moral do's and don'ts is totally rejected. Right and wrong are two sides of the same coin, and we could not know what one is without the other, any more than we could know what it is to be alive without the certain reality of death. In some circumstances, a certain form of behaviour will be right, not because of any divine decree, nor even because it has been a long-standing tradition, but because it is the natural way to behave in that circumstance; and with different times and situations will come the need for different behaviour. We could say that, in Taoist terms, when the *yang* is in the ascendant, *yang*-like qualities will be required; and when the *yin* is in the ascendant, *yin*-like qualities (or, to make the matter more confusing, *yin* may be needed in a *yang* situation, and *yang* in a *yin*). Whichever is required, a person will, if behaving naturally, act accordingly.

We can consider the straightforward example of aggression. In the West, we should be inclined to debate whether or not it is morally justified. Taoists would argue that this is an unnatural representation of the situation. It is impossible to say whether aggression is right or wrong, for the simple reason that in some circumstances it is natural, in others, not. On a games field, for example, or when facing a homicidal maniac, or in time of war, aggression would be in place; in a classroom of young children, or in a council chamber, or in a hospital ward, it would be out of place. In itself it is a neutral quality, neither good nor bad: in a phrase made famous by Nietzsche, but known to Eastern philosophers for two millennia before he coined it, it is *beyond good and evil*.

What this phrase means is the key to understanding Eastern ethics at its highest peak (although this may seem to some a value judgment). It is a phrase that reflects both Indian and Chinese thought, but I shall discuss it in its Hindu context. In their view of justice (*dharma*) there are, as we have seen, no absolute prohibitions or imperatives. Appropriate behaviour varies with social role and stage of life. It is right for a student to be celibate, and right for a householder not to be celibate. It is right for a soldier to kill an enemy, right for a citizen not to kill an enemy. Irresponsibility is acceptable among adolescents, unacceptable among the old.

As in all ethical systems, there is in Hinduism an identification of sources of norms for human behaviour: tradition (needed for social stability) and interdependence (needed for social cohesion). The sanctions, as we saw above, are consequences, not guilt or retribution. However, those who try for liberation outgrow these norms. Instead of seeking, as in most other religions, to live according to a received pattern, they practise bodily, mental and emotional self-control, with the aim of achieving personal harmony and peace. They believe that all can achieve this aim by stabilising the lower aspects of the person – the body, mind and personality – and reaching the ground of being, which is reality, consciousness, happiness (*sat chit ananda*).

When this state is reached, they leave behind the dualities, or pairs of opposites, such as heat and cold, light and dark, hatred and love, misery and pleasure, since to be one with the ground of being means losing one's personal ego, which is the source of all dualities. In its place is absorption into that which is impersonal and one in all individuals (akin to, but not identical with, Jung's sense of the collective unconscious). Thus liberated, a person is bound by no rules or duties but acts spontaneously from joy and for the welfare of others. This can lead to political action, as with Gandhi, to teaching, as with Ramakrishna, to celebration in music or poetry, as with Nanak or Tagore, to work for the poor, as with Vivekananda, or with the mentally ill, as with Meher Baba.

Liberation is, then, in a phrase, awareness of *non-dual reality* (the water-drop entering the sea) and is incompatible with assertion of personality or injury of others. This is the state beyond good and evil.

The significant feature of this state is not that it leads to disregard of benevolence to other sentient beings but that benevolent acts – and any others that may be termed morally desirable – are viewed as an intuitive expression of the experience of oneness with all beings, rather than as a painstaking observance of rules for which rational arguments can be offered. It embodies Nietzsche's objection to morality as obedience, but not merely because, as he argued, this is an immature, non-autonomous form of morality; rather, the Hindu concept, which is found again in Taoism, describes a deeper level of experience than the dualistic state, which, even for Nietzsche, remained the context of moral decision-making.

Great care must be taken in its application. It is not a state into which everybody arrives at birth, but one that can be achieved only after gaining enlightenment. Until then, it is helpful to observe norms of behaviour, while recognising that these relate only to the lower levels of existence. We have in fact in non-dualistic Hinduism a form of thought not unlike Meister Eckhart's, quoted on page 138. It is not easily understood and may be misinterpreted as an immaturely anarchic attitude to morals. Those who are immature may in fact abuse it, claiming the right to ignore moral rules without having arrived at the state where the rules effectively evaporate: hence the Hindu emphasis on the enlightenment that first needs to be gained. Those who are enlightened express their moral freedom not selfishly but along the lines described above.

There is a story about Jesus, not included in the New Testament, that he saw a man working at his daily job on the Sabbath. Jesus himself had said to his critics, after he had healed a man on the holy day, 'The Sabbath was made for man, not man for the Sabbath' (Mark 2: 27), which sounds not dissimilar to Nietzsche's advocacy of autonomy when making moral decisions. On this occasion, however, Jesus said: 'If you know what you are doing, you are blest; if you do not know, you are cursed.' Action taken with the sole purpose of flouting received rules has no justification in this enlightened way of thinking. St Augustine, in his Seventh Homily, summed up morality as 'Love [God] and do what you will.' If we were to perform an act of reductionism and replace the first phrase with the counsel, 'Follow your intuition, which you discover in the ground of being', this approach is not far removed from that of Advaita Vedanta. In the light of various modern directions taken by theologians, this does not seem too far-fetched a consideration and will be given further examination in Chapter 18.

How far the world in general is ready to dispense with moral absolutes is a matter of individual judgment. Relativism is in some quarters a philosophy to be fought and ousted. The important point to consider about moral relativism is not that it necessarily leads to a *laisser-faire* approach to moral decision-making but that it denies the existence of moral absolutes, on the grounds that accepting these only leads to further insuperable problems, such as where is the source of their authority, and how to respond when two of them clash (like, for example, the *right to life* versus the *right to choose* apropos of abortion). No sane person denies that child molestation is wrong: but it is wrong not because God, or the law, or tradition says so, but because nobody is likely to find a situation in which it would be right. To be in the state beyond good and evil is to be beyond the level of needing to debate the rights and wrongs of any moral matter in the first place.

16 Nature and community

'The earth is the Lord's, and the fulness thereof; the world, and they that dwell therein.' Thus wrote the Psalmist (24:1) some 2½–3 millennia ago. The sentiment has a noble ring to it and has been expressed over the ages by religious people of many varieties. With or without the reference to God, the idea of the perfection of nature and the perfectibility of human society has gripped philosophers and scientists, poets and peasants alike. It seems that, despite overwhelming evidence to the contrary, most people try to view the world and its ways with optimism, shunning the existentialist 'anguish, abandonment and despair' expressed by, among others, Jean-Paul Sartre.

THE PROBLEM OF EVIL

What we now need to discuss is the extent to which any idealistic picture, such as that expressed in the quotation above, accurately reflects the reality as it is perceived by exponents of Eastern thought. How important is the natural world in their thinking? Is it unambiguously a vehicle of the divine, so that Earth and 'Heaven' can be one? And, whatever conclusion may be reached about that, is it feasible to aim at creating a human society that either reflects the divine order or seeks to give palpable expression to the myths of a distant golden age? Are the Utopian visions that surface from time to time, like Tennyson's 'one far-off divine event, to which the whole creation moves', to be viewed as realistic expressions of what the future may hold, or are they no more than whistling in the dark, as his earlier words in the same poem ('In Memoriam') suggest: 'Nature, red in tooth and claw'?

So far as the theistic approach to these questions is concerned, it is difficult to avoid the characterisation of consistent ambivalence (to coin yet another oxymoron). All three theistic religions, but especially Christianity, are in fact on the horns of a dilemma, an uncomfortable position arrived at through the attempt to maintain two contradictory ideas within the same *Weltanschauung*, (world view), whatever common sense may suggest to the contrary. On the one hand is the belief that the world 'and the fulness thereof' are the product of the creative power of an omnipotent God; on the other, that this same God is all-loving. Alongside this dual concept, account has to be taken of the manifest existence of what is normally characterised in shorthand terms as 'evil', in both the world of nature and that of human affairs. The refusal by the theistic religions to dispense with the concept, linked with their inability to ignore the practicality, have created the dilemma of dilemmas for theistic metaphysics: the 'Problem of Evil'. Because of this problem, any kind of theistically based Utopian vision for either nature or society has always been clouded and, other than in the world of myth, effectively shattered.

The escape from the dilemma has been found by resorting to one of, if not the, most elementary of the world's myths: the account of the primordial state of paradisial bliss experienced in the Garden of Eden, where the nature of the loving God who created it was perfectly reflected in the behaviour of all the species it contained, including, especially, human beings. In that garden, no tree was stifled by ivy, no rabbit killed by a stoat, and the human occupants lived harmoniously together, unwarped, it seems, by sexual desire. This idyllic (*sic*) state of affairs endured until the first act of human disobedience, which resulted in the discovery of their sexuality by the two progenitors of the human race, who were consequently expelled by God from the garden, and sin, or evil, entered the world of both nature and human nature (Genesis 3).

It was from human bondage to sin that, according to Christian mythology, Jesus, 'the second Adam', delivered the human race by living a life of total obedience to God his Father, including the vicarious sacrifice of his life, so creating the opportunity for all to achieve salvation through faith in his person and in his redemptive works. They are then invited to believe (although some are more liberal in their thinking) that, because Jews and Muslims (to say nothing of followers of Eastern religions or philosophies) do not accept the redemptive power of Jesus, these non-believers remain under the power of sin and are consequently doomed to whatever fate awaits those in that state (a crucial issue, both metaphorically and literally, to which we shall return in Chapter 18).

Much has, of course, been written on this matter, and any study in depth will require consulting the Bibliography. What seems transparently clear, however, is that the 'problem' is of the theologians' own making, a consequence of putting the theological cart before the existentialist horse. The attempt to combine the concepts of divine omnipotence and divine benevolence within the statement of His nature is doomed to failure on the grounds of common sense alone. As the philosopher Hume pointed out, either God *can* change things (that is, remove the 'evil') but will not, in which case He is not benevolent; or He wants to change things but cannot, in which case He is not omnipotent.

Any dispassionate view of the world must lead to the conclusion that, whatever is the relationship between the different species and, in particular, between members of the human species, benevolence is not the key. Ivy, by its nature, stifles trees; stoats, by their nature, kill rabbits; and people exploit one another for selfish ends so that, in extremes, genocides occur. The key to human behaviour is, as Darwin's discoveries reveal, not benevolence but survival. Those so-called benevolent acts that do occur do so only when they assist, or at least do not threaten, the survival of the perpetrator or his/her kin. Even acts of self-sacrifice can be subsumed under this generalisation, as Hobbes (himself the kindliest and most generous of men) indicated in *Leviathan*.

Theists who have persisted in maintaining that God's omnipotence and His love are not mutually exclusive have adopted a variety of escape clauses. Some, like the Christian Scientists, have taken the radical step of denying the existence of matter altogether. This denial has the useful consequence that one does not need to worry about the bacteria that may cause, say, meningitis, since no such bacteria are held to exist. Others, with Zoroastrianism and Manichaeism, have argued that the world is the battlefield for a war between two gods, one good, one bad (or between God and Satan). The former will ultimately prevail, but the latter continues to express his nature in the various manifestations of evil that we encounter.

More widely accepted (among philosophers, at any rate) is the argument of the Book of Job that it is only because we cannot see the broad picture as God sees it that we introduce the word 'evil' when describing either the condition of the world or the behaviour of its inhabitants. Leibniz, who regarded this as the best of all possible worlds (since it was the creation of a perfect God), argued that what we term evil is necessary in order to throw into relief what we term good, as shade is necessary in order to bring relief to a picture. This concept is reminiscent of Chuang Tzu's relativism, described on page 100, although more difficult to come to terms with here because of its link with an allegedly benevolent creator, who presumably lacks the deviousness inherent in Leibniz's picture. The suggestion that one child dies of meningitis in order to appreciate more fully the survival of one who does not seems grotesque. This will no doubt be how the situation is perceived by many of those involved in such a tragedy, but that is a different matter from accepting it as planned by a loving God who, being omnipotent, could have ordered things otherwise. Few human beings would devise such an insidious scheme: for a *god* to do so is insufferable.

A fourth answer to the problem, given by many Christian apologists, beginning with Origen (185–254) and especially explored by Thomas Aquinas, is that evil exists because human beings, having been given by God the blessing of free will, have consistently abused this luxury. The trouble with this argument (for theists, at any rate) is that it leaves the way open for predestinarianism, since an omniscient God must have foreseen that this is precisely what would happen. Logically, it makes God ultimately responsible for the evil that has resulted from this abuse.

THE EASTERN VIEW OF NATURE

In Eastern philosophy, the main burden of the problem is removed because no expression of it is shackled with the theistic image of a God with anthropomorphic qualities; in particular, there is no attempt to combine omnipotence and benevolence with respect to God's nature. Popular expressions of Hinduism and Buddhism, and religious forms of Taoism, certainly include such anthropomorphic images; but these are not central to their respective belief systems, and in any case they are not representative of the highest expressions of these philosophies, which have been our main consideration. In particular, the Eastern view of nature as a manifestation of *brahman*, or the ground of being, or of the *Tao*, does not lead to any attempt to attribute to it qualities such as might be found in an ideal human being. Their perspective on nature is in fact similar to that of Meister Eckhart, who said in his Eleventh Sermon:

> Here is the unity of blades of grass and bits of wood and stone, together with everything else ... All that nature tries to do is to plunge into that unity, into the Father-nature, so that it may all be one, the one Son.

The *Bhagavad-Gita* (XIII:19/20) states:

> You must know that both material Nature and the Spirit are without beginning, though changes and qualities spring from Nature. Nature is declared the cause of anything that concerns action, means or result, while the Spirit is the cause of experience in pleasure and pain.

Nature is thus characterised in these writings as a sum of many parts which, acting and reacting harmoniously together, express that which, in Isaac Newton's words, 'is very consonant and conformable with itself'. That is, the world is not a combination of disparate features that can be labelled 'good' or 'evil', 'of God' or 'of the Devil', but is a unified organism, authentic and autonomous, containing features such as trees, and lakes, and flowers, which can be, in Wordsworth's phrase, 'the bliss of solitude', and features that disturb and even repel, such as the pit viper and the tapeworm. It is pointless to make a moral judgment about nature: nature is, and human beings are part of it.

Those familiar with the Gaia hypothesis will find this thesis congenial, as will followers of Teilhard de Chardin, who wrote in his *Phenomenon of Man*:

> The stuff of the universe, woven in a single piece according to one and the same system, but never repeating itself from one point to another, represents a single figure. Structurally it forms a Whole.

It is a pathetic fallacy, however (to quote a technical term), to envisage a personal relationship with nature; nature, as evolution confirms, is indifferent to individual representatives of any species, including the human: and Indian philosophy supports this perspective. Each self may lose his or her personal identity in the Whole, whether before or after death: but the union which thus occurs is spiritual, not – as is basic in most romantic descriptions of union with nature – emotional.

The *Tao Te Ching* (chapters 5 and 7) expresses with peculiar bluntness this rejection of human personal qualities in relation to the Tao:

> Heaven and earth
> > are not like humans.
> The Tao does not act like a human.
> They don't expect to be thanked
> for making life,
> so they view it without expectation.
> Heaven and earth are like a pair of bellows:
> they are empty, and yet they can never be exhausted. . .

> Heaven and earth
> > are enduring.
> The universe can live for ever,
> because it does not live for itself.

> And so both last – outliving themselves.

This is from the Sacred Arts translation; others are even blunter with the opening statement. Waley, Lau and Feng/English all translate it as 'Heaven and Earth are ruthless', adding that 'they see all things as straw dogs' (or 'dummies' in Feng/English). Thus there is no point in our romanticising about nature, apart, perhaps, from trying to extol it in poetry. Nature *is*; each of us is part of it; and any attempt that we may make to alter it (which, in theistic terms, may include the desire to 'redeem' it), will ultimately prove disastrous, not least to ourselves. The wolf will never lie down with the lamb, cats will always kill mice, and human ingenuity will only speed up the growth of wheat, or the laying of eggs, by changing the natures of the crop or the birds. One does not need to be a trained ecologist to recognise the implications of this thinking, which points the way to a simpler and – although this is admittedly a value judgment – more 'natural' existence than is generally found in modern technology-dominated cultures. If human beings, like lemmings sniffing the sea, prefer these cultures whatever the price, nature will be indifferent, enduring after technology with all its accoutrements has come and gone.

UTOPIA

If, as I suggested above, the Eastern view is that the wolf will never, as in Isaiah's vision (11:6), dwell with the lamb, can we nonetheless hope that, turning to an earlier vision (2:4), human beings will 'beat their swords into ploughshares'? To use a New Testament concept, can the 'Kingdom of God' be established among people here on Earth?

This has throughout history been the aim of any theocracy (literally, 'government by God'). When the kingship was established in Israel, the rulers were viewed as vicegerents of Jehovah, charged with the task of establishing and enforcing His laws among the people; and, when the monarchy disappeared after the Exile, the government remained just as, if not even more, theocratic. The concept is intrinsic to Islam, and numerous Islamic states are today ruled according to the code of the Qur'an – which, with the substitution of the Torah for the Qur'an, is the aim of contemporary Jewish fundamentalists in Israel. Medieval popes, especially Gregory VII, attempted to realise the theocratic ideal, which was shared, although with different interpretations, by Calvin in Geneva and in Cromwell's Commonwealth. The important point to note about all these theocracies is that the codes that they enforced were based on the laws expressed in their sacred scriptures, all of them, of course, extremely ancient, so that the question of how far different times need different customs was, and is, consciously or otherwise, disregarded (see Chapter 17). Equally questionable is, of course, the assumption that, because the codes are to be found written in what are held to be sacred scriptures, they were ever necessarily the ideal expression of government.

The closest parallel to any of these theocracies among followers of Eastern philosophies is to be found in the Tibet of the Dalai Lamas, where the chosen one is accepted as head in both the religious and secular spheres, and the laws of the country, together with the daily lives of the people, reflect the teachings of Buddha as interpreted and modified by that country's native religious traditions. Elsewhere, Confucius spoke of the need for his countrymen to follow 'the way of Heaven'; but, as we saw, this is a phrase that can hardly be interpreted theistically: he was referring to the perfect way which can be gleaned intuitively, strengthened by the archetypal myth of an ancient golden age. It would be a risible misnomer to designate Confucius's ideal as a theocracy, however emphatically he described the perfect ruler as both appointed from Heaven and the touchstone of the nation's values.

However, theocracies are only a literalistic interpretation of the means by which society may be brought to be a mirror of divine perfection, and many people believe that the latter is possible without having recourse to the former. The issue we face is whether Eastern philosophy shares this Utopian vision: not, that is, as an ideal to be realised in Heaven, or *nirvana*, or by entering into *samadhi*, but among the communities of men and women eking out their daily existences in the world of practical affairs. Leaving aside wolves and lambs, cats and mice, how far can it be anticipated that human beings, even those of the same class, race and creed, may eventually live harmoniously together?

One short answer to this question is a stark 'not at all'. People may certainly join together with a common purpose and, on the surface at least, work together to that end; but this is saying no more than that sometimes, as Hobbes asserted, people find it in their interests to cooperate with others. So far as Indian philosophy is concerned, the world of human affairs is characterised, inescapably and unalterably, by *maya*, and any attempt to transform this condition is as doomed to failure as trying to make a wasp stop stinging or persuade a tiger to become a vegetarian. The world of human affairs is transient and unsatisfactory to the core. People may, as part of their karmic duties, tinker with it here and there, and perhaps generate a little happiness; they may feed the hungry and give alms to the poor, rectify the occasional injustice and remove the odd tyrant, but this is the equivalent of building dams in the hope of changing the law of gravity.

Confucius was more optimistic about the possibility of creating an ideal society than were his Indian counterparts. He believed, with Plato, that education for all would both mirror the ideal heavenly world and provide the means for bringing it to pass in the present one. But he was enough of a realist to acknowledge that this was never likely to be the experience of more than a minority of the population, who would probably (as he was) be the object of suspicion on the part of most of the remainder. Even in contemporary America, with 2½ millennia of learning to add to that of Confucius's China, no politician has the slightest chance of success if he/she gains the reputation of being an academic, or egg-head, as they picturesquely say (hardly surprising when half of them deliberately ignore the evidence of reason and declare 'the theory' of evolution to be both heretical and immoral; to them the schoolboy witticism must apply, that 'all men spring from apes but some have not sprung far enough').

The Taoist philosophy is that people should be left to themselves, not induced to conform to some received ideal. To live intuitively is to live beyond the law, and the best rulers, as the *Tao Te Ching* states continually, are those who make themselves inconspicuous, ideally by doing nothing at all. With nothing to disobey, there can then be no law-breakers, and the whole penal system falls into disuse. Decriminalise drugs, and half of police time will in any case be freed to deal with crimes that harm others rather than the offenders themselves. Subsidise and improve public transport, and increase tax on private vehicles, and there is the strongest possible incentive to reduce congestion on the roads. It is no coincidence that Thomas More himself described his Utopia as a state 'where everything is well ordered with very few laws'.

It is all a matter, as Chuang Tzu would have said with a shrug, of what people really want out of life. If it gives them satisfaction to think that they are 'doing something' about social problems, fine: they may not achieve much, but they will feel better in themselves. From where he sat (probably fishing), the ideal society was his own, in communion with the *Tao*. If this meant doing without luxuries and the conveniences brought about by technology, he would have judged this a small price to pay.

The Eastern view of society, then, runs counter to that of the West, with its emphasis on progress and change, either for its own sake, or, in its religions, as a step towards the establishment of God's Kingdom on Earth. As a direct consequence of this perspective, we find in these religions what is often termed 'the social Gospel', and there is a school of theistic thought named Political Theology. Eastern philosophers would, on the whole, view these emphases as well-intentioned but misguided. The activities to which these

Western considerations lead – involvement in social and political affairs – belong, in most Eastern philosophical and religious thought, to a lower order of existence.

It may well be, as Mahatma Gandhi, for instance, illustrated, that one who has reached a higher plane may still wish to spend time and energy at the lower level. He said in one of his speeches:

> If I have to be reborn, I should wish to be reborn as an 'untouchable', so that I may share their sorrows, sufferings, and the affronts levelled at them, in order that I may free myself and them from that miserable condition.

Primarily, however, the Eastern emphasis is that this will be most surely achieved by seeing the divine (God, *brahman*, the *Tao*) in the whole of creation, and living in harmony with it. When this has been achieved, if there is any truth at all in the central Eastern assertions about the Fourth State, or *nirvana*, or embracing the forces of *yin* and *yang*, or going with the flow of the *Tao*, this harmony will become a centre that will embrace others in ever-widening circles. This form of quietism is found in these words from the *Tao Te Ching* (chapter 2, Waley's translation):

> Therefore the Sage relies on actionless activity,
> Carries on wordless teaching,
> But the myriad creatures are worked upon by him: he does
> not disown them.
> He rears them, but does not lay claim to them,
> Controls them, but does not lean upon them,
> Achieves his aim, but does not call attention to what he
> does.

Western social reformers are likely to argue that, if he does not call attention to himself, he will make little impact on a world whose major events are financed and controlled by big business, which could not survive without attention. Lao Tzu's response would have been: wait and see.

17 Authority and faith

Every religion needs a *raison d'être*: justification for the message it proclaims, the life-style it commends, the ritual it practises and the orders that it accepts. In a word, it needs to be able to demonstrate where its *authority* lies.

The 'received' sources of this authority in the theistic religions are threefold: scripturality, or the authority of holy texts; canonicity, or the authority of tradition; and, less enthusiastically because of the alleged 'fallen' nature of human beings, 'natural theology', or the authority of the individual reason and conscience (in contrast to the 'revealed theology' of the first two sources). All three, in their different ways, are held to bear witness to the will and purpose of the divine. In earlier centuries, Christians believed that this witness could also be found in a fourth source, the world of nature, a view expressed in such hymns as 'All things bright and beautiful' and 'All things praise Thee, Lord most high'; but, in the post-Darwinian age, with nature revealed, in the words of Tennyson already quoted, as 'red in tooth and claw', the tendency, apart from in the mystical tradition, has been to characterise nature, alongside the human race, as having 'fallen', so that any evidence which it presents for the divine is deemed to be fatally flawed.

The problem with all three bases of authority among the theistic religions (although I shall again concentrate on Christianity) arises from their inconsistency, both internally and *vis-à-vis* the others. **The Bible**, for instance, contains moral injunctions in diametrically opposing directions on virtually every feature of human behaviour. Shall we drink wine? Turn to Psalm 104:15 and we are told that God has given it 'to gladden the heart of man'; go forward to Proverbs 20:1, and it is 'a mocker ... whoever is led astray by it is not wise'. Should we participate in acts of war? 'All who take the sword will perish by the sword', said Jesus (Matthew 25:52); but Paul argues that the ruler 'does not bear the sword in vain; he is the servant of God to execute his wrath on the wrongdoer' (Romans 13:4).

On this matter, the **Tradition** of the Church has been equally ambivalent: on the one hand, Thomas Aquinas taught the concept of a just war (just cause, just means, just ends), while most Quakers take the pacifist stance. (No Christian tradition has, however, formally supported the idea of *jihad*, or Holy War against the infidel, as advocated in Islam.) On the role and status of women in the Church there is, ironically as it happens, considerable consistency. Both the Bible and Tradition express an attitude on this elementary moral issue that is found repugnant by most contemporary upholders of the Faith, who, in this instance at least, prefer to follow the authority expressed by reason and conscience. Few still observe Paul's admonition that 'women should keep silence ... for it is shameful for a woman to speak in churches' (I Corinthians 14:34–5); or agree with Tertullian that woman is 'the devil's gate', or with St Jerome that she is 'the root of all evil'; or ask with Odun of Cluny 'who would wish to embrace *"ipsum stercoris saccum"*?' (loosely translated 'a stinking bag of manure'). They may, however, be glad that the Council of Trent (1545–64) agreed, by a majority of three, that women possess souls.

On matters of doctrinal belief and Church orders a similar lack of consistency is to be found. The Great Schism of 1054 occurred primarily because of differences of interpretation between Eastern and Western Churches about the status of the Bishop of Rome: *primus inter pares* or vicegerent of Christ? The key issue of the Reformation was the extent to which authority on matters of faith and order lay primarily with the Pope and the councils, or with holy scripture. Among the two leading reformers, Luther and Calvin, there was a further subdivision over the authority of scripture: granted that practices and beliefs should be dropped if they were contrary to biblical teaching, what should be done about matters about which it was silent or ambivalent? Bishops or presbyters; the meaning of 'is' in 'This is my body'; icons in churches; and, later, infant or believers' baptism: all these and numerous other issues brought about divisions between those who were, without exception, looking for their authority in either the Bible or the Church. For them, the question was whether authority should be sought in *the Bible* as interpreted by the Church, or in *the Church* as interpreter of the Bible. (The aim in either case was the philosophically dubious one of discovering 'the truth', a matter to which we shall return on page 176.)

Anyone who has read the foregoing chapters will be aware that on this matter – more, perhaps, than on any other – the Eastern religions/ philosophies speak a different language from their theistic counterparts, as will be clear if we recall their attitude to each of the authoritative sources referred to above.

SACRED WRITINGS

Virtually all the Eastern schools have their authoritative texts (Zen is an obvious exception), but the basis of their authority differs from that found in theism, where the holy scriptures are held, inconsistent or otherwise, to be the unchallengeable Word of God. Their authority springs from this unnervingly simple assumption, so that anyone wishing to dispute a passage will have to give just cause why previous readings should be questioned: this is not impossible, of course, given the complex history of biblical textual analysis, but it would be a bold critic who asserted that the Bible was wrong on any matter.

This is not, on the whole, the case with Eastern texts. An exception is the *Bhagavad-Gita*, which some commentators approach with a reverence found otherwise only when Jews and Christians are discussing their Old or New Testaments, or Muslims their Qur'an: the title of the *Gita* in some editions as 'The Song of God' certainly seems to place it on a higher plane than the mythological narrative that it undoubtedly is, and which most Hindus hold it to be. So far as the Vedas generally are concerned, their authority lies not in being the 'Word of God' (even though some Hindus may so describe them) but in their antiquity. The fact is that, over some four millennia, their authoritative role as guides to the spiritual life has been proved by countless millions: that is, what they suggest has been found to work. Being so extensive, and having been written over many centuries, the teaching is not always uniform: but no Hindu finds this an insuperable problem, or one that needs the kind of tortuous explanation that biblical fundamentalists engage in when confronted with discrepancies in their holy book. The two accounts of creation found in Genesis 1:1–2:3 and 2:4–24 would simply be viewed as precisely that: two accounts of creation. Only when it is asserted that sacred writings are by the hand of the inerrant God does this discrepancy become a problem; few Hindus would give a second thought to the two accounts of the slaying of Goliath, one giving David as his killer (I Samuel 17), the other (II Samuel 21:19) stating that it was Elhanan the son of Jaareoregim the Bethlehemite (causing the addition of 'brother of' before 'Goliath' in some ancient versions of this text).

There are Hindus who nonetheless feel that too much reverence is accorded to some of the Vedas, just as there are modern representatives of the theistic religions who approach their sacred texts more critically than do their fundamentalist colleagues. The danger with anything that is written down, as Zen Buddhists never cease to remind us, is that it tends to become the message rather than the – sometimes faulty – medium. The danger with the Zen attitude, of course, is that, with nothing written, there is nothing from the past with which to compare and contrast present experiences. It seems that we simply have to become accustomed to the logical conclusion (which happens to accord with the existentialist situation) that fallible man will never produce an infallible authority on any matter, least of all on religion.

This viewpoint is even more marked in Buddhism than in Hinduism. We have seen that a major division occurred in Buddhist ranks between those (the Theravada) who hold that Buddha's words, as expressed in the Pali Canon, were alone eternally definitive for beliefs and practices, and those (the Mahayana) who held the experience and understanding of the spiritual dimension to be a continuous process, so that it was unnatural to confine the guidelines within a single framework, given once and for all. Theists would prefer the term 'revelation' to 'guidelines', but Buddhists have always viewed the experience as originating in people's hearts rather than descending from 'on high'; consequently, the reverence accorded to their writings arises not from their being the product of the hand of God but from their association with a leader who had deep spiritual insight, from which others may draw inspiration.

In China, the emphasis is even clearer: the great books, the so-called 'classics' (*ching*), such as the *Tao Te Ching*, the *I Ching*, *Chuang-Tzu*, the Analects of Confucius, and Mencius, are read and honoured out of respect for their authors and their teaching. A student of Confucius or of Taoism would no more speak of their writings as being divinely inspired (except in the most general of senses) than would a Western student of Shakespeare, Goethe or Dante. These classics are simply viewed as noble works reflecting the minds and insights of men possessed of deep wisdom; over the centuries, their rare understanding of the complexities of the world has been recognised, and some of their wisdom gained by their readers and followers. The authority of their works is therefore authenticated by the benefit that others have derived from them.

TRADITION AND EXPERIENCE

A similar difference can be identified between East and West regarding the authority of *tradition*: in fact, so far as the East is concerned, its status is similar to that of their writings. Any teachers or *gurus*, *rishis* or seers who have at any time, whether in their lives or in their utterances, offered directions that others have found spiritually helpful are likely to be accepted as guides and mentors. What we do not find is any equivalent to the Roman Catholic Curia, or the concept that one particular person speaks with uniquely divine authority. On the contrary, the decisive authority accepted by all the Eastern schools studied (with the possible exception of the Jains) is *individual experience*.

Here we reach the heart of Eastern philosophy, and the focal point of the differences between it and its Western counterparts. While neither Buddhists, Hindus, Confucianists or even Taoists ignore their ancient writings, or the utterances of their sages and seers (including, as we shall note in Chapter 18, teachers of traditions other than their own), no absolute authority is accorded to them. We are unlikely to find anyone raising aloft the *Bhagavad-Gita* or the *Tao Te Ching* like a chief constable's handbook, as do fundamentalists of the Jewish, Christian and Islamic persuasions. Nor do we find any human being accorded the status of infallibility as with His Holiness the Pope: even His Holiness the Dalai Lama, with a far longer pedigree of sacredness, expounds his Tibetan Buddhist beliefs not as divine commands requiring universal obedience but as having, in his experience, proved their worth; and he freely adds that others may prefer a different way to the mountain top (as remarkable a statement as would be papal advice for people to go the way of the Protestants if it suited them).

Individual experience, then, is the supreme authority in Eastern philosophy and religion: it is the ultimate determinant of the value of particular spiritual exercises, methods of meditation, forms of ritual (if any), and rules of life. Guidelines on all these are readily available, and many follow them because they know that others have proved their efficacy; but in no way are they mandatory ('mandatory guidelines' would in fact be as oxymoronic as 'compulsory options'). The test is what a person knows within him- or herself; and in this context 'knows' embraces all facets of a person, not just the cognitive: not only the mind, but also the will, the feelings, the social sense and what we term the conscience. It is all that is represented in the third source of authority for the theistic religions, and more.

Many followers of the Judaeo-Christian tradition would doubtless be sympathetic to this emphasis. They might well agree with Dag Hammarskjøld, former Secretary-General of the United Nations Organisation, who described the language of religion as 'a set of formulas which register a basic spiritual experience' (*Markings*, 1964). Nevertheless, few outside the mystical tradition would be willing to regard that experience as self-authenticating, with only secondary regard given to either the Bible's or the Church's teaching. Few, that is, would be totally happy with these words of Bede Griffiths (*Return to the Centre*, 1976):

> There is an experience of being in pure consciousness which gives lasting peace to the soul. It is an experience of the Ground or Depth of being in the Centre of the soul, an awareness of the mystery of being beyond sense and thought, which gives a sense of fulfilment, of finality, of *absolute truth*. (My italics)

That last is a bold phrase, and it raises the first of two major questions over the claim of experience to be the supreme authority: how can anyone be sure that his or her experience is not a delusion; and even if it is not, how can anyone else, to whom the experience may be described, be sure of this? How can anyone else in fact be sure that he/she is not being treated to an act of make-believe, born of a deranged or overstimulated mind? Why should we pay more attention to a *guru* who claims to have entered *samadhi* than to a woman who claims with equal conviction that her long-dead uncle gives her daily advice from his seat on top of her wardrobe?

Of course it is necessary to be cautious when interpreting another person's experience, just as it is necessary not to interpret coincidences as portents (as some viewed the lightning that struck York Minster when the radical David Jenkins was made Bishop of Durham), or to make statements along *post hoc ergo propter hoc* lines ('before Margaret Thatcher became Prime Minister, AIDS had never been heard of'). Experience may, or may not, be self-authenticating: *interpretation of experience certainly is not*. We are consequently led to a central issue in Western philosophy: the problem of verification.

If we were discussing the latest scientific findings in a particular field, this would not be a problem: set up test conditions, and check them out. But how does one verify the affirmation that a person has entered *nirvana*, or has reached the stage 'beyond good and evil', or has achieved union with the *Tao*? There are certain factors that can help one in making any kind of assessment. The first is that the experience should not be ephemeral, but enduring; the second, that it be generally in tune with the experiences of others, so that they can sympathise if not empathise; and the third, the realisation that 'there are more things in Heaven and Earth, Horatio, than are dreamt of in your philosophy': the interpreter must be honest – and humble – enough to appreciate that the experience is not invalidated simply because he/she has not shared it. If we add to these an assessment based on the behaviour of the individual concerned ('By their fruits shall ye know them': Matthew 7:16), we may begin to feel that some kind of verification has been possible. Phenomenologically speaking, any person's experience must ultimately remain a mystery to others, but this need not rule out an approximation of the assessment process. It certainly seems a good deal less unrealistic than the blind acceptance of either the inerrancy of Holy Scripture or the infallibility of the Pope.

With this in mind, there seems no valid reason to write off as aberrations either the Buddha's claim to have achieved *nirvana*, Lao Tzu's description of his state of harmony with the *Tao*, Shankara's achievement of enlightenment and entry into the Fourth State, or – to move into the present – Fritjof Capra's vision, recounted in his book *The Tao of Physics*, of the Dance of Shiva. We are in the end confronted with the haunting assertion of the Upanishads, quoted earlier in the book: 'He who knows thus merges his Self in the Self – yea, he who knows thus.' It is impossible not to be gripped by the authority – perhaps the absolute authority – of those words.

FAITH

The second issue that relates to this individual source of authority is its relationship to the concept of *faith*. In the theistic religions, this quality, often described as a gift, is generally held to be of infinitely greater worth than knowledge, even with the broad interpretation of that word described above.

We need first to be clear what it is that we are referring to by the word. Webster's dictionary outlines eleven different meanings and usages, but three of these epitomise the issue. First, we may speak of the Christian or Jewish Faith, by which we mean the sum total of beliefs associated with that particular religion. Second, we use faith in the general sense of having confidence in a person or process. Third, there is what Kierkegaard described as 'the leap of faith': the commitment of one's life to a particular path, or person, or principle, for which no initial test of validity is possible. The leap of faith is a leap into the dark. Theists generally speak of faith in God in these terms: 'betting your life that there's a God', as St Augustine expressed it; less dramatically, the Letter to the Hebrews (11:1) described it as 'the substance of things hoped for, the evidence of things not seen'. Kierkegaard himself wrote in his *Journal* that faith is God-given: 'Man is capable of nothing, it is God who gives everything, who gives man faith.' For most Christians, it involves faith in the salvatory effectiveness of the sacraments, 'the means of grace'; but their supreme act of faith is belief in the redemptive work of Jesus. Through faith in his vicarious sacrifice, they receive assurance of the forgiveness of their sins and entry into 'the life everlasting'.

While Eastern philosophies express ideas akin to the first two meanings outlined, there is no place in their teachings for this third usage. In fact, the only word for faith used in either the Chinese or Indian texts discussed in earlier chapters is the Sanskrit *shradda*. In Hinduism, this refers, however, not to a condition of completion as in Christianity, but to the state of mind of those who, although having not yet achieved *moksha*, believe that they will eventually find it, as others have before them. It is therefore a psychological condition, a quality of patience, a drive or determination to follow the path to enlightenment. *The Bhagavad-Gita* (XVII:3) states:

> Faith [*Shradda*], among human beings ... is characterised ... according to a man's dominant tendencies. Now listen. The faith of each individual corresponds to his temperament. A man consists of the faith that is in him. Whatever his faith is, he is.

It then goes on to delineate various human characteristics, with their characteristic types of faith, according to the three *gunas*, or fundamental qualities, described on pages 25–6. The important point about Hindu teaching is that, once *moksha* has been realised, the enlightened one has passed beyond faith to a state of knowledge. It is described (*EPR* 328), in a phrase with which Kierkegaard would hardly have disagreed, as 'a working hypothesis': but, whereas for him this remains the limit of any human being's journey, the achievement of the union between *atman* and *brahman* effectively declares *shradda* redundant.

In Buddhism, faith, in the third sense outlined on page 174, is out of place. As with Hinduism, the concept of receiving forgiveness and consequent absolution is in any case alien to the doctrine of *karma*, with its inexorable process of cause and effect. That the slate should be wiped clean 'through faith alone' would therefore seem offensive: whatever the spiritual rewards that are sought, they will not be gained by anyone else's efforts other than one's own.

Shradda in Buddhism refers to an inner attitude of devotion to the Buddha himself: meditating on his words and life, and seeking to emulate his journey to *nirvana*. It is accepted as the basis of the first two steps of the Noble Eightfold Path – perfect view and perfect resolve: that is, it is a means by which the mind is rid of extraneous thoughts and brought to a state of stillness as a preliminary stage of the path to *samadhi*. It is also viewed as one of the five spiritual powers, *balas*, which Buddhists are called on to develop in order to make *moksha* possible. In this context, *shradda* means the power of faith to thrust aside false beliefs; but what is highly significant is the nature and status of the other four powers. These are: *virya* (exertion), *satipatthana* (mindfulness), *samadhi*, and – highest of all – *prajna*: the wisdom that leads to the knowledge which brings liberation.

There is no concept of 'blind faith' here: in fact, apart from in the Pure Land School (see below), to proceed on this basis would be viewed by Buddhists as contrary to the founder's teaching. This fact would not in itself rule out the taking of such a step since, as we saw earlier, Mahayana Buddhists certainly do not view his teaching as being necessarily the final word on any matter: but to teach otherwise on so important a matter would be to create a major hiatus with the earliest beliefs and practices. The Catch-22 aspect of this situation, ironically, is that it was against blind faith in his own teaching that Buddha – along with later masters – was warning his followers. We are left with the logical dilemma of not having blind faith in teaching that included the admonition not to have blind faith in the teaching.

The Pure Land School in China does lay greater emphasis on *shradda*, and is in fact often described as a 'Way of Faith'. As we saw, however, on page 77, the faith that is invoked in this school is faith in the name of Amitabha as the means of bringing a person to the 'pure land', from which entry into *nirvana* is guaranteed. By reciting his name, the mind is cleared of the five hindrances to meditation and spiritual growth: sensual desire, ill-will, sloth and torpor, excitedness and worry, and doubt. Paul Williams, in *Mahayana Buddhism* (p.216), states:

> In other words, faith provides both the cognitive basis and the volition for spiritual growth. Faith is faith that certain things are the case, and because of this, certain behaviour is appropriate. The result of appropriate behaviour is enlightenment, a transcendence of faith to a knowing of those things which were previously only believed.

Even at its most explicit, faith is therefore seen as a stage on the journey to knowledge (in its comprehensive sense), not journey's end.

With Chinese philosophy we enter even further into the world of verifiable experience. Confucius refused to speculate on matters concerning which the theistic religions advocate faith: he would have paid little regard to the quotation from Hebrews cited earlier. The Taoist philosophy is similarly not based on speculation. We cannot know the *Tao*, but through our experience of the *Te* we can infer its being; and through the twin forces of *yin* and *yang*, we see it manifested, both in the natural world and in the world of human affairs. To be at one with the *Tao* is not, therefore, a matter of faith or of speculation, but of simply acting naturally by following one's intuitive processes.

Perhaps this idea is reflected in Matthew Arnold's phrase 'the Sea of Faith': it has some place in the modern Christian movement of that name, and those who follow the Christian path according to their own perceptions rather than those of traditionalists and fundamentalists should not feel too alienated by the relegation of faith by Eastern philosophies to an early stage of the spiritual quest. If this is so, they may be heartened by these words, written 900 years ago by one of Christianity's greatest theologians, St Anselm, in *Proslogium*:

I do not seek to understand in order that I may believe, but I believe in order that I may understand.

It is doubtful that any Eastern teacher would have disagreed with those sentiments: the authority for anything that such teachers might affirm arises not from their having taken a leap in the dark but from what they have come to know to be the case in their own experience. Faith without works may, as St Paul asserted (James 2:17) be dead; but faith plus works yet without knowledge would still, in the view of any Eastern teacher, be only halfway to enlightenment.

18 Coexistence or coinherence?

Hardly a chapter in this book has lacked a reference to an issue that, in its way, draws together all its themes: the possibility of union between all religions. From time to time throughout history there have been mergers between particular schools, such as that in the sixteenth century involving Hindus and Muslims, leading to the emergence of Sikhism. And therein lies the irony of such attempts at syncretisation: instead of bringing Hinduism and Islam together, the outcome was the creation of yet another religion. Whether this consequence is viewed with gloom or delight will depend largely on one's response to the question under discussion: the fact is that any organised attempts to bring about union between religions, as opposed to the lengthier process of natural mutation, tends only, it seems, to lead to greater diversification. A 'non-denominational Church' would simply be an additional denomination.

If the merger of any two schools results in not one but three expressions of belief (and to be fair to most of those Hindus and Muslims referred to, the outcome, in general if not in detail, was foreseen) how realistic is it to envisage a union of all the schools of thought mentioned in this book? For some, such a situation would no doubt be a nightmare rather than a Utopian vision, but the question here is whether it could ever be more than a pipe dream (a nightmare to non-smokers). Is it the case that, as William Blake wrote in 1788, 'All Religions are One'; and if in general we gave assent to that question, would that imply that we were agreeing with the proposition, 'All religions are true'?

There are a number of human foibles that would need to be overcome even to begin a serious debate on these propositions. The most basic of these is tribalism, the blinkered state of mind that comes about in those who, whether geographically or psychologically, suffer from near-sightedness, barricaded from both the physical world over their doorsteps and the world of ideas beyond their tabloids. Talk to the smallholders of Little Birch, Hereford, and they will still say that the inhabitants of Much Birch, two miles down the road, are 'queer'. Talk to the average *Sun* reader (if that is not yet another oxymoron) and he will write off the black races as delinquent (although probably in more Anglo-Saxon terms).

In religion, tribalism evinces itself in the view that only one group, the one to which I (*sic*) belong, has the right message. Its theme song was penned some decades ago:

> We are the chosen few:
> All others will be damned;
> There is no room in heaven for you –
> We can't have heaven crammed.

The attitude of those needing the security of such a closed world view is unlikely to include any appreciation of anyone on a different path. The blinkers provide both protection and ego-enhancement, and become virtually indestructible. It may justly be remarked that we are not here concerned with such people, who are in any case unlikely to be reading this: but their presence and influence cannot be ignored, any more than one can ignore racists, sexists or extreme nationalists. The fact is that the main problems facing the human race relate, directly or indirectly, to tribalism, a disease found in religious, as well as secular, circles.

Most people who have experienced life in a multi-cultural setting – one, that is, that takes them beyond their immediate surroundings – are likely to have a wider view on the issue. They probably, as I mentioned in the Preface, received some instruction at school about the beliefs of different cultures, and they may well have at least achieved an attitude of 'live and let live'. They will no longer sing:

> The heathen in their blindness
> Bow down to wood and stone

any more than their opposite numbers in Asia or Africa will sing, after observing a service of Holy Communion:

> The Christians in their folly
> Kneel down to grape and grain.

Since the first World Parliament of Religions in Chicago in 1893, however, there has been a worldwide attempt by all religions to reach an understanding of other religions that goes beyond caricature. One remarkable outcome of this development is this statement, made by the Second Vatican Council in 1966, in its *Declaration on the Relations of the Church to Non-Christian Religions*:

> The Catholic Church rejects nothing that is true and holy in these religions … In Hinduism, men probe the mystery of God and express it with a rich fund of myths and a penetrating philosophy … In the various forms of Buddhism the basic inadequacy of this changing world is recognised and men are taught with confident application how they can achieve a state of complete liberation … The Church also regards with esteem the Muslims who worship the one, subsistent, merciful and

almighty God [and] venerate Jesus as a prophet . . . Given the great spiritual heritage common to Christians and Jews, it is the wish of this sacred Council to foster and recommend a mutual knowledge and esteem.

These words reflect a remarkable advance in the thinking of the Roman Catholic Church, influenced by the extraordinary Pope John XXIII. They indicate that the non-theistic religions are not alone in having the ability to appreciate others' values. To acknowledge the strength of another school of thought is not, however, the same as agreeing to join with it as one entity. For this to be possible, there must be a mutual recognition that each is seeking the same goal, so that neither looks on the other as having gone astray.

It may be that the different groups have reached a point of agreeing to coexist, and this is certainly an advance on the bemused contempt with which the first colonialists in India treated most Hindu beliefs and practices, or the exiling of Jews from Christian countries, or the Muslim *jihad* (holy war). However, coexistence between religions does not mean that any of them wishes to take another's philosophy into its own system, any more than the coexistence of the United States and the Soviet Union meant that either of them wished to share the other's political system. At this level, pluralism (which is coexistence in another guise) still leaves open the view that any particular religion alone embraces the basic truths, leaving others struggling to make the grade.

The theistic religions have the greatest difficulty here, since each of them expresses confidence in its own possession of 'the truth'. The Jewish scriptures continually affirm the conviction that the Hebrews are God's chosen people. John's Gospel quotes Jesus as saying, 'I am the way, the truth, and the life: no man comes to the father but by me.' Muslims daily recite the prayer, 'There is no God but Allah and Muhammad is his prophet.' If there is to be more than coexistence between them, it seems that either a modification or a reinterpretation of these claims is essential.

Eastern religions are not without similar claims, however. K. S. Murty, in his *Revelation and Reason in Advaita Vedanta* (1959), wrote:

> Modern exponents of Hinduism should make it explicit that such state-ments as 'All religions are true' are made only on their own authority, and do not represent the orthodox Hindu tradition.

It was this same tradition that pronounced Buddha to be *nastika* 2½ millennia earlier, and, whatever modifications may have occurred over the centuries, continues to be expressed. Even the liberal sharing of ideas between Bud-dhism, Taoism and Confucianism in China (mentioned on page 87) is criticised by some Buddhists, who hold that there is an orthodox Buddhist philosophy, which cannot (or should not) be 'watered down' in this way.

The main problem, then, is not that of agreeing to differ but of finding common ground: and here the theistic religions have certainly been the more recalcitrant. Concentrating again on Christianity, it is noteworthy that the published papers of the first World Parliament of Religions, *The Dawn of Religious Pluralism*, end with one entitled *Christ, the Unifier of Mankind*. This approach is reflected in the title of a book by R. Panikkar (1964): *The Unknown Christ of Hinduism*. The view expressed in both these writings is one that many Christians are happy to hold: that other religions may well express important truths, but the worth of these is assessed by the extent to which they reflect the teaching and person of Jesus, since he alone is the Son of God, the ultimate revelation of the divine. The problem here is self-evident, and we shall return to it later. The dilemma is sharpened, however, by a further affirmation that Christians are wont to make: Jesus is actually 'contained' in other religions, so that, to a greater or lesser extent, they can all be adjudged to be Christian, whether they know it or like it or not.

It is difficult to view this attitude, often expressed with the utmost sincerity and goodwill, as little more than impertinent, a view expressed peremptorily by Hans Kung in *On Being a Christian*:

> It would be impossible to find anywhere in the world a sincere Jew, Muslim or atheist who would not regard the assertion that he is an 'anonymous Christian' as presumptuous.

This, then, is not the way forward: not, at any rate, if the religions are to move beyond coexistence to coinherence. What that way is needs a recapitulation of the properties of a religion, which were discussed in the opening chapter. The questions to ask are, first, how far any of them can already be found in different forms within one religion (again with Christianity as the main example); and second, to what extent there is already broad agreement, on any category, between religions.

We can immediately eliminate the issue of *buildings*. There is a universe of difference between St Peter's in Rome and a Friends' Meeting Place anywhere, yet each is a building within which Christians assemble. Whether, then, we prefer temples, shrines or backyards in which to worship or meditate may be accepted as largely a matter of aesthetics, or taste: both can coinhere within one religion.

The same is the case for the *social element* in religion. People will tend to meet with others towards whom they feel some affinity as human beings, and it is not therefore surprising to find, say, mostly professional people in one congregation (such as a suburban Anglican church) and primarily working-class people in another (such as an inner-city Pentecostal church). In the Christian ranks can be found activists of all political parties, royalists and republicans, rich and poor. They may argue strongly with each other on social and political matters, yet remain united under the Christian umbrella. The same situation is to be found in all the religions discussed here, although perhaps divisions in India over the question of caste create more of a challenge to unity in Hinduism than does any Western social problem to Christian unity.

On *ethical* matters there is broad agreement in principle between and within religions, less so on specific practices. All condemn killing (although Buddhists include the killing of animals), stealing, lying and certain expressions of sexuality. It may justly be said that none of the religions has really come to terms with the crucial issue of the role and status of women, but this is a universal problem, not confined to the religions. It is not an issue over which there is likely to be a new schismatic movement, and within Christianity, rightly or wrongly, those who approve of female priests or ministers can freely transfer from a church that is unsympathetic on this issue to one that is, and vice versa (as happened when the Church of England accepted women priests). The current situation is one that is certain to change in the years ahead, in some religions more rapidly than others, and this process will no doubt test the goodwill of some religious affiliates: but not, one feels, to the point of creating new formal divisions in the ranks.

On individual moral issues such as abortion, euthanasia, use of drugs or foetal research there exist depths of disagreement both within and between religions. The important point is that these disagreements can be expressed under a single religious umbrella. The authoritarian approach on these matters on the part of the Roman Catholic Church might suggest that varieties of opinion are denied to its members, but one needs only to observe the attitude of many Catholics to artificial forms of birth control, condemned by the Pope but practised by millions, to recognise that even in that Church differences of opinion are not *religiously* divisive. A religion can embrace both the rule-governed and the autonomous, as it can contain pacifists and warriors, playboys and puritans, the bountiful and the miserly.

One further category need cause few alarums in the quest for a universal religion: that of the *practical and ritualistic* aspects of religious belief. On the face of it, there is a world of difference between, for example, Zen, with its assessment of ritual as generally counter-productive to *satori*, and the Orthodox Church in Christianity, for which it is central. But just as Quakerism can maintain a Christian stance despite its rejection of all formal liturgy, including the sacraments, so it seems that those who set their faces against liturgical activity anywhere may still be subsumed within a body for most of whose members ritual is a pathway to the divine. Zen and Christian Orthodoxy could coinhere, as Zen and Buddhism coinhere, provided the basic spiritual aim is the same.

This brings us to the nub of the problem, which relates primarily to the *doctrinal and philosophical* category of a religion, but also, since the remaining categories are in many respects interdependent, the *experiential and emotional* and, more directly (because they provide much of the content to doctrine), the *narratives and myths*. In these three areas there is so wide a range of ideas and beliefs that any attempt to view them as a harmoniously coinhering whole must seem totally unrealistic. At one extreme are simple peasants in a Hindu temple, watching the continual sacrifice of goats with the aim of gaining karmic merit by smearing themselves with their blood; at the other is the Tibetan monk, spending hours in deep contemplation before a wall in the hope of achieving *dzogchen*. Elsewhere are Muslims, who believe that their holy book, the Qur'an, is not only Allah's perfect guide to individual human behaviour but also, since it is the word of Allah, the ultimate statement on a nation's laws and punishments for crimes; in contrast, followers of Zen in Japan view these and similar writings as no more than provisional and inadequate (because man-made) guides on any of these or other matters. There are religious people who make no decisions without consulting their own special deity, whether Shiva, Vishnu or Amitabha; others who seek a personal encounter with the one divine being who is above all others, whether Brahman, Jesus or Allah; and still others who have moved into the mystical heights beyond all deities and doctrines.

The interesting fact is that, varied as these expressions of belief certainly are, they can all be found in any single religion and therefore, other things being equal, need not constitute an insuperable barrier to unity. As in Hinduism, so in Christianity, there are expressions of the four approaches. Catholic peasants in South America will throng to touch the statue of the Virgin as it is carried through the streets at festival time; other Christians worldwide will pray freely to their own patron saint in the belief that he or she is in constant attendance on them; most Christians pray to God through Jesus and believe that he speaks in turn to them; and there remain mystics in Christianity whose spiritual path involves no images, no conversation, no personalised God.

We may accept the view of followers of Advaita Vedanta that these four expressions of belief represent four rising levels of religious experience: the question is whether they can all be contained within one universal religion. There seems little problem with the first two: if it helps people in their spiritual lives – whether or not these are assessed as being at a 'low' level – to venerate the spirit of a tree, or to pray constantly to St Christopher, there seems little ground for excluding them from the company of others who view these as examples of superstition: just as a school contains both the bright and the dim, so a religion can include in its midst both the enlightened and those in semi-darkness (or even near-obscurity). The test is not where a person *stands* spiritually but the direction in which he or she is looking.

It is when we reach the two higher stages on the Advaita Vedanta scale that we face the starkest problems in the quest for unity, and we need to examine it directly. Theists hold the spiritual life to be basically one of communion with a God or divine figure as they have been taught to understand Him (since the demise of the Earth goddess, there is no female expression of the deity in the theistic religions). We must be clear about the implications of this belief. One requirement for any theistic conception of God is that He be designated with characteristics that are identifiable at the human level. This means that any qualities ascribed to the deity will be expressions of what is already found among human beings, although at an infinitely more rarefied level. He will be a God of justice, or of compassion, one with supreme power and perfect reason, purposive, in harmony with His Selfhood, and so on. The *Bhagavad-Gita* (XI:44) unambiguously expresses this anthropomorphic image of God:

> As a father to his son, as a friend to his friend,
> As a lover to his beloved, be pleased to show mercy, O God.

One would not need to look far in either the Old or New Testaments, or in the Qur'an, to find parallels to this description. The heavenly Father addressed in these writings has all the qualities one would seek in a perfect parent. This may be difficult to imagine by those whose parents were malign, but most people can latch on to this image, and others like it, and so familiarise themselves with the deity with whom they seek to communicate.

The fourth stage of spirituality moves beyond this personalised characterisation. It is the union of 'I' and 'Thou', at which point, in Buber's words quoted earlier, 'God is no more.' The God of the theists is one about whose characteristics one can argue and debate, altering emphases here, modifying the image there. Is He more a just than a merciful God? Is His truth more important than His love? Does His providence mean that all is predestined, or has He granted free will? This is the stuff of theological and philosophical debate, in which sharper minds may triumph over the rest: but those who seek the final stage are looking beyond these human foibles to a state of absorption in the ground of being: beyond rationality, beyond virtue, beyond good and evil. Meister Eckhart (*Fragments*) wrote:

> The divine One is a negation of negations, and a desire of desires. What does 'One' mean? Something to which nothing is to be added. The soul lays hold of the Godhead where it is pure, where there is nothing beside it, nothing else to consider.

It is this sense of oneness with the absolute, the union of *atman* and *brahman*, the harmonising of oneself with the *Tao*, that has recurred throughout these writings. There is no religion in which, in some way, it fails to find expression, even though it is normally found alongside images of a personal deity, as in the *Bhagavad-Gita*. Could we not, then, envisage a world religion in which all are accepted as travelling on the right path, but at different levels?

There are affiliates of most religions who, secretly perhaps (because of the value judgment that it embodies) have no great problem with this universalist attitude. The problem lies in the value judgment that the state of absorption is spiritually 'higher' than the worship of a personal, albeit almighty, God. The validity of this judgment would be denied by most theists, strengthened and confirmed by their scriptures, on which, together with interpretations accumulated over the centuries, their creeds and beliefs are largely based.

Judaism has its own distinct problem here, since being a Jew implies membership of a particular race besides following a particular religious tradition. With the other two theistic religions there are different, but what seem to be insuperable, problems for anyone looking for their participation in a world religion: both affirm the uniqueness of the truth taught by their founders, Muhammad and Jesus. In Christianity, we have seen that this view is taken a step further, since it is not only in what he proclaimed that Jesus is held to be 'above all others', but in his person. More than a prophet, more than an *avatar*, more than a Shankara or a Buddha, Jesus was God incarnate, claiming 'He that has seen me has seen the Father' (John 14:9).

Most Hindus, particularly of the Advaita Vedanta school, will have no problem with that claim, since they can associate it with many of their own persuasion who have attained *samadhi*, and who have realised the union of *atman* and *brahman*. In fact, in one Advaita Vedanta centre known to the author, pictures of Jesus and Buddha can be found alongside those of Ramakrishna and Swami Vivekananda, founder of the Ramakrishna order of monks. Buddhists will have to make some adjustments in order to come to terms with the Christian claim, since they reject its implied concept of God; but, if interpreted as a claim to have achieved Buddhahood and to have realised Buddha-nature, many could freely live with Jesus's words. Confucianists might well interpret the claim as emanating from one whose life in its totality reflected the 'way of Heaven'; and Taoists could view him as one who, like Lao Tzu himself, was in full harmony with the *yin* and the *yang*, so that the *Tao* was reflected in all that he said and did.

There are Christians who can live with this interpretation, agreeing that, while the person of Jesus is their own guide along the spiritual path, others, although making the same journey, have a different one. Those with this broad view remain, however, a minority of the Christian body, and the dominant expression of that faith retains the claim to uniqueness. We may forecast that, with the ever-increasing interaction between East and West, this isolationist attitude cannot finally prevail, but this remains a matter of speculation. What is certainly the case is that there is no hope whatsoever of the unity of all religions – coinherence as well as coexistence – so long as this solipsistic approach prevails. The belief that Jesus is uniquely the Saviour of the World (rather than one example of many saviours throughout the millennia) and that he uniquely rose from the dead (rather than joining with many in entering *samadhi* or gaining *nirvana*) cannot survive in any universal religion: not, that is, if this belief is accompanied by the assertion (which millions make) that this belief is essential for salvation, or full enlightenment. It may happen that a substantial number of Christians become so dedicated to the universalist perception that they cease to call themselves Christians, perhaps (although less likely) joined by Muslims and Jews taking a similar step. What is more certain is that none of the fundamentalists of any theistic religion, and few Roman Catholics in Christianity, will do so. If that be the case, Christianity will survive mainly as either biblical or ecclesiastical fundamentalism, with ominous political implications.

What would be the basis, or bases, of a world religion? The way forward may be suggested by these words of Bede Griffiths (*Return to the Centre*):

I have to become a Hindu, a Buddhist, a Jain, a Parsee, a Sikh, a Muslim, and a Jew, as well as a Christian, if I am to know the Truth and to find the point of reconciliation in all religion.

We may judge these to be far-sighted sentiments, but most people are likely to find life too short to achieve any understanding in depth of all these expressions of belief (*most people* find it time-consuming enough becoming conversant with one religion). Since, however, one is not expecting to realise the aim overnight, the achievement of a greater universal awareness of religions may be viewed as a laudable first step towards it. The broadening of the RE syllabus in schools, described in the Preface, should then be recognised as a key element in this process.

A greater problem is that of the differences between the religions in both the imagery of their expression and the vocabulary they use. Continually throughout this book, for instance, it has been necessary both to explain the meanings of certain words and to 'demythologise' certain exotic concepts. The first task is not exceptionally difficult, but it means overcoming extra problems at the earlier stages of study. The second is more complicated, since the understanding of imagery and iconography requires some appreciation of the culture within which a particular religious or philosophical perspective has taken shape. It is this latter difficulty that led even so far-sighted a writer as William Johnston to conclude (in *The Inner Eye of Love*) that the impetus towards a world religion must come from within the framework of single religious traditions.

This has been the experience of the present writer, and the final task is to state one view of what might be the central features of a world religion, with all its streams coming together in one river (with the added assumption that the river flows into a universal sea).

From **Buddhism** may be learned the underlying consideration that is the fact of *anicca*: nothing endures, and this is the thread that directs all that follows. From **Judaism** we learn how to remain loyal to our convictions, despite suffering and even persecution. From **Islam** comes consistency: the conviction that the whole of life must be an expression of our beliefs. From **Jainism** we may learn how to have compassion for all sentient beings, including our fellow humans, who should never be treated as a means to an end but always as ends in themselves. In **Confucianism** we find the emphasis on self-control – nothing in excess – and the call to follow the best we know, 'the way of Heaven', in all our doings. From **Christianity** we may find the motivation to fight social wrongs, strengthened by the vision of the kingdom of God, a world in harmony with itself. In **Hinduism**, the most specifically religious of all religions, we discover the path to spiritual enlightenment and learn how to say from inner experience, '*Tat tvam asi*'. From **Zen** we derive an appreciation of the intuitive side of our natures, and the realisation that the whole universe lies within our own being. From **Taoism** we learn about the naturalness of the way, how to cooperate with nature rather than exploit it, and to realise its forces within ourselves. From *yin* and *yang* comes the realisation that the harmonious life is one that goes with the flow, recognising that there is both a time to be assertive and a time to be quiescent.

This way allows each person to find his or her own path. It calls for no prophet, no holy book, no creed, no moral code, no God, but for meditation, harmony with others, oneness with the natural world, and the acceptance of the transitoriness of all things except the ground of being, by whatever name this ultimate reality is designated. To be one with the ultimate is the goal of the journey; it is acknowledged in theism by Jewish Kabbalists, Islamic Sufis and Christian mystics, as well as in the non-theistic religions by Hindus seeking *samadhi*, Buddhists looking to *nirvana*, and Taoists achieving harmony with the 'watercourse way'.

In gaining this perspective, some sources have proved more enriching than others, but no expression of the numinous, however rarefied, is totally worthless. Perhaps the primary aim of all religions may be most succinctly expressed by way of a secular source. Wordsworth defined poetry as 'emotion recollected in tranquillity'. It seems rather that the basic need of all members of the human race is *tranquillity recollected in emotion*. That, at any rate, seems to be the main explanation for the universal phenomenon of religion.

Bibliography

Books quoted or mentioned in the text:

Armstrong, K. *A History of God* (Heinemann 1993).

Billington, R. *East of Existentialism* (Routledge 1990).

Buber, M. *I and Thou* (T&T Clark, second edition 1958).

Capra, F. *The Tao of Physics* (various editions).

Chang, C. *Original Teachings of Zen Buddhism* (Harper Row 1969).

Chang, J. *The Tao of Love and Sex* (Wildwood House 1977).

Chardin, T. de *The Phenomenon of Man* (Collins 1959).

Chryssides, G. 'God and the Tao', *Journal of Religious Studies*, 19, pp.1–11 (article)

Cleary, T. *The Essential Tao* (HarperCollins 1991).

Collins, S. *Selfless Persons* (Cambridge University Press 1982).

Conze, E. *Buddhist Thought in India* (Allen & Unwin 1962).

Feng, G.-F. and English, J. *Lao Tzu: Tao Te Ching* (Wildwood House 1973).

Feuerstein, G. *The Yoga-Sutra of Patanjali* (Inner Traditions 1990).

Foy, W. (ed.) *The Religious Quest* (Routledge 1988).

Gadon, E.W. *The Once and Future Goddess* (HarperCollins 1989).

Gimbutas, M. *The Civilisation of the Goddess* (HarperCollins 1991).

Gombrich, R. *Theravada Buddhism* (Routledge 1988).

Graham, A.C. *Chuang-Tzu: the Inner Chapters* (Mandala 1986).

Griffiths, B. *Return to the Centre* (Collins 1976).

Hammarskjøld, D. *Markings* (New York 1964).

Harvey, P. *Introduction to Buddhism* (Cambridge University Press 1990).

Hospers, J. *Introduction to Philosophical Analysis* (Routledge 1956).

Huxley, A. *The Doors of Perception* (various editions).

James, W. *The Varieties of Religious Experience* (Fontana 1977).

Johnston, W. *The Inner Eye of Love* (Harper & Row 1978).

Kierkegaard, S. *The Journals of Kierkegaard, 1834–1854* trans. Dru, A. (Fontana/ Collins 1958).

Kung, H. *On Being a Christian* (Fount Paperbacks 1978).

Kwok, M.-H., Palmer, M. and Ramsay, J. *The Illustrated Tao Te Ching* (Element 1993).

Lau, D.C. *Lao-Tzu: Tao Te Ching* (Penguin 1963).

Marshall, C. *I Ching* (Carlton 1994).

Murty, K.S. *Revelation and Reason in Advaita Vedanta* (Harper Row 1959).

Needham, J. *Science and Civilisation in China* (Cambridge University Press 1954–74, five vols).

Otto, R. *The Idea of the Holy* (Oxford University Press paperback 1958).

Palmer, M. *The Elements of Taoism* (Element 1991).

Radhakrishnan *Indian Philosophy* (Allen & Unwin, second edition 1962); see also *East and West* (1955) and *An Idealist View of Life* (1935, reissued Mandala 1988).

The Rider Encyclopedia of Eastern Philosophy and Religion (Hutchinson 1989).

Robinson, J. *Honest to God* (SCM 1963); see also *Exploration into God* (SCM 1967).

Smart, N. *The Religious Experience of Mankind* (Scribners, third edition 1983); see also *The World's Religions.*

Tessier, L.J. (ed.) *Concepts of the Ultimate* (Macmillan 1989).

The Tibetan Book of the Dead (various editions); see also: Rinpoche, S. *The Tibetan Book of Living and Dying* (HarperCollins 1992).

Vivekananda *Raja Yoga* (Ramakrishna Vedanta Centre).

Waley, A. *The Way and its Power* (Allen & Unwin 1934); see also Addiss and Lombardo, S. *Tao Te Ching: Lao Tzu* (Hackett 1993).

Waley, A. *The Analects of Confucius* (Unwin Hyman paperback 1988).

Watts, A. *The Way of Zen* (Penguin 1957).

Watts, A. *The Watercourse Way* (Arkana 1975).

Wilhelm, R. and Baynes, C.F. *The I Ching* (Princeton University Press, third edition 1967).

Williams, P. *Mahayana Buddhism* (Routledge 1989).

Wu, L. *Fundamentals of Chinese Philosophy* (University Press of America 1986).

Zimmer, H. *Philosophies of India* (Princeton University Press 1969).

Two essential source-books for primary sources:

Radhakrishnan and Moore *A Source-Book in Indian Philosophy* (Princeton University Press 1957).

Chan, W.-T. *A Source-Book in Chinese Philosophy* (Princeton University Press 1963). This may be used alongside the comprehensive *A History of Chinese Philosophy* by Fung Yu-Lan (two vols, Princeton 1983).

For Buddhist Pali (i.e. Theravada) sources:

The Dhammapada trans. Carter, J.R. and Palihawadana, M. (Oxford University Press 1987).

See also:

Collinson, D. and Wilkinson, R. *Thirty-five Oriental Philosophers* (Routledge 1994 – but does not include Chuang Tzu).

Clarke, J.J. *Oriental Enlightenment* (Routledge 1997: an essential guide to the history of Eastern thought in the West).

The monumental *Companion Encyclopedia of Asian Philosophy*, eds Carr, B. and Mahalingam, I. (Routledge 1997) arrived too late to be used for this book. Be aware that this is a *companion* to an encyclopaedia, i.e. articles rather than alphabetically arranged summaries.

Index

absolutism, moral (versus relativism)
  157–60
advaita: see non-dualism
Advaita Vedanta 24–5, 29–30, 33–7, 65,
  88, 94, 135–6, 159; and levels of
  religion 184–5
agape 120
aggregates: *see skandhas*
Agni 41–2
agnosticism 14–15
ahimsa 47, 84, 152
alaya-vijnana: see storehouse
  consciousness
alms-giving 68–9
Amidism 72
Amitabha 72, 77, 81, 176, 183
Analects of Confucius 88, 93, 119–25,
  172
anatman: see anatta
anatta 55, 56–7, 59, 63, 132, 136, 144–5
anicca 54, 56–7, 61, 70, 113
animism 10
anitya: see anicca
Anselm, St 16, 177
anti-anthropomorphism 101
Apostles' Creed 150
Aquinas, Thomas 7, 16, 88, 163, 169
Aranyakas 21
arhat 72, 155
Aristotle 7, 70, 122, 126, 130
Arjuna 22
Armstrong, K. 15
Arnold, M. 176
artha 32
aryamarga: see supramundane path
arya-satya: see Four Noble Truths
asana 27
asanga 79, 82
ashtangika-marga: see Noble Eightfold
  Path
astika: see orthodoxy
Atharvaveda 21
atheism 12, 14–15; in Buddhism 140; in
  Jainism 45
ati-yoga: see dzogchen
atman 25–6, 30, 33–4, 48, 58–9, 65, 88,
  135–6, 143–4, 147
Augustine, St 159, 174
Aurobindo, Sri 20
austerity: *see tapas*
authority (for belief) 169–74
Avalokiteshvara 72, 82
avasthas 35
avatar 29–30, 40–41, 185
avidya 33, 67
awareness: *see vijnana*
axial age 52

Bahm, A. 86
balas 175–6
Baldwin, S. 98
Barbaspati-Sutra 44
*Bardo Thodol: see Tibetan Book of the
  Dead*
Beethoven, L. 142
behaviour, moral ch.15 *passim*
Benares Sermon 56
Bevan, A. 1
beyond good and evil 100, 158–9
Bhagavad-Gita 20, 24, 36, 54,
  89, 113, 143, 147, 164, 171–2, 176,
  184
bhakti: see devotion
bhikshus, bhikshunis: see monks/nuns
  in Buddhism
Bible, the, authority of 169–70, 184
Blake, W. 178
Bodh-gaya 53, 56

bodhichitta: see chitta
Bodhidharma 74
bodhis 53–4
bodhisattva 72–3, 81–2, 155
bodhi-tree 53, 74
Boehme, J. 10
Bon 78–9
Bonhoeffer, D. 132, 141
Brahma 22, 41
brahman 22, 25–6, 29–30, 33–4, 36, 48,
    55, 58, 65, 88, 90, 92, 132, 136–7, 144,
    147, 164, 168, 175, 184
Brahmana 21, 29
Brahmanism 20, 41
Buber, M. 18, 92, 138, 184
Buddha 41, 43, 48; his person 68, 73, 84,
    90, 92, 113, 134, 137, 174, 176 (chs
    6–8 *passim*)
Buddha families 80–2
Buddhaghosa 61
Buddhahood 51, 73, 79, 144, 185
Buddha-nature 76
buddhakulas: see Buddha families
Buddhism 19, 21, 87, 93, 103, 105, 118,
    131, 140, 157, 180, 185–6; *see also*
    Theravada; Mahayana
Burke, E. 151
bussho: see Buddha-nature
Butler, S. 1

Calvin, J. 87, 166, 170
Capra, F. 109, 137–8, 174
carvaka: see charvaka
caste 39–40, 84, 181
chakras 61, 80, 82–3
Ch'an Buddhism: *see* Zen
ch'ang 94
Chang, J. 105
Chan, Wing-Tsit 102
charismatic movement 77, 106
Charvaka 43–5, 60, 70, 142, 145
Chesterton, G. K. 138
Ch'i 91, 105, 130–32; in Chu Hsi 132–3,
    148
chih 122–3
Chinese Buddhism 74–8
ching 72, 88, 105
chit 30
chitta 57, 65, 79, 81, 136
Christianity 9, 19, 51, 72–3, 77, 84, 138,
    156; and ethics 154, 170, 176, 183,
    185–6; on government 125–6, 131
Christian Science 163
Chuang Tzu 76, 92, 95, 97–103, 106,

112, 137, 140, 148, 153, 163
Chryssides, G. 137
Chu Hsi 118, 132–3
chung 120, 126
chun-tzu 121, 126–7
citta: see chitta
Civilization of the Goddess, The 15
classical period in Hinduism 20
Cleary, T. 107
Collins, S. 59–60
conditioned arising 57–60, 80
Confucianism 74, 87, 102, 105, 107, 109,
    114, ch. 12 *passsim*, 149, 151–2, 186
Confucius 52, 88–9, 92–3, 99, 115,
    117–26, 166–7, 172
conscientiousness: *see zhong*
consciousness: *see chit*
conventional truth 59, 84
Conze, E. 145
I Corinthians 139, 150, 170
cosmological argument 16
craving 62
'creative ambiguity' 87
Cromwell, O. 166

dakini 78–9
Dakshinachara 23
Dalai Lama 81–2, 166, 172
dana: see almsgiving
darsana 61
darshanas: see systems
Darwin, C. 16, 46, 101, 118, 154, 162
deism 10–11
delusion: *see maya*
demythologising 186
dependent arising: *see* conditioned
    arising
Descartes, R. 16, 87
descents: *see* avatars
destiny, human 146–50
devas 41–2, 67
devotion 22, 50
Dhammapada 59
dharana 28
dharma 32, 61, 73, 82; as justice 158–9
dharmakaya 90–1
Dharma-Shastra 24
dhyana 27–8, 47, 65–6, 72, 74, 148; *see
    also* meditation
diagram of the supreme ultimate: *see T'ai-
    chi-t'u*
Diamond Vehicle (in Buddhism) 71, 79
Diener, M. 76
dreamless and dreaming sleep 35

dualism, Hindu: *see* Dvaita Vedanta; in contrast with mysticism 139, 142; apropos the soul 142–5
duhkha 53, 55, 61–3, 73, 86, 148, 151
duty (Confucian): *see i*
Dvaita Vedanta 29
dzogchen 79–81, 83, 183

Earth goddess 15, 183
Ecclesiastes 31
Eckhart, Meister 10, 20, 138, 159, 164, 184
education (in Confucianism) 125, 127
eel-wrigglers 55
embryonic breathing 105–6
enlightenment: *see* moksha
entering the stream 66–8, 72, 82
Epic period (Hinduism) 19–20
essence: *see ching*
ethics, Eastern 152–60; compared with Western 182
evil, problem of 161–3
evolution/involution 26, 133
Exodus 13
experience as basis of authority 173
Ezekiel 52

faith 9, 174–7
fasting 63, 68–9
fetters 66–7
First Cause 11
Fischer-Schreiber, I. 72
Five Agents, theory of 116–17, 133
five hindrances 65
Five-Pecks-of-Rice School 104
five relationships (Confucian) 123–4, 131
ford-crossers: *see jinas*
four awakenings of mindfulness 64–5, 175–6
Four Noble Truths 61–3
four signs of Buddha 52–3
four states 35
Fourth State 28, 35–7, 54, 65, 94, 135–6, 144, 148, 168
Fox, G. 138, 153
freewill and fatalism (in Hinduism) 39
Friedrichs, K. 29
fu 91–4
fundamentalism, Protestant 153, 172: *see also* charismatic movement

Gaia hypothesis 164
Gadon, E. 15

Galatians 154
Gandhi, Mahatma 20, 22, 40, 158, 168
gati: *see* modes of existence
Genesis 3, 10, 162, 171
Gimbutas, M. 15
Goddess *see* Earth goddess
golden rule 5, 120
Goldwyn, S. 151
Gotama 24
Graham, A. C. 98
great vow 47–8
Green Movement 5, 96
Gregory VII 166
Griffiths, Bede 173, 185–6
ground of being ch.13 *passim*, 164
gunas 25–6
gurus 26, 86, 140, 157, 172–3
Guru Rinpoche 78–80

Halbfass, W. 21
Hammarskjold, D. 173
Hammurabi, code of 6
Harvey, P. 84
Han Fei-tzu 94
heathen 15
Heaven (in Confucianism) 119, 130–1, 147–8; and hell 149–50, 156; as Paradise (Islam) 144
Hebrews, Letter to 174–5
Heidegger, M. 60, 101
Heine, H. 149
henotheism 12, 42
heterodoxy: *see* unorthodoxy
Hinayana Buddhism: *see* Theravada Buddhism
Hinduism, Hindus 8, 12–13, chs 3 and 4 *passim*, 48, 51, 54, 58, 64, 70–1, 74, 84, 100, 118, 131, 135–6, 139–40, 143, 147, 157, 171, 178, 180, 182, 186
Historical Records 89
Hobbes, T. 129, 145, 154–5, 162, 166
ho ch'i 104–5
homoeopathy 113
Honest to God: *see* Robinson, J.
Hospers, J. 2–3
hseng shen: *see* mutual arising
hsiao 121, 126
hsien 89, 103–4
hsin 123
Hsun Tzu 128–30
humanism in China 86–7
human nature 142–6
Hume, D. 12, 62
Huxley, A. 78

Huxley, T. H. 14

i 122–3, 127
I ching 88, 107–8, 113–16, 131
illusion: *see maya*
immortal: *see hsien*
immortality: of the soul (versus
  resurrection of the body) 149–50; in
  tao chiao 103
Indra 41–2
inner alchemy: *see* inner elexir
inner chapters 97–8, 100
Inner Deity Hygiene School 104
inner elexir 105, 114
Isaiah 52, 165
Islam 9, 19, 138, 149, 166, 169, 186
Itihasa 22

Jaimini 28–30
Jainism 21, 32, 44, 53, 55, 64, 68, 70,
  148, 157, 186
James, W. 135, 137
Jaspers, K. 52
jen 120–3, 126
Jenkins, D. 173
Jeremiah 52
Jesus 12, 15, 44, 53–4, 68, 72, 92, 134,
  150, 159, 162, 169, 175, 180–1, 183,
  185
jihad 84, 169, 180
jinas 45–6, 48
jiriki 77
jiva (*ajiva*) 46, 48
jnana 32
Job 137; on evil 163
I John 120
John, Gospel of 180, 185
John of the Cross 138
John XXIII, Pope 180
Johnston, W. 134, 186
Judaism, Jews 9, 19, 41, 45–50, 54, 84,
  138, 150, 170, 184–5
Julian of Norwich 138
Jung, C. G. 38

kabbalists 187
Kali 12, 41
kama 32
Kama Sutra 24
Kanada 24–5
Kant, I. 17, 87, 120, 131, 154
Kapila 25
karma 25, 32, 37–40, 42, 45–6, 54, 58,
  60, 64, 67, 70, 79–80, 153, 155–6; *agami-*

karma 38; *prarabda-karma* 38;
  sanchita-karma 38
karman: see karma
Keats, J. 1, 9
kensho 74
kevala 45, 47, 49, 55
Kierkegaard, S. 39, 109, 174–5
Kingdom of God 165–6
King Lear 46
I Kings 13
knowledge: *see vidya, jnana*
koan 75
Krishna 12, 22, 113
kundalini 28, 83
Kung, H. 181
K'ung-tzu: *see* Confucius

lame 82
Lao, D. C. 107
Lao Tzu 52, 89, 101, 106, 110, 141, 168
Law, W. 138
lay persons (in Buddhism) 68–9
legalistic school in China 85, 129–30
Leibniz, G. 163
Leviticus 5
li 99–100, 120–3, 126, 130; in Chu Hsi
  132–3
Lin Yutang 87
logic, Jainite 48–50
logical positivism 109
logos 90–1
Lokayata 44
loving kindness: *see jen, agape*
loyalty: *see chung*
luminosity: *see ming*
Luther, M. 35, 53, 103, 170

Madhva 29
Magic Jewel School 104
Mahabharata 20, 22
Mahakashyupa 75
mahavakya 34
Mahavira 45, 52
Mahavrata: *see* great vow
Mahayana ch. 8 *passim*; in China 74–8;
  in Tibet 78–83; 85, 136, 144, 155–6,
  171
male–female union, twin polarities 73,
  83, 104–5
manas 57, 79
mandala 81–2
Manichaeism 163
mantra 36, 75–6, 81
Mao Tse-Tung 126

Mark, Gospel of 159
Marks of Existence 54–63
Marshall, C. 115
Marx, K. 156
materialism 14–15, 145, 147: *see also* Lokoyata
matriarchy 15–16, 23, 109
Matthew, Gospel of 169, 174
maya 25, 30–1, 35–6, 44, 54, 86, 147, 151–2, 166
meditation 28, 64–6, 70, 73; in Zen 75–6, 130
Meher Baba 20, 159
Mencius 98, 118–19, 121, 123–4, 126–31; on human nature 127–9, 155, 172
Meng-tzu: *see* Mencius
menpekikunen 74
merit 68, 77; Pure Land 78
middle way in Buddhist ethics 70
Mill, J. S. 101, 122–3, 154
Mimamsa 28; Mimamsa-sutra 28–9
ming 94
modes of existence 67
Moguls 40
Mohism 85
moksha 25, 30–1, 35–6, 40, 42–3, 48, 58, 135, 144, 152–3, 156, 175
monism 142
monks/nuns in Buddhism 68–70, 73
monolatry 12
monotheism 13, 42
moral argument for God's existence 17
More, Thomas 167
Moses 6, 13, 15, 157
Mo Tzu 122–3
mudra 82
Muhammad 5, 15, 68, 134, 180, 185
Muslims 84, 153, 157, 162, 171, 178, 180, 185
Mussolini 1
mutual arising 111
mutuality: *see shu*
mysterium fascinans 11
mysterium tremendens 11
mysticism 10, 26, 76, 134–6, 138–9, 183, 187

Nagarjuna 51, 57–9, 61, 71, 79, 82, 87, 136
names, school of 85–6, 125; rectification of 124
Nanak 158
Napoleon 78

nastika: see unorthodoxy
natural being in Taoism 95, 155
nature 95–6;/naturalism 141; Christian view 169; Eastern view 163–5
Needham, J. 113, 133
Nehru, Pandit 39
nei-tan: see inner elexir
neo-Confucianism 103, 118, 131–3
neo-Platonism 150
Newton, I. 11–12, 128, 164
Nichiren Buddhism 73, 83
Nietzsche, F. 75, 139, 147, 159
nirvana 45–6, 54–6, 58, 60, 70, 72, 136, 139, 148, 152, 166, 168, 174, 187
niverana: see five hindrances
niyama 27
Noble Eightfold Path 62–6, 70, 72, 145, 175
non-dualism 35–6, 159
nothingness: *see tzu-jan*
non-violence: *see ahimsa*
Nyaya/Nyaya-Sutras) 24
Nyingmapa school, Tibet 78

obedience: *see ti*
Odun of Cluny 170
OM 36
OM MANI PADME HUM 81
Once and Future Goddess, The 15, 183
one's own power/power of the other: *see jiriki; tariki*
ontological argument 16–17
Order, the: *see Sangha*
Origen 163
orthodoxy: Christian 182; Hindu 24
Otto, R. 3, 11
outer elexir (alchemy) 105, 114

pacifism 64
padarthas 24–5
Padmasambhava: *see* Guru Rinpoche
pagan 15
Pali (canon) 56, 63, 67, 73, 171
Palmer, M. *et al.* 89, 106
Panchen Lama 82
panentheism 14
Panikkar, R. 181
pantheism 9–10, 16, 34
paramartha-satya: see ultimate truth
parinamavada: see evolution/involution
parinirvana 55
Parshva 45
Paul, St 121, 124, 139, 150, 154, 169–70, 177

permanent, the: *see ch'ang*
philosophy, Chinese literation: *see zhe-chue*
philosophical Taoism: *see tao-chia*
piety: *see hsiao*
Plato 29, 124, 126–7, 132, 143–4, 147, 149, 155, 167
Plotinus 150
Polycarp 14
polytheism 12, 32
political theology 167–8
Pope, A. 129, 134
Pope John Paul II 153, 172
postmodernism 128
prajna 176
prakriti 25–6
pranayama 27
pratitya samutapada: see conditioned arising
pratyahara 27, 28
precepts: *see shila*
propriety: *see li*
Proverbs 169
Psalms 161, 169
p'u 92–3
punya: see merit
Puranas 22
Pure Land Buddhism 71, 76–8, 85, 176
Purgatory 149
purusha 25–6
Purva-Mimamsa 28–9
Pythagorus 29

Quakers: *see* Society of Friends
Qur'an 166, 176, 183–4

Radhakrishnan, S. 20, 158, 185
Rama 13
Ramakrishna 20, 158, 185
Ramanuja 30, 143
Rand, Ayn 6
Ramayana 20, 22
reason and intuition, in *yin/yang* 109–10
rebirth 38, 140, 149 *see also samsara*
refuge formula 67–8
relativism in Jainism: *see syadvada*; in Chuang Tzu 99–102; moral 157–60; sceptical 100–1
religion, characteristics of 1–8, 48, 134
religious taoism: *see tao-chiao*
resurrection of the body 149–50
return(ing): *see fu*
revelation 73
Rigveda 21, 32, 39, 42

Rinzai school in Zen 75–6
rishis: see seers
ritual, Zen attitude 75–6
Robinson, J. 13–4, 139
Roman Catholics 82, 172, 180, 182
Rousseau J.-J. 127, 129, 154–5
Ruach 91
Russell, B. 142

sadhana 81–2
samadhi 27–8, 34, 54, 65–6, 135–6, 139–40, 147, 152, 166, 173, 175, 185, 187
Samaveda 21
samsara 38, 40, 42, 45–6, 58, 64, 67, 80, 152
samskara 38, 54
I and II Samuel 171
samvriti-satya: see conventional truth
samyojana: see fetters
Sangha 62–3, 68–9, 82, 84
Sankya 25
sannyasin 35
Sanskrit 20–1, 34, 54, 56, 63, 69, 144
Sartre, J.-P. 92, 127, 147, 161
sat chit ananda 34, 158
satipatthana: see four awakenings of mindfulness
satori 74–5, 182
Scholastic period in Hinduism 20
scriptures, authority of 156, 170–2
Schleiermacher F. 17
Sea of Faith (movement) 176–7
seers 19–20, 25, 28, 30, 140, 157, 172
Sen, Prof. S. 42
sexual pleasure: *see kama*
Shaivism 20, 41
Shakespeare, W. 142
Shakti, Shaktism 23, 41: *see also* Kali
Shakyamuni 52, 74–5
Shankara Adi 30, 35–6, 51, 74, 84, 135, 137–8, 174, 185
Shaw, B. 112
Shelley, P. B. 36–7
shen: *see* spirit
Sheol 150
shih-i 108
shila 63
Shiva 12, 22, 35, 41, 44, 83, 183
shu 120, 126
Shun, Emperor 93, 125
shunyata: see void
Siddhartha Gautama 52
Sikhism 178
sila: see shila

skandhas 62, 65, 79
sky-clad, white-clad 47
Smart, N. 1–6
social gospel 167–8
Society of Friends 4, 10, 48, 77, 169
shradda 175–6: *see also* faith
shrota-apanna: see entering the stream
Soto school of Zen 75–6
Spinoza, B. 9
spirit 105
spontaneity 94
spring and autumn annals 108, 119
storehouse consciousness 79–80
suchness 79, 83, 94, 136
suffering: *see duhkha*
Sufis 138, 187
Sukhaviti 77
supramundane path 53–4, 72
supreme ultimate: *see T'ai ch'i*
sutra 23, 68, 73
syedvada 49–50
syncretism 145
systems, orthodox, in Hinduism 24–30, 45

Tagore 158
T'ai ch'i (Ch'uan) 106–7, 130, 133
T'ai-chi-t'u 111–13
Tantra 23, 26, 32, 41, 71, 82–4, 105, 136, 144
Tao 88, 90–6, 98–9, 110, 112, 119, 137, 146, 164, 184
tao-chia 8, 88, 93, 103, 132, 137–8
tao-chiao 8, 88, 93, 103–6, 148
Taoism 26, 34, 74, 76, ch. 9 *passim*, 87–8, 103, 115, 118, 130–1, 136–8, 141, 145–6, 148, 152, 155, 157, 167, 185–7
Tao Te Ching 87–96, 98–9, 110, 112, 119, 137, 146, 164, 168, 172, 176
tapas 46, 48
tariki 77
tathata: see suchness
tat tvam asi 34–5, 186
te 88, 93, 98
Teilhard de Chardin 164
teleological argument 16
Tennyson, A. 161
ten thousand things 91, 108
Teresa, Mother 112, 155
Teresa, St 138, 142
termas 79
Tertullian 170
theism 11–12, 16, 139, 141–2, 171, 174, 180–1, 183

theocracies 165–6,
Theravada Buddhism 8, 68, 71, 73–4, 77, 85, 145–6, 155–6, 171
Three Baskets: *see Tripitaka*
Three Jewels 62–3, 66, 68–70
ti 121
Tibetan Book of the Dead 80–1
Tibetan Buddhism 71, 73, 78–83; theocracy in 166
tirthankaras: see jinas
Torah 166
tradition and authority 169–70, 172–4
trilakshana: see Marks of Existence
Tripitaka 57, 69, 73
trishna: see craving
trust (in Confucianism): *see hsin*
t'sien: see Heaven (in Confucianism)
turiya: see Fourth State
tzu-jan 94–5

ultimate truth 59, 84
universalism 139–40
unorthodoxy (in Hinduism) 21, 23, 51, 84, 180
Upanishads 19, 21–2, 34–5, 54, 134, 143, 174
uposatha: see fasting
Utopia 165–8, 178
Uttara-Mimamsa 28–9

Vaishnavism 20, 41
Vaisheshika (Vaisheshik-Sutra) 24–5
vajrayana: see Diamond Vehicle
Vallauri, M. 22
Vamachara 23
Vasubandhu 61
Vatsyayana 24
Vedanta: *see* Advaita Vedanta
Vedas 20–2, 28, 34–5, 38, 41, 84, 171
Vedic period 19, 40
vegetarianism 64, 84
vidya 32–3
vijnana 57, 79
Vishnu 12, 22, 41, 43, 183
Vishtadvaita Vedanta 30
visualisation: *see sadhana*
Vivekananda 20, 35, 136, 142, 153, 159, 185
void, the 57–9, 79–80, 82, 93, 136, 145

waking state 35
Waley, A. 108
wan wu: see ten thousand things
Watts, A. 110, 112–3

Way, the: *see* Tao
Way of Heaven 119, 166, 185
Way of Realisation of the Truth 105
Way of Right Unity 104
Way of Supreme Peace 105
wealth: *see arhat*
wei-tan: see outer elexir
Weil, S. 33
well-field system 129–30
Wheel of Life 80–1
wheels of energy: *see chakras*
Wilde, 0. 97–9, 102
Wilhelm's *I Ching* 115
Williams, P. 176
wisdom (Confucianist): *see chih*
women, status of in Buddhism 69–70; in Christianity 169–70, 182; in Confucianism 123–4
Wordsworth, W. 33, 137, 155, 187
World Parliament of Religions 136, 179, 181
Wu, L. 86–7, 106, 125–6, 133
wu-hsing: see Five Agents
wu-lun: see five relationships

wu wei 92–3, 98–9, 151

xiao: see hsiao

Yajurveda 21
yama 27
Yin Hsi 89
yin and *yang* 11, 31, 41, 83, 90, 92, 105, ch. 11 *passim*; definition 107–9; and sexual harmony 110–11, 120, 122, 130–1, 133, 136–7, 141, 148, 152, 158, 168, 176, 185, 187
Yoga 25–8; Bhakti 28; Hatha 28; Jnana 28, 131; Karma 28, 131; Raja 27–8; Tantric 28
Yogachara school 71, 79, 82
Yoga-Sutras of Patanjali 23, 27–8
yogi(s) 26, 36, 48

zazen 74, 76–7
Zen 8, 26, 65, 67, 72–3, 79, 85, 92, 99, 103, 157, 170, 182–3
zhe-chue 86
zhong 123
Zoroastrianism 11–12, 15, 52, 163